"Larry is the real deal. His st[...]

are nevertheless real. His goal is to accurately share the events of his life and not to worry about the repercussions. This is Larry. He is not management material because his internal moral and professional compass is set to 'do the right thing,' which has been tested and developed over his life. Larry's story about his experience along the Southwest border is the unfortunate byproduct of money, violence and corruption that is the 'War on Drugs.' This story is not a theatrical portrayal or a TV movie, it's just one part of the complicated reality of the drug world on the border. While many people find these stories entertaining to watch on our digital devices to people like Larry, they are haunting tales. Let this poor country boy from Kentucky take you down the 'rabbit hole' of the tragic reality that is the drug business and the border." -- Robert W. Meza, Retired Special Agent FBI

"The stories Larry relates to the reader are real. He demonstrates that hard work, trust and integrity have positive results. He lets us know that not all Criminal Justice personnel are bad." – Bryan Cook, Retired Supervisory Special Agent, U.S. Department of Justice, DEA.

"I am truly grateful for your service to your community. It is an honor to serve as your President and to work each day to improve the lives of the American people. Your encouragement inspires me and gives me great hope for the future of our Nation." – President Donald Trump

ii

Fighting my Greatest Enemy: Myself

Trust in God/Confia en Dios

An Inspired True Story by a DEA Agent

Larry Ray Hardin, Author and Writer

Dianne DeMille Ph.D., Writer

November 2019
Dianne's Consultant Services
Anaheim, CA

Paperback ISBN 978-1-7336350-8-0

iv

v

Foreword

I have been with the University of Phoenix for over 16 years, and I was one of the first Lead Faculty Area Chairs for the Criminal Justice Program. I have over 32 years of law enforcement experience. I retired from government service after serving 25 years with the United States Department of Justice as a Supervisory Special Agent with the Drug Enforcement Administration (DEA). I served four years with the Naval Investigative Service (NIS) Office of Naval Intelligence now known as the Naval Criminal Investigative Service (NCIS) as a Special Agent, and three years with the San Diego Police Department (SDPD) for the City of San Diego as a sworn Police Officer.

I have known Larry since he first started to work for DEA in San Diego. Larry is from the Kentucky mountain hollers of the western Appalachians. He is from God fearing, hard working parents. Larry's father was a man of few words who believed that a man's words and handshake were as valid as a signed and witnessed contract. Larry did not fall far from the tree.

The stories Larry relates to the reader are real. He demonstrates that hard work, trust and integrity have positive

1

results. He lets us know that not all Criminal Justice personnel are bad. Like all walks of life there are always a few bad apples. I highly recommend that you read "Fighting my Greatest Enemy: Myself." To experience how a country boy from the hollers and hills of rural Kentucky dealt with one of the deadliest Law Enforcement tasks in American History.

----- Bryan Cook, Adjunct Professor for University of Phoenix, Retired Supervisory Special Agent, U.S. Department of Justice, DEA

In Memory of

Domingo Julio Gomez Franco

During the summer of 1998 at the American Embassy in Bogota, Colombia, Vice-Consular Officer Catalina Moreno Hardin learned that the Spanish Embassy was inviting foreign embassy officers and their guests to their festivity. Catalina contacted the Spanish Embassy and talked to a Guardia Civil, Julio Gomez Franco.

Julio and Catalina instantly began talking about how they missed their families in Spain. Catalina told Julio that she was the daughter of Pedro Moreno Jaramillo, a retired Guardia Civil. She mentioned that her husband was a DEA Agent assigned to the American Embassy. He told Catalina that he and the other Guardia Civils would like to see her at the festivity. She said, "Can I bring my DEA husband with me?" Julio quickly replied, "Yes, if he brings me a DEA hat."

Several days later, Catalina and Larry arrived at the Spanish Embassy. Approaching the large front main entrance door, they were welcomed by the Spanish Ambassador and his

3

bodyguard, Guardia Civil Julio Gomez Franco. Quickly, the Ambassador kissed Catalina on both sides of her face.

Larry immediately thought, Is this guy going to kiss me too?

As Catalina and Larry greeted the Spanish Ambassador, the Ambassador noticed that Larry had a black hat, with embroidered gold letters of DEA Bogota, in his left hand.

Julio expressed warm greetings with Catalina while Larry spoke in English to the Ambassador about DEA. She said to Julio, "My husband has your DEA hat." He quickly responded with a grin on his face as he stared at the DEA hat in Larry's left hand.

When Larry was about to make a conversation with Julio to give him the DEA hat, the Spanish Ambassador took it out of Larry's hand and put it on his head. The Ambassador, laughing, told Larry in English, "Thank you for the DEA hat."

The Ambassador resumed welcoming the other guests to the Spanish Embassy while wearing the DEA hat.

Larry looked at Julio, saying, "I'm sorry, brother. The Ambassador seized the DEA hat from my hand. I promise you are going to get a better-looking hat." Julio smiled.

Catalina learned thoroughly from the other Guardia Civil and the Spanish employees that Julio was a courageous and unique man. He was generous, a loving husband and father, and looked out for those who counted on him, including the Ambassador. He worked hard to protect the Ambassador and his co-workers.

On November 26, 1998, a Guardia Civil contacted Catalina and told her that Julio was assassinated on the streets in Bogota.

On November 28, 1998, Catalina and Larry arrived at the old 18th-century Catholic church in Bogota to give their last respects to Julio. The church was overflowing with law enforcement, military, and personnel from all the Embassies and Consulate offices in Colombia. (Espana elpais.com/Agencias Bogota - 27 NOV 1998 – 00:00 CET, Un guardia civil el la embajada en Bogota muere de un tiro en un atraco.)

Catalina and Larry sorrowfully met with Julio's sad weeping wife and his wonderful son as they sat together next to Julio's casket. Larry showed the DEA hat to Julio's son. Catalina said to Mrs. Gomez, "This is Julio's hat that my husband promised him. We are extremely sorry." The boy glanced at his mom. Larry then lay down the hat in the young boy's hands. With approval from

5

his mom, Julio's son slowly put the hat on his head. He then looked up at Larry.

Larry suddenly sees Julio's eyes in his son.

Catalina and Larry slowly turned around to face Julio's casket. They silently prayed for Julio and his family. Then they slowly walked away for the last time. Within minutes, several people from the Rociero Group were singing, La Salve Rociera, "Ole, Ole!"

Julio, you are at peace.

Author's Note

The stories you are about to read are true. Some names of individuals and companies have been changed for their protection. Incidents, events, and conversations have been recreated with the aid of reports, personal diaries, author's memory, and interviews with people involved.

As a reader of these inspiring stories, you can be assured you are not getting just another theory or opinion; but the truth of "Why there is no war on drugs." You will find the answers right here in these pages, but some of you will continue to ask the questions in the search for answers.

About a year ago while in San Fernando, Cadiz, Spain, Pedro Fernandez-Lopera, a retired High School Professor, encouraged me to meet with his friend Antonio Lagares. Antonio is a well-known Spanish Author and writer. Pedro said, "I want you to meet with Antonio Lagares, he is a great friend, and he's interested in meeting you."

The next day Pedro took me to a wonderful place for tapas "Bodegon Rocio." He gave me a book from Antonio. Antonio's book is about Venta Vargas[1], a true story of the people (Las

7

Cañaillas) of San Fernando. While waiting on Antonio at Bodegon Rocio restaurant, Pedro and I drank Cruzcampo and Estrella de Galicia beers and ate some tapa de Jamon. Antonio finally arrived.

After drinking a few more Cruzcampo and Estrella Galicia beers, Antonio and Pedro agreed that I should write and publish my book in Spanish, also. I reached up to get the small DEA lapel pin attached to my black leather jacket. I ask Antonio, "Give me your right hand."

Antonio thinks we are going to shake hands on my new Spanish book. I stuck the DEA lapel pin into his hand, squeezing my hand on top of his hand, pushing down on the lapel pin to draw blood. "Ouch," says Antonio. I looked at Pedro. But Pedro would not give me his hand. I said, "This is my promise to you and Pedro in blood the book will be translated in Spanish." Pedro was trying to interpret my English into Spanish (Andalusia), but it was too late. Pedro had already

The Spanish El Toro Flag

8

drunk too many beers. Pedro was probably thinking to himself, "This DEA agent is loco."

After deciding what name to use for the title of the Spanish book, Pedro suggested, "Confia en Dios."

My wife, Kathy, strongly agreed with Pedro with the title of the Spanish book should be: Fighting My Greatest Enemy: Myself; Trust in God: Confia en Dios.

Acknowledgments

I want to thank God for my parents, Ray Hardin, Junior and Elizabeth G. Johnson Hardin, both of whom have gone home to our Lord Jesus, for their power of love, patience, and sacrifices for our family.

In July 2016, I told Momma, "I am writing a book on corruption in law enforcement at the Mexico border and the evil of drugs I faced while working with DEA."

Momma said, "You won't get in trouble with DEA?"

"No, Momma," I told her.

"I can't wait to read your book, Larry Ray," said Momma.

Momma died January 14, 2017 at my sister Sherry Geneva's home. Momma didn't live long enough to read my book.

I did read part of the book's manuscript to Daddy before he died at home on February 4, 2018. Daddy, hiding behind the pain, smiled as I read to him from the manuscript of *Growing up in Kentucky*.

I also want to thank Ann Hazelwood, my cousin, for her hard work in proofreading these stories. She dedicated a lot of her

11

time to the book and hopefully helped in bringing the truth to the public.

And, thanks to my cousins, Mary Bell Warner and Diane Smith, who provided a lot of family photos. I am grateful for Ann, Mary Bell, and Diane's willingness to take on this task.

And finally, I want to also recognize my wife, Kathy, for her love, friendship, knowledge, a lot of patience, and support on behalf of this true story.

"Thanks to everyone" is not enough. It truly could not have been done without my family, relatives, friends, and former co-workers in the law enforcement community.

About the Author

Larry Ray Hardin

Larry DEA without the face mask

This book is my story about growing up in Kentucky and my experience with law enforcement. After serving over thirty years, I retired from the Federal government, United States Department of Justice, as a Special Agent with the Drug Enforcement Administration (DEA).

I initially served with the Immigration and Naturalization Service (INS) as an Adjudicator Officer; as a Correctional Officer with the Federal Bureau of Prisons; and over six years in the military service, primarily with the Marine Corps. I hold a Master of Arts in Business Management and a Master of Arts in Human Resources Development.

Currently, I teach criminal justice to U.S. military students and their family members throughout Europe, Spain, and San Diego, CA. I am a licensed Private Investigator (PI) and operate my own private investigating business as the President and Chief

13

Executive Officer (CEO) of L.R.H. Investigations in San Diego, California.

I volunteer to visit with military veterans, law enforcement agents, and officers in hospice in the San Diego County area. Also, I am a consultant and lecturer on law enforcement, international/domestic terrorism, and intelligence methodologies. I am also a co-author and writer of my first book, *Path of the Devil - - Camino del Diablo, Based on True Events of A DEA Agent and Two Private Investigators.*

Introduction

This book is the true story during the time I served as a DEA agent in San Diego, California, the Southwest Yuma Arizona and Mexico border, and Bogota, Colombia.

The story relates three investigations in different locations throughout the country, Central America, South America, Colombia, Asia, and Europe. I was determined to bring down three notorious major drug trafficking organizations operating along the southwestern border of the United States and Mexico.

The First Investigation

Investigative reporter for the Albuquerque Journal learned from former DEA agents that twelve gatekeepers form "a syndicate of the major drug cartels operating in Mexico"[2] along the border between United States and Mexico, from Tijuana, Mexico/San Diego, California to Matamoros, Mexico/Brownsville, Florida.[3]

The syndicate controls specific regions for smuggling narcotics and drugs into the U.S. and transportation of weapons to Central and South America. The cartels "coordinate bribes at the

15

national level, oversee money laundering operations and negotiate the shipment of drugs at the international level."[4]

One of the criminal cases I conducted took place in Yuma, Arizona and San Luis, Mexico. I initiated a conspiracy Organized Crime Drug Enforcement Task Forces (OCDETF) investigation targeting a Mexican cartel, one of the twelve gatekeepers.

Through information obtained from my Confidential Informants (CIs), Sources of Information (SOIs), and Private Investigators (PIs), I found myself making connections of three brothers who ran a drug cartel with Colombians and Chinese criminals. Their businesses connected throughout the United States and the world. The three Garcia brothers were known as El Lobo (Jaime Garcia), El Camaron (Javier Garcia), and El Loco (Joselito Garcia).

My informants and sources were extremely knowledgeable of the Garcia brothers and their family members' criminal activities within Mexico and the United States. As a result, I was able to target the brothers' cocaine, heroin, and marijuana distribution network as my initial ploy.

16

With the help from my informants, sources, and the Private Investigators (PIs), I found approximately 40 major Mexican, Colombian, and Southwest Asian drug traffickers, considered to be from the highest echelon in manufacturing and distribution of narcotics. I was able to identify the major traffickers' connections with the Garcia brothers' criminal activities and links to corrupt cops and federal agents at the Southwest Arizona border with Mexico.

About 30 Drug traffickers were related by blood or marriage to the Garcia brothers, and some were in the law enforcement community, primarily at the U.S. and Mexico Port-of-Entries (POEs) in San Luis, Arizona, and Algodones, Mexico.

The CIs, SOIs, and PIs talked about the Garcia brothers' utilizing underground tunnels, produce trucks, shrimp trucks, and other vehicles to transport large quantities of heroin, cocaine, and marijuana from San Luis, Sonora, Mexico, to the United States. The brothers were known to DEA since the early 1970s as the largest trafficking Mexican organization in San Luis, Sonora, Mexico.

17

The Garcia brothers' organization was family-oriented and functioned as a supply source for contract couriers. The brothers utilized their legitimate agriculture produce and shrimp business in San Luis, Sonora, Mexico and in the United States, as fronts for arranging and trafficking multi-kilograms of narcotics.

The Second Investigation

Marijuana Cultivation and Distribution

I initiated a conspiracy Organized Crime Drug Enforcement Task Force (OCDETF) as a joint investigation with Yuma U.S. Customs and Arizona Southwest Border Narcotics Task Force (NTF) targeting a marijuana cultivation and distribution organization in Arizona and throughout the United States, Hawaii, and Canada.

The criminal investigation is unique in that it consisted of two primary and equally important objectives. The first objective was to identify those individuals responsible for marijuana cultivation and distribution throughout the United States and Hawaii. The second objective was to infiltrate the center of Pat Weed's, a University of California, Berkley Professor, and Earl

18

Lick's, a former aide to President Regan staff, marijuana and distribution organization where I could identify the cotton and citrus farms used as marijuana cultivation.

Experiences from my investigations, surveillances, and collections of intelligence to build the cases present a compelling story leading to what became of the Garcia brothers' connection with corrupt Customs and Immigration officers. I identified Pat Weed and Earl Lick to a marijuana and distribution organization using cotton and citrus farms as marijuana cultivation.

The Third Investigation

Manufacturing Meth and Distributing Organization

An Arizona Southwest Border Narcotics Task Force officer and I initiated a conspiracy OCDETF investigation targeting a criminal organization with suspected connections to the Cornbread Mafia and Hells Angels manufacturing methamphetamine (meth) and distributing organization. This meth investigation was unique for two reasons.

DEA, FBI, and other law enforcement agencies in Yuma, Arizona had previously conducted several criminal investigations to identify the illegal activities of Joe Cactus, a Cornbread Mafia member, and Nick Star, an agriculture produce grower. Second, Joe Cactus is documented in the law enforcement community as a career criminal residing in Yuma, Arizona, and is suspected a mentor of the Las Vegas criminal underworld. Some of Cactus' illegal activities included the production and distribution of meth and the involvement in the importation and distribution of cocaine with the Garcia brothers.

I later identified from my sources and other law enforcement officers that Joe Cactus' manufacturing of methamphetamine (meth) and distributing network in Yuma was working with the Cornbread Mafia in Nevada and Hells Angels in California. The intensity of targeting some of Cactus' buddies in the Cornbread Mafia and Hells Angels – and in some instances, the fun time – relate how these events shaped my life dealing with corruption at the Arizona and Mexico border POE.

I quickly learned who could be trusted working on the U.S. and Mexican border; the Confidential Informants (CIs), Sources of Information (SOIs), Private Investigators (PIs), federal agents, local state officers, and police officers in the law enforcement community.

"Those who walk righteously and speak what is right, who reject gain from extortion and keep their hands from accepting bribes, who stop their ears against plots of murder and shut their eyes against contemplating evil - [16] *they are the ones who will dwell on the heights, whose refuge will be the mountain fortress. Their bread will be supplied, and water will not fail them."* (Isaiah 33:15-16 New International Version).

Growing Up in Kentucky

Momma and Daddy's last photo

I am the oldest of eight children. I was a tall, skinny guy who did not talk much but spoke excellent Southern grammar. Momma said that she gave birth to me first, then Jeffrey Dewayne, twins Brenda Sue and Linda Lou, and Debbie Jean at home. Sharon Geneva, the seventh sibling, wishes to remain anonymous, so I'll refer to him as "my little brother," and James Daniel (nicknamed Doodle Bug) were born at the hospital.

In June 1977, Doodle Bug was age 11 when Daddy found him lying on the garage floor. He had accidentally hung himself inside the garage. My little brother and I tried to save our brother's life. My little brother gave Doodle Bug mouth to mouth resuscitation, and I pushed down on his chest. Soon the ambulance arrived.

In the hospital emergency room, Momma said that when she rode in the ambulance, she kept looking at Doodle Bug's face, praying to God to save him. But Momma said, "God's voice whispered in my heart, saying HE gave his only son." Several times Momma heard God's voice as she begged Jesus to save Doodle Bug.

I asked the emergency room nurse if I could see my baby brother. Alone, I entered the small white cold room. In the middle of the examination room, I saw Doodle Bug's face, and a white linen sheet covered his body lying on a silver metal table. I leaned over his face and whispered in his ear, "I love you. I'm sorry." Doodle Bug's face looked so peaceful and beautiful lying on the table. I believe my baby brother heard me.

Several years later, Daddy and I were fishing on one of Mr. Wheelers' ponds. Daddy mentioned how Daniel enjoyed going fishing with him at this same pond. Suddenly, he said, "After Daniel died, I cried a lot and missed him so much. I kept questioning God: Where is Daniel?"

Daddy looked at me and said, "One day, I was in the bedroom, alone and crying so much about how Daniel accidentally

24

took his own life. I heard my Dad (Grandpa Hardin) yelling at me from outside the window above the Water Maple trees; "Junior, why are you asking where Daniel is?"

Daddy said, "I couldn't see my dad above the trees, but his voice was so clear coming from there, and dad said again, 'Junior, why are you asking HIM where's Daniel?"

Then he said, "I could strongly feel Dad was no longer above the trees but walking up the driveway towards the house. But I couldn't see him."

"I tried to look for my Dad, but I couldn't see him. Suddenly, I heard Dad's voice so loud and clear again as he came close to the outside bedroom window," he said.

"'Where is Daniel?' my Daddy yelled."

"He is over there with Ima (Grandma Hardin)"

Then he said, "I looked over behind Dad's voice to see if Mom and Daniel were there. I could hear Mom and Daniel laughing, but I wasn't able to see them. Dad told me, 'Stop asking where's Daniel. Daniel is okay."

Then Daddy said, "I never asked God, 'Where is Daniel' again."

25

Momma and Doodle Bug

Momma said the death of little Doodle Bug broke our family circle. Momma and Daddy grieved the rest of their lives for the way Daniel died. Momma died January 14, 2017 and went to heaven to see her baby boy James Daniel Hardin, Doodle Bug. Daddy joined Momma and Daniel on February 4, 2018.

Daddy, Ray Hardin Junior, had a second-grade education. He couldn't go to school because he had to work on the farm at the age of seven. Daddy couldn't read but knew his math and puzzles, and he rarely lost a game of checkers.

Daddy told me, "I was chewing tobacco at age five." Daddy's brother, JT, started to chew tobacco at age four. Daddy worked in the tobacco and cornfields and later, following behind a mule pulling a plow.

Daddy worked most of his life as a farmer in Taylorsville and later as a welder in Louisville. When Daddy finished working at his regular job in the daytime as a welder, he started working in the tobacco fields in the evenings with some of my brothers and sisters. Daddy quickly learned that the best way to earn extra money for the family was to sharecrop for other farmers in tobacco fields. Some of my siblings and I worked in the tobacco fields in the daytime.

Momma, Elizabeth Gertrude Johnson, worked hard washing clothes in a tub, cooking on a wooden stove, ironing, cleaning, and taking care of us every day. Keeping us clean and fed was Momma's life. She bought most of our clothes from second-hand stores, or she got free clothes at the church. She made sure our clothes were always clean for church and school. Momma said, "You can be poor, but you can be clean."

Momma took care of us. She cooked two meals each day, early breakfast and early supper. We didn't have many material things but always had food on the table – mostly white and brown beans, potatoes, flour and water gravy, and pan cornbread. Sometimes Momma made potato sandwiches for our lunches when we were going to the Catholic school.

Momma always talked about how her brothers and sisters wore old worn-out clothes. Momma said, "Sometimes we went without eating three meals a day to nothing. We were lucky to have

27

one meal a day: water gravy. I remembered when we were so poor and often moved from rental to rental throughout Nelson County while mom and dad were looking for jobs."

Most of Momma's brothers and sisters were born in New Haven and Bardstown, Kentucky. She was the second oldest of ten children. Momma's oldest brother Joseph Earl died at childbirth. Following Joseph Earl were my Momma, Elizabeth (died at age 80), Mary, Charles (died at age 68), Joe (died at age 68), Dorothy, Ernie (died at age 66), Mary Margaret, Judy, Herman (Andy), and Billy (died at age 61). Momma's dad was always traveling away from home looking for a job, leaving her mom and the children alone to take care of themselves. mom and the children alone to take care of themselves.

Momma told us, "I learned to take care of my little brothers and sisters before I was age 13. My dad went to prison for about five years for making moonshine. While Dad was in prison, Mom left me and my sister, Mary, with our brothers and sisters alone at home for

House where Larry Ray was born

28

days while she looked for extra money to pay the rent and buy food. I remembered going days without seeing Mom and not knowing where she was. My little brothers and sisters cried because they were hungry," said Momma.

"While my dad was in prison, and Mom was out looking for a job, I had to take care of my brothers and sisters. When we were alone, hungry, cold, and afraid, I prayed our Lord's Prayer," Momma said.

Momma told stories about God and explained how HIS son, Jesus, died on a cross because Jesus loves us. Sometimes before I went to bed, I would see Momma holding a Rosary in her hands praying to Jesus' mother, Mary. Momma sure loved Mother Mary.

Also, there were times Momma told ghost stories that she learned from her mom and relatives.

Growing up, Momma taught my brothers and sisters how to pray Our Lord's Prayer. "Our Father who is in heaven. Hallowed be Your name. Your kingdom comes. Your will be done, on earth as it is in heaven. Give us this day our daily bread. And forgive us our debts, as we also have forgiven our debtors. And do not lead us into temptation but deliver us from evil. For yours is the kingdom

29

and the power and the glory forever -- Amen" (Matthew 6:9-13 New American Standard Version).

A Single-barrel 12-gauge Shotgun in my Hands

Daddy

I was age six when Daddy put his single-barrel 12-gauge shotgun in my hands and taught me how to use it. He stood behind me while I slowly raised the shotgun to my left shoulder and squeezed the trigger. I remembered hearing a loud noise, and then Daddy laughing picked me up off the ground.

With Daddy's patience, I began learning to shoot at empty coffee cans and some beer bottles next to the creek behind the outhouse where I lived. The old farmhouse had no bathroom, nor running water. It had an outside well and an outhouse. Sometimes the woods were my toilet, and I used the creek to wash my butt.

I quickly learned that Daddy's shotgun helped put food on the table, could help you stay out of trouble, and kept you from getting hurt. After shooting his 12-gauge shotgun that year, I wanted my own shotgun for Christmas.

Late in the evening on Christmas Eve, I looked out the small wooden framed window waiting to see Daddy drive up the dirt road covered with snow. He was late getting home from his welding job in Louisville. Staring out the window waiting for Daddy, I suddenly heard someone enter the kitchen yelling, "Ho, Ho, Ho."

Where was Daddy? I didn't see him driving up the dirt road. Momma was in the kitchen, not saying anything. I wondered why Momma wasn't saying, "Help me, Larry Ray."

Being scared of the "Ho, Ho, Ho," I slowly peeked into the kitchen to see if Momma was okay.

It was dark and cold outside when Santa Claus finally arrived at our house.

Wow, there's Santa Claus, standing next to Momma wearing worn-out dark grey dirty pants, a grey shirt, and Santa black boots that are awfully dirty.

I quickly noticed that Santa Claus was not wearing anything red. But his hair was red like Daddy's. I was wondering, *That's strange. Santa Claus has white cotton wrapped around his face and a brown burlap feed bag over his shoulder.*

Santa Claus looked at me with his bright blue eyes, like Daddy's, and said, "I have something for you kids."

Santa Claus's voice sounds like Daddy's.

He reached his dirty hand into the burlap feed bag and slowly pulled out a toy wooden plane. "This is for you," Santa Claus said to me.

I said, "Santa Claus, where is my 12-gauge shotgun?"

He said, "Sorry, not this year." I guess Santa Claus knew I was age six and still not ready to have my own shotgun.

Too Dangerous to Walk Alone

When I was age six, I had to miss my first year of school because Momma said our home was too far back in the woods from the school bus stop. Momma said, "It is too dangerous for you to walk alone from the house to the school bus and walk back to the house. You can go to school once we move to the city. Momma said, "You and Jeffery can go to school together." Momma also said that Daddy would be closer to his job in Louisville.

32

After that first year in the old farmhouse next to the creek, Daddy moved us to Louisville, Kentucky. I then started going to school. I was age seven and in the first grade.

From 1st through 4th grade, Jeffrey, Brenda Sue, and Linda Lou, and I went to Catholic schools. Most of the time, Momma walked us to school. On Sundays, we all walked to church, except for Daddy. He stayed home to rest.

In school that first year, I was always in trouble with the Catholic Nuns for fighting with the other students. The Nuns hit me across the hands with a long wooden ruler and pulled my ears. Jeffrey only watched as the Nuns whipped me. Sometimes I saw Jeffrey smiling while they were hitting me or pulling my ear.

At home, I tried to explain to Momma that the other kids in school were making fun of my brother and sisters. The other kids laughed at us when we ate our potato sandwiches in the lunchroom, and also about how we dressed.

I told her, "Momma, I had to fight those kids out on the playground." That was why the Nuns whipped me. I think Momma understood how other kids could be cruel.

Kissing Her on the Cheek to get my Money

One day at Grandpa's house, Daddy's sister, Aunt Betty Jane, asked me, "Larry Ray, you want to make some money?"

Aunt Betty Jane told Daddy that RT was looking for help to work at his tobacco field. RT Jennings was a local farmer, and he owned a small grocery store in the community of Big Plum Creek. Aunt Betty Jane looked at Daddy and said, "I'll watch over Larry Ray."

I was excited and thinking; Wow! I am going to earn some money.

My first job to make money was chopping out the weeds on RT's tobacco field. I was eight years old.

Aunt Betty Jane and I worked all day in the tobacco field, next to the creek, chopping weeds. It was in mid-July, and the weather was hot and humid. Later in the afternoon, I got very hot and a little dizzy from the sun. Aunt Betty Jane looked at my red face and said, "Larry Ray, you go over there and sit down under the old Elm tree right now, while I continue to chop out the weeds from the tobacco."

Under that old tree, I was dreaming about all the Big Red soft drinks and bags of salted peanuts I could buy. I loved putting peanuts inside my Big Red soda drink. I learned that from the older boys that lived on Big Plum Creek Road when we went to RT's grocery store.

Aunt Betty Jane took care of me. Later at the end of the day, at RT's grocery store, she never mentioned to RT or Daddy what happened to me at the tobacco field. At the grocery store, Mrs. Nancy Jennings said, "Do you want your $5, Larry Ray?"

I said, "Yes, Mrs. Jennings."

"Okay, then come here and kiss me on the cheek, and I'll give you the $5." I looked at Daddy to see if it was okay.

I earned $5 chopping out weeds, and I had to kiss Mrs. Jennings' on the cheek to get my money. After I got my money, I ran out of the front door of the country grocery store like a dog chasing a rabbit.

The next day, Daddy took me to Crazy Red surplus clothing store in Mount Washington. He picked out a pair of blue jeans and a brown short sleeve shirt for me. He said, "Follow me."

When I walked to the cashier, Daddy told me, "Pay for the pants and shirt."

I thought he was joking. Then, I realized the clothes were not for Jeffrey but for me, and that I was going to pay for the pants and shirt with my own money.

I couldn't believe he wanted me to spend my $5 to pay for the pants and shirt. I was thinking; I kissed Mrs. Jennings' on the cheek to get my $5. I was going to buy a lot of Big Red soft drinks and salted peanuts with my money. Daddy is supposed to pay for these, not me.

The owner of the surplus store, Crazy Red, was waiting behind the counter for me to pay for the pants and shirt. *I never knew why people in Mount Washington called him Crazy Red.* I gave my hard-earned $5 to Crazy Red. He put the clothes in a brown paper bag and gave me back some coins and the bag.

After we left Crazy Red's surplus store, Daddy stopped at a small grocery store to buy a beer and fishing bait. I realized I might have enough money to buy a Big Red soda that cost five cents and a bag of salted peanuts for two cents.

Wow! I have enough change from my $5 for a Big Red and a bag of peanuts. This is great!

I never forgot the first $5 I earned. I had worked so hard that summer day in the tobacco field, and I got so hot and dizzy. Aunt Betty Jane took care of me. She did most of the work, chopping out the weeds in the hot sun while I watched her, lying under the old Elm tree.

At age 8, I learned the value of money from that experience. But most important, Aunt Betty Jane was watching over me as a mother protecting her child.

Big Plum Creek Road

Jesus Take Care of My Family

In December 1965, I was age 11 when my family moved from Louisville out on Big Plum Creek Road to Mr. Harry's old wooden-frame three-room house.

Mr. Harry's Old House

Once we left the city and moved into Mr. Harry's old cold house, Momma wanted us to go to a Catholic church. In the city, we walked to church, but in Big Plum Creek, there was no Catholic church. The nearest Catholic church was in Taylorsville, about 12 miles from Mr. Harry's old house.

Momma took us in her small grey Falcon car, and later the old black 1960 Chevrolet, to Saint Joseph Catholic Church in Taylorsville.

Jeffrey and I became altar boys helping the priest at Sunday morning Catholic Mass. That was the only time my brother and I

38

could drink the left-over red wine. Jeffrey liked the wine, but I didn't.

Daddy was a Southern Baptist Christian, and he didn't want to go to a Catholic church. I don't think he liked it when he saw some of the priests drinking beer and cursing at the Catholic churches Friday night Bingo parties and at some of the picnics. He also didn't feel comfortable with the Catholic Mass. He stayed home on Sundays, for a day of rest, while we were in Catholic Mass. I guess that was Daddy's day to relax.

When he wanted to be alone, he walked behind the house or sat under a tree and prayed to God. That was his church. Sometimes when Daddy thought he was alone behind the house or in the woods, I overheard him talking to God and to Jesus.

At nights, after I went to bed, in the next bedroom where I slept, I could hear him praying to God, saying, "Jesus take care of my family." Sometimes, I heard Momma praying to Jesus and to Mother Mary.

Beans and Cornbread

Old Mr. Harry's house had electricity but did not have heat, a bathroom, or running water. Jeffrey and I got firewood from the woods next to the house for Momma to cook her beans and cornbread and to keep the house warm in the winter.

Momma would cook a pot of potato soup, beans, and homemade bread on the woodstove. For the rest of the meals, she would use her gas stove.

We got water from the outside well when Momma needed to wash clothes and for our weekly baths in the winter.

Sunday suppers were special. We had fried chicken or fish. Daddy would cook our Sunday supper to give Momma a break from cooking.

Keep your Eyes on the Front Door

During the winter months, Jeffrey and I would sometimes forget to bring firewood into the house for the wooden stove. Daddy's brother, Uncle JT, always had firewood on his front porch for the cold days.

One cold early morning, I woke up and remembered that I didn't get the firewood for Daddy to start the stove to warm the house. In bed, I poked Jeffrey on the arm and said, "Come on, we've got to get up and go over to Uncle JT's porch to get some firewood. If I don't, Daddy is going to whip me."

My other two youngest brothers stayed in bed. But I told Jeffrey, "If you don't come with me, I'm going to beat you up later."

Jeffrey and I quietly crept out of the house like a mouse and slowly walked toward Uncle JT's house. I had taken wood off of our Uncle's porch several times in the past. I saw smoke coming out from JT's chimney. *Wow. JT is already out of bed.*

I whispered, "Jeffrey, keep your eyes on the front door and the windows. If you see JT's face looking out the window, make a whistle like a jaybird!"

It was a cold and dark with no lights on inside my Uncle's house, as I approached his front porch in the early morning, I was thinking; *Uncle JT went back to bed.*

I slowly crept up on the porch like a squirrel looking for some nuts hidden in the firewood. I grabbed some wood and left

41

without making a sound. I was quiet as a field mouse and thinking; *Uncle JT is sound asleep like a baby.*

Daddy was looking for some firewood to start a fire just as I returned with the wood. Later that morning, he and I went outside to feed the pigs. Uncle JT yelled at Daddy, "I saw Larry Ray sneak up on my porch this morning and take some of my firewood. I also saw Weenie (Jeffrey's nickname) hiding behind the tree. I thought about shooting my shotgun over that boy's head when Larry Ray snuck up on the porch. Those boys of yours would be running home screaming with no firewood if I shot my shotgun."

I couldn't believe Uncle JT was telling Daddy that he was watching me take his firewood. Where was Jeffrey? Wow! I said to myself; Jeffrey was supposed to be watching JT's front door and window. I am going to beat him up.

Uncle JT was chewing tobacco and smiling as Daddy looked at me and told his brother, "I'll talk to you later, JT."

After Daddy talked to me about stealing the firewood and whipped me, I made sure I always had our wood in the house. Later that afternoon, I chased Jeffrey outside and hit him several times to get back at him for not watching out for Uncle JT. Jeffrey and I were very close growing up.

Wait till your Daddy gets Home

Momma never whipped us; she only yelled, "Wait till your Daddy gets home."

Daddy did the whipping with switches or his belt. He would wait until we were in bed to whip us for not listening to Momma. My whippings

Momma after having 8 children

were usually for beating up my brothers and sisters. While he was whipping me, I screamed and begged, "I won't do it again, Daddy."

Most of the time, while he was whipping me on my butt and legs, I faked the pain. I cried and screamed, but not for very long. Jeffrey used to scream as if Daddy was killing him with his belt or switch when he was getting hit on the butt and legs.

Brenda Sue and Linda Lou would dance like chickens losing their heads and screamed like wild cats before they got a whipping from Daddy. With all that dancing and screaming, you

43

would think Brenda Sue and Linda Lou would be crying. But after the whipping, Brenda Sue and Linda Lou would run off to play or fall asleep.

Debbie Jean always begged Daddy not to whip her. He would not whip her very hard, maybe a couple of licks across the legs. Debbie Jean always said to us, "Daddy won't whip me hard because I have red hair like him." Debbie Jean had long red hair like Daddy's short red hair. Maybe it was Debbie Jean's red hair that kept him from whipping her very often. I guess Debbie Jean was right.

Sherry Geneva knew how to stay quiet when Daddy was whipping the rest of us. She was a good baby sister most of the time, but she was a mean and stubborn little girl when she didn't get her way at home or school. She always sucked on her two fingers even when she wasn't hungry. My little brother and Doodle Bug watched and sometimes laughed at all the drama from the rest of us getting our daily whippings.

I also got whipped if anybody mistreated my brothers and sisters because I didn't protect them from bullies at school or in the neighborhood. Most of the time, Brenda Sue would defend her sisters fighting the other girls, and I would protect my brothers fighting the other boys.

I understood why Daddy whipped me when I hit my brothers and sisters. But I didn't understand why he whipped me when I took Uncle JT's firewood since he had plenty of it on his front porch.

Old Mr. Harry's house had a kitchen, a bed in the living room for Momma and Daddy, and another small bedroom for me and my brothers and sisters.

Doodle Bug and my little brother were close to each other. The little brothers were fighting all the time, even when we all slept together in an old feather bed at Mr. Harry's old house. My sisters slept together in another feather bed.

We lived there for five years in Mr. Harry's old house. By the third year, Mr. Harry did finally add another bedroom for us boys.

The Stinking Outhouse

Mr. Harry's old house had sulfurous well water that smelled like rotten eggs, especially in the hot summer. Momma washed our clothes in the sulfurous water every day.

45

Hardin Family Photo

My family shared the outside sulfurous well water with Uncle JT and his three daughters. JT lived across the street in a two-room house with Big Plum Creek running behind it.

The water from the sulfurous outside well stunk so bad that on a hot day, I had to pinch my nose to swallow it. The well water was not so bad in the cold winter months. Uncle JT loved drinking the nasty sulfurous well water. He always said, "It's good for you. Keeps you young and healthy."

The old house was built next to a little creek where I sometimes took my baths in the summer.

The stinking outhouse remained the same. *Smelly*! I had to use the *pee pot* under my bed or pee out the window when it was too cold to walk outside. The boys' new bedroom had a small window. Jeffrey and I would sometimes pee out the window for the fun of it. We didn't like to pee in the *pee pot* under our bed or go outside, especially when it was cold or rainy. Jeffrey and I were also lazy to put our clothes on and go outside to pee.

One evening, when Momma was outside walking by the boys' bedroom window, she saw me "peeing in the wind." Momma yelled, "Stop that peeing out the window. I'm telling your Daddy."

I yelled back, "Momma, it's not me; it's Jeffrey."

After Daddy's whipping, Jeffrey and I used the smelling pee pot under the bed, or went out into the woods, or used the outhouse, even when it was cold or rainy.

During the summer, I used the woods behind the outhouse to poop and pee. In the summer, I used the nearby creeks and ponds to wash up, making sure my butt was cleaned. I hated a smelling butt.

Weird Screams that Echoed in the Darkness

Jeffrey and I forgot to get Momma's outside sulfurous well water before we went to bed one November cold night. About 4:30 a.m., the next early cold morning, Daddy yelled, "Get out of bed and get your Mom's wash water."

He didn't have to yell a second time. Jeffrey and I ran outside in the cold early morning with two empty buckets. It was so dark and cold that the well water inside the hand pump was almost frozen. I tried to stay warm, with one hand holding my jacket wrapped around my chest because some of the buttons were missing while pumping the cold water with the other hand. Jeffrey was standing behind but very close to me, waiting for me to give him a bucket of water. Jeffrey said, "Hurry up, Larry Ray. I'm cold and scared that I might see a ghost."

I gave Jeffrey a full bucket of water, and as I was attempting to fill another bucket, he screamed, right in my ear. I turned around and looked at Jeffrey's face to see what made him scream like that. He suddenly screamed again, louder, and dropped the bucket of water when he took off running as fast as he could. He was screaming for Daddy to help.

"Jeffrey, what's wrong?" I yelled.

I couldn't understand what was happening to Jeffrey. Then I heard something behind me making weird noises. I saw a white ghost standing next to the coal pile. I was shocked and could not move my body to run. I kept looking at the ghost, waving his arms

48

up high in the air and making weird screams that echoed in the cold morning darkness. I was freaking out! *Momma's ghost stories were true!*

I needed to run to get away from the screaming ghost, so I dropped my partially filled bucket and followed Jeffrey. He had already disappeared in the darkness, and I slipped and fell on the water he spilled. I was lying on the cold, wet ground screaming for help. Then I started yelling for Daddy to help me. While trying to get up from the wet, muddy ground, I looked around, and the screaming ghost was flying towards me. *The ghost is going to carry me in the woods and kill me.* I was scared and thinking, *Where is Jeffrey? Did the ghost get him?*

I finally got up off the ground and took off running towards the house, with my hands up in the air, and continued to scream for Daddy to help me. Then I heard Momma laughing inside the house. I turned around to see if the ghost was following me and saw it was Daddy taking off a white sheet.

After that night, I never believed in ghosts again nor Momma's ghost stories.

They will Kill Again

I was age 12 when Daddy finally gave me a single-barrel 20-gauge shotgun for Christmas. That summer, I walked in the woods behind the house in the early mornings and late evenings with my shotgun looking for squirrels or rabbits to eat for supper.

I remembered one day when we returned home from grocery shopping in Louisville, and I saw old Mr. Harry standing in our front yard yelling: "Hey Junior, your black dog tried to kill one of my hogs."

Daddy said to Mr. Harry, "Okay. Show me the hog."

After seeing the hog, he looked at me and said, "Go find Pepper."

Pepper was a big beautiful black German Shepherd that I loved, and Pepper loved me. He was intelligent and protected me, my brothers and sisters from anyone who came to our home.

My brothers and sisters yelled, "Pepper, Pepper. Where are you?"

I wondered; Where is Pepper? He always gets excited when I return home. But I couldn't find him.

Jeffrey yelled, "Here's Pepper. He's under the house."
50

After I called Pepper several times, he slowly came out from under Mr. Harry's old house; He had dark dried blood all over his face. I immediately knew Pepper did something wrong because of the blood, but I didn't believe he would try to kill Mr. Harry's hog.

After finding Pepper, I ran to see what Daddy and Mr. Harry were doing at the hog pen. I saw a hog's back leg eaten down, almost to the bone. The hog was alive but slowly dying from the loss of blood from his leg. I heard Mr. Harry say, "Junior, you need to get rid of that dog."

I tried to convince myself Pepper did not do this to the hog, even if Pepper had blood on his face. I heard Daddy say, "Okay, Harry."

He and I sauntered slowly back to our house.

Once we returned to the house, Daddy looked at Pepper's face covered in dried blood. He looked at me and said, "Put a rope around Pepper's neck." Daddy walked into the house.

I sadly thought; Pepper is going to die for what he did to the hog.

51

Pepper stared at me as I put the rope around his neck. I believed Pepper knew he did something wrong at the hog pen.

He returned with my Christmas gift, the 20-gauge shotgun. He didn't have to say why he had the shotgun. Once I saw it in Daddy's hand, I knew Pepper was going to die. Daddy took the rope from my hands, and Pepper slowly followed him towards the woods. Pepper suddenly stopped and turned around for the last time to look at me, as if to say, "I'm sorry, Larry Ray, I love you, goodbye."

Daddy pulled on the rope, and Pepper followed him slowly until they disappeared in the dark woods.

Why did Pepper try to kill the hog? Now, he is going to die for what he did to Mr. Harry's hog.

Seeing Pepper alive for the last time, I was thinking about what Grandpa Hardin said, "When a dog kills a chicken or any other farm animal and taste the blood, the dog is no good anymore. The dog will kill again."

I kept staring into the dark woods, praying Daddy would change his mind about killing Pepper and bring him back home.

After a few minutes, I heard a loud noise from my shotgun. I continued to pray that he did not kill Pepper. I suddenly saw him walking back out of the woods without Pepper. I was disappointed and thinking; *Daddy did not change his mind. He is returning home without Pepper. He killed Pepper*

I asked him, "Where is Pepper?"

He handed me the shotgun and said, "Pepper is gone."

I couldn't cry for what Pepper did to that hog. But I did cry because I will always miss Pepper.

I was age 13 when Pepper died. Daddy never mentioned him again. Before he died, one year after Momma died, I asked him about Pepper. He said, "I tied Pepper to a cedar tree, and then Pepper looked up at me."

He never said anything else about Pepper.

Later in life working with DEA, I remembered Grandpa Hardin's words again when I tried to understand why a human being could kill and kill again. I learned that human beings are much the same as animals. When evil people hurt and kill other good people, the wrong people will hurt and kill again unless justice is quick. Years later, I remembered a homeless man living on the streets said, "What man has been waiting for on earth is righteousness and justice; it can be found only in God's kingdom."

For the next five years living at Mr. Harry's old house, I grew up running barefooted on Big Plum Creek Road and swimming and fishing in the creeks and playing in the woods during the summers.

Daddy, little brother, Jeffrey Dewayne, & Larry Ray

Once Jeffrey and I learned how to fish and to dog paddle at Noah Moore's water hole, we went fishing and swimming naked almost every day in the summer. Little brother and Doodle Bug later joined us after they learned how to fish and swim.

I was still missing my dog, Pepper. He loved playing in the water and running through the woods with me.

The School Bus Incident

The Taylorsville yellow school bus stopped at Mr. Harry's old house to pick up the Hardin kids (seven of us) each day during

54

the school months. Momma was so happy to see us go to school and to be alone with Doodle Bug in the old three-room house.

The yellow school bus was an opportunity for me to socialize and fight with kids living on Big Plum Creek Road and the other kids connected to Plum Creek and Little Plum Creek roads. If I was not fighting with the kids on the school bus, I was screaming and yelling like everyone else on the bus.

It seemed that if there were any problems of mischief and bad behavior on the school bus, Mr. McGee, the old white-haired bus driver, would only focus on the Hardin kids, especially Jeffrey and me. I don't understand why Mr. McGee focused on us when Momma said we were good boys.

I remembered a day that Mr. McGee had Jeffrey and I sit behind him so that he could watch us closely from his big mirror hanging down over his head. I couldn't understand why he watched Jeffrey and me so carefully when the other kids on the bus screamed and yelled at each other, too. I guess Jeffrey and I were fighting too much with each other and with the kids on the bus.

Jeffrey and I sat behind Mr. McGee for about a week while

he watched us through his big

mirror. Did Mr. McGee believe

that I would do something stupid

on the bus to get a whipping at

school and Daddy whipping me

later at home?

Jeffrey Dwayne & Larry Ray

One day, when Mr. McGee failed to watch me closely from

his mirror, two older boys gave me a small red firecracker and a

match. The older boys didn't say anything but smiled. Jeffrey and

I were sitting behind Mr. McGee, and he didn't see the older boys

give me the firecracker and a match. Wow, I was excited and

thinking; *I never had a firecracker. When I get home, I'm going to*

scare my sisters or Mr. Harry's hogs.

Suddenly, an evil thought came to me. I whispered in

Jeffrey's ears. "Hey, hold the firecracker in your right hand. When

the school bus starts moving, and the old man is not watching us,

I'm going to light it. Now don't forget Jeffrey, throw it under the

seat behind you, not to the front. You need to throw it fast from your hand because it could blow your fingers off. Daddy would kill me if you lost a finger."

I looked up slowly towards Mr. McGee to see if he was watching me in his mirror. I was wondering how the old man could watch me, the other kids, and drive the school bus at the same time. *Wow. The old man doesn't know what I plan to do in the next few minutes.*

After traveling a few miles on Big Plum Creek Road and getting close to Mr. Harry's old house, I said, "Jeffrey, remember when I light the firecracker, you don't throw it under Mr. McGee's seat. You need to throw it towards the back, not in front of you." I repeated it to Jeffrey several times to throw the firecracker under the seat behind him.

Jeffrey said, "Okay. I understand. I'm ready." Jeffrey held the firecracker in his right hand.

I lit the firecracker without any problems. I said, "Jeffrey don't hang on to the firecracker, it's burning, throw it under the seat behind you now. If you don't, it will blow your hand off."

Instead of throwing the firecracker behind him under the seat, Jeffrey threw it under Mr. McGee's seat. Before I could say,

57

"Jeffrey not towards the front," the firecracker landed under Mr. McGee's driver seat.

Wow. It was a loud explosion, like shooting my 20-gauge shotgun. It numbed my ears. Mr. McGee hit the brakes immediately, and the bus came to a squealing stop. I noticed some of the kids were flying towards the front of the bus.

After all the screaming and crying from the other kids stopped, Mr. McGee slowly got up from his seat. He looked at Jeffrey and me. Then I quickly looked at Jeffrey. I said, "What happened?"

Jeffrey reached down and picked up the burned match from the floor. It was stupid, and I thought, *Jeffrey, you shouldn't have pick-up the burned match from the floor.*

Mr. McGee saw Jeffrey with the burned match in his hand. Jeffrey started screaming out loud, "It wasn't me."

It was too late. Mr. McGee grabbed Jeffrey's hair and pulled him up from the seat. Jeffrey screamed for his life, saying, "It wasn't me that had the match! it wasn't me!" I looked at Jeffrey crying and begging the old school bus driver not to hit him. He needed to keep his mouth shut. I kept my mouth shut while Jeffrey

58

continued to scream. I was scared and thinking; *Mr. McGee is going to kill Jeffrey. Jeffrey is going to say it was me that gave him the firecracker. I will beat Jeffrey up if he said it was me.*

Mr. McGee pushed Jeffrey back down on the bus seat. The old bus driver was agitated; his head and hands were shaking. He told Jeffrey and me to get off the bus now. Lucky for me, the yellow school bus stopped in front of Mr. Harry's old house. Jeffrey and I jumped off the bus. We didn't have too far to walk.

I didn't mention what happened to Jeffrey on the school bus to Daddy or Momma. Neither did my little brother, or my sisters talked about how Jeffrey threw a firecracker under old Mr. McGee's seat. If Daddy and Momma found out what happened on the bus, I would beat my sisters up but not my little brother.

The next day, my school buddies told me Jeffrey was screaming in the Principal's Office when he got hit on the butt by the paddle– Jeffrey never mentioned who gave him the match and firecracker. He later told me in the school hallway that the Principal whipped him on the butt ten times with a wooden paddle. Jeffrey said, "Daddy whips a lot harder than the Principal did."

Wow. I was thinking; Jeffrey was at the school Principal's Office, getting a whipping (10 hits on the butt) for throwing a firecracker under Mr. McGee's seat. If he only didn't pick-up that burned match from the bus floor, it could have been me getting a whipping from the Principal.

I was proud of my brother for not telling the Principal who helped him light the firecracker and throw it under Mr. McGee's seat. When Daddy found out later from Debbie Jean what happened on the school bus, Jeffrey never mentioned it was me who gave him the firecracker. He told Daddy it was an older boy who gave him the firecracker and the match.

For the remainder of the school year, Jeffrey and I sat behind Mr. McGee on the bus ride to school.

Five Died at Childbirth and One an Accident at Home

Grandpa Ray Hardin &
Grandma Sara Ireland Hardin

Grandpa and Grandma Hardin had 17 kids at home. They were Southern Baptists and believed in having a large family to help out on the farm. Grandma had five babies who died at home during childbirth, and one little boy died in an accident. At age five, little Jimmie climbed up on a large white kitchen cabinet, reaching for a homemade pie when the cabinet fell on top of him. Several days later, little Jimmie died at home from internal bleeding. Grandpa and Grandma didn't know little Jimmie was bleeding inside from his injuries.

There is a list of Grandma's children in Hardin's family Bible. They are Ray Hardin Junior, my Daddy, (died at age 86), Susan Ellen (died at age 72), JT (died at age 84), Ruby, David, William (died at birth), Harold (died at birth), Anna Lee (died at birth), Joe Luis (died at age 56), Betty Jane, Nannie, Sara Lee (died at age 50), Earnest (died at birth), Ronald (died at age 53), Mary

Elizabeth (died at age 59), Jimmie (died at home age 5), and Hazel (died at birth).

Daddy said all of his brothers and sisters did not go further than first grade in school, except Mary Elizabeth. Daddy said, "I couldn't go to school because my dad needed me and my brothers and sisters to work in the corn and tobacco fields." Grandma also needed the girls to help at home. Mary Elizabeth did graduate from Taylorsville High School.

Black Mule Called Jack

Daddy said when he was age five, his dad (Grandpa Hardin) used a black mule named Jack to plow the corn and tobacco fields. He remembered Grandma, Susan, and he followed behind his dad to move rocks and broken tree roots plowed up by Jack. He told me, "Dad would whip Susan and me if we didn't move the rocks out of the fields. Mom never whipped us."

Old Jack worked from sunrise to sunset, plowing the fields. When the sun started to disappear, he was tired of working all day and wanted to go home to his stall to eat and rest. Daddy remembered old Jack would saunter when he and his dad followed old Jack.

He told me, "I guess old Jack was telling Dad he was tired, hungry, thirsty, and done working. He needed to get some rest and be ready to plow the next day in the fields." Susan followed closely behind Mom as she went home to get the wood stove ready to cook supper.

Once in the barn, Daddy explained, "My job was to get the water and feed for Old Jack. Before I finished taking care of old Jack, I saw Dad slowly walk out of the barn towards the house.

"Later, my sisters Susan, Ruby, and Betty Jane would help Mom when she was having more babies at home. And, when my sisters were not working in the fields, they were at home with Mom cleaning, washing, cooking, and getting well water to wash and drink."

Daddy told me, "My dad didn't have money to pay for someone to help him on the farm. Without hired help, he needed Mom, my brothers, sisters, and me to work in the corn and tobacco fields."

"I started to chew tobacco at age Five. Dad chewed, so I wanted to chew. I didn't see any of my sisters chew tobacco, but I wouldn't be surprised if they didn't try to chew," he explained.

Daddy was sure that Grandma chewed tobacco, but he never saw his mom spit on the ground or in the spit bucket.

The Smell of Cow Poop and Taste of Warm Milk

I visited my grandparents often on Ray White's farm on Big Plum Creek Road a few miles from Mr. Harry's old house. During the summer school break, Jeffrey and I would be helping Grandpa Hardin milk cows and push green poop out of the milk barn every day in the morning and evening. I was age eight, and Jeffrey was age seven when we started carrying milk buckets to the cooler and cleaning cows' poop.

I quickly learned that cows love to poop while Grandpa pulled on their big fat udders. Once, when Grandpa gripped the udders of one of the milk cows, he squirted warm milk on Jeffrey and me. Sometimes Jeffrey and I would be covered with warm milk and cow poop from our face down to our shoes. Heck, I even had warm milk and cow poop splattered on my eyes and inside my

64

mouth. Milk and cow poop were all over me; on my shoes, clothes, and face. Today, I guess that's why I like the smell of cow poop and the taste of warm milk.

Russel Smith was a farmer who lived on Big Plum Creek Road. Sometimes I helped him during the summer hauling hay and chasing his steers to the barn. He once said, "Don't worry about the warm cow poop on your mouth; it's green grass from the fields."

"Grass poop?" I asked.

"The cows only eat grass and some corn, but not meat," Russell told me.

Jeffrey and I loved Grandma's sausage and flour gravy, lard biscuits, and hog bacon she cooked for breakfast every morning on her wood-burning stove. Jeffrey and I didn't like shoveling cow poop, but we loved Grandma Hardin's old hard brown biscuits with home-made blackberry jam after returning late at night from coon hunting.

I remembered one morning Grandpa and Grandma were killing some chickens at the woodpile. Grandma was getting ready to cook fried chicken for supper. Jeffrey and I were watching

Grandpa pulling the heads off the chickens while Grandma pulled the feathers off. Grandpa said, "Boys pick up the chicken heads."

I told Grandpa, "Nope."

I turned around and started to run towards Uncle Ronald. I was going horse-back riding with Uncle Ronald. Wow! Grandpa quickly picked up a small chicken head and hit me on the back while I was running towards the horse. I hated picking up the chicken heads.

As a young boy and later as a teenager, throughout the summers, I worked for farmers on Big Plum Creek Road hauling hay, repairing fences, cutting tobacco, and cleaning out poop from cows and horse stalls, pig pens, and chicken houses. Cleaning out poop from Mr. Pop's chicken house and Carroll Ray's hog pens and horse stalls were the worst jobs I ever did while working on the farms.

Sometimes, I later helped out at RT Jennings' country grocery store on Big Plum Creek Road, cleaning up the store and putting grocery supplies on the shelves. I also earned a little extra money cutting grass for Mrs. Jennings. I didn't have to kiss Mrs. Jennings' anymore to get paid. I was too big for that.

Working on farms during the summers helped me earn enough money to buy a bike and a lot of Big Red soft drinks and bags of salted peanuts. When I reached age 16, I got my driver's license. Momma gave me her old black 4-door Chevy car. After earning gas money, I hit the roads with my brother Jeffrey and our buddies Joey, Russell, and Barry on Friday and Saturday nights to go to Taylorsville, looking for girls and drinking beers.

Once I started driving, Grandpa Hardin would ask me to take him to the doctor in Taylorsville for a medical checkup. One time, when Grandpa had his old late 1960's green Chevy pickup, he let me drive to the stockyards in Sheep-Town (Shepherdsville, Kentucky) with his hogs to sell to other hog farmers.

Grandpa was so scared of my driving, but he continued to ask me to take him to the doctor's office in Taylorsville and the stockyards in Shepherdsville. I'm not sure why he was afraid of my driving. Momma did say, "Larry Ray, you need to learn how to drive on the right side of the road." Grandma Hardin didn't seem to care about how I drove her to the doctors' office or the grocery store.

I always tried to stay out of trouble with the town cops in Taylorsville. Many times, while driving there, the town cops would stop me because they said I looked like a kid in the driver's seat. The cops would say, "Boy, you look under 16 years old. That's why I stopped you. Do you have any alcohol in your car?"

I said, "I don't think so."

But it didn't stop the cops from looking inside my car. Sometimes they would find moonshine and beer under the car seat. I always told the cops the moonshine and beer weren't mine.

The cop would tell me, "I have to take it. I'm not going to give you a ticket for having the beer and moonshine. But boy, don't you know you can't have beer in Spencer County? It's a dry county. Now tell me where you bought the moonshine?"

I said, "What moonshine?"

"Okay, this time I'll let you go."

I don't know why some of the town cops would stop me and ask for my drivers' license when they already knew I could drive legally. Maybe they just wanted my beer and moonshine. If some of the cops couldn't find any alcohol, they would give me a ticket for reckless driving or speeding on the main street. I asked them, "Can I pay the traffic ticket now?"

Sometimes, the cops let me pay in cash, whatever the amount I had on me. I never thought the Taylorsville cops were corrupt; it was normal for cops to make a little money and drink my beer and moonshine.

Killing on Thanksgiving Day

Grandpa Hardin and the rest of the family gathered on Ray White's farm out on Big Plum Creek Road every year on Thanksgiving Day to kill about five to eight hogs. Each member of the family had a job for processing the hog meat. For example, Uncle Bill would shoot a 22 long rifle bullet into the hog's skull, then Daddy would immediately cut the hog's throat to drain out the blood.

Once the blood was drained from the hog's body, Uncle

David would use a tractor to drag the hog to the hot tub. After a few minutes of

Grandpa Ray Hardin, Ray Hardin Jr., & JT Hardin. Back: David Hardin & Ronald Hardin

dipping the hog in the hot tub, our aunts and cousins, including me, would scrape the hairs off with a small knife. After removing the hog's hair, David or Ronald would hoist it up high, where Daddy would cut the meat into large sections. Uncle JT or Uncle Earl Warner would distribute the large sections of the hog meat to other family members to cut into smaller sections for sausages, pork chops, and ribs. The fat from the hog was used for cooking lard (fat grease).

This is Evil

In the late evenings after milking the cows and cleaning cows' poop from the barn, Jeffrey and I would follow Grandpa Hardin and Uncle Ronald into the woods with their two coon dogs.

70

Wow! I was going coon hunting. While the dogs chased a raccoon (coon), possum, fox, or any other animal through the woods, creeks, and fields, Grandpa and Ronald would stop walking and sit down on a tree log or whatever they could find and wait for the dogs to stop hunting.

Grandpa, with his old gas lantern next to him, would reach in his small white tobacco pouch and whatever paper he could find, roll up a cigarette and begin telling us about evil ghosts wandering through the woods or at the Robinson's family 19th-century graveyard that was on the farm. When we returned home late at night, after eating some of Grandma's cold hard biscuits and home-made blackberry jam, Jeffrey and I would be in the chicken feather bed before Ronald jumped into bed.

Just as I was falling asleep, Ronald would say, "You want to hear some ghost stories about the graveyard (old Robinson family cemetery)?" I said, "No."

After a few ghost stories, Ronald would fall asleep, and Jeffrey and I would begin to hear strange noises, like someone walking around upstairs in the old logged house.

71

There was one night when I was age 16, Uncle Ronald asked us, "When I get up in the morning do you and Jeffrey want to help me dig up one of the graves in the Robinson family cemetery to find bones and artifacts?"

I said, "Yes."

Jeffrey said, "No."

Ronald went to sleep, leaving the oil lamp burning all night next to the bed. I guess Ronald was scared of his own ghost stories.

Grandpa and Grandma Hardin's Home

The next day at the Robinson's family cemetery, Ronald was using a shovel to dig up dirt from an unknown grave. I was laughing and thinking; *Uncle Ronald is like a fat groundhog, throwing dirt out from the grave everywhere.*

"Wow!" I said out loud, "Hey Ronald, are you going to find some really old bones and stuff in the grave?"

Ronald had dug about two feet down into the grave when I noticed a white marble tombstone lying flat on the ground next to

72

the hoe. I wasn't able to read the inscription on the tombstone. I started to dig next to Ronald, and then I heard Grandpa yelling at us, "Stop digging and leave the grave alone."

Ronald and I immediately stopped digging. I looked up from the grave and saw Grandpa walking toward me. Grandpa pushed the dirt back into the grave, and I took off running because I knew Grandpa was a good rock thrower.

Grandpa was mad at me for the rest of the day.

Later that night in bed, I heard someone slowly coming downstairs, walking as if they were tiptoeing. Our bed was under the stairs, and I was wondering; *Aunt Sara Lee or Aunt Mary Elizabeth are probably going to the kitchen to get a drink from the water bucket or eat something off the table. But why are they tiptoeing?*

Then, I sensed someone walking up to the bed. I pretended to be asleep. I started to feel heat all over my body. The heat was not burning my skin; it was burning me inside my body. I was praying and telling myself, *What is happing to me? Something deep inside of me is telling me not to open my eyes.*

73

In a strange, unrecognizable crying voice with a lot of pain, the voice whispered, "Larry, please open your eyes; it's Sara."

I suddenly heard an inner voice saying, *"Don't open your eyes."*

I questioned myself; Could it be Sara Lee? But why aren't Ronald and Jeffrey not hearing the crying voice and feeling the heat?

I refused to open my eyes to see who it was.

The crying voice said, "Larry, you have something in your ear."

Wow! That someone is touching my ear.

I immediately reached up and touched my ear. *Now, whoever Sara is, she knows I'm awake.*

Suddenly, Sara moved close to my face and said, "Larry, this is Sara, please wake up."

Wow. The heat from Sara felt hotter than the sun, yet it was not burning my skin. I believed it was an evil spirit named Sara. I just kept praying and thinking; I don't want to open my eyes and see the evil spirit.

The heat was getting so bad, but it didn't burn me. Sara continued begging and crying for me to open my eyes. With God's blessing, I didn't open them.

Then, I heard Grandpa's alarm clock waking him up to go to the milk barn. Whatever it was next to my bed, it moved away quickly and ran upstairs. I no longer felt the burning heat. I tumbled out of bed and ran to my Grandparent's bedroom. I tried telling Grandpa and Grandma what just happened, but Grandpa didn't want to hear it.

Grandpa said, "I've got to get up and go milk those cows."

Grandma went to the kitchen to start making breakfast.

After helping Grandpa milk the cows and clean the poop off the floor, I had a strong feeling to walk up to the graveyard behind the milk barn before going in to eat breakfast. At the gravesite, I looked at the hoe on the ground where Ronald left it. Something was telling me to pick up the white marble tombstone next to the grave and read the inscription.

I was scared and thinking; What happened last night? What am I going to see on the other side of the tombstone? I'm afraid.

With a lot of effort, I raised the marble tombstone upright from the ground. Now, I could read the words. Sara Robinson died in 1863. Is that the same Sara who was crying and telling me to open my eyes last night?

I dropped the marble tombstone on the ground and ran back to the old farmhouse. I never stayed all night at Grandpa's home again.

I believed Grandpa knew I met an evil spirit that night. I was wondering; I'll bet that's why Ronald left the oil lamp burning all night. It happened to him. He heard the Devil.

When I did visit my grandparents throughout the years, I felt an evil spirit watching me. My grandparents lived in that farmhouse for almost 20 years.

A Gun Pointed at Me

I was about age 19 old when my buddy Joey Conniff and I met a girl at the public park sitting at a picnic table by herself. *Wow, she's not so beautiful, she's a little heavy around the waist, but she has big breasts!*

I yelled at her, "Do you want to join us? We're just riding around drinking beer."

"Sure!" She said, laughing.

Joey moved quickly into the backseat and did not say a word as she jumped in the front seat.

We talked and joked around in the car for a while. I didn't even kiss her or touch her breasts. Later that night, when I was taking her home, she told me, "I don't want to go home. I want to stay with you."

I said, "No. I have to go home."

I pulled up to the house, and her parents, Little Judy and Big Clarence, were standing in the driveway. Little Judy, about 4 feet tall and 110 pounds, had a small handgun, pointed at me.

I told the girl, "Your mom has a gun. Why does she have a gun pointed at me?"

The girl started crying, saying, "I'm afraid. I don't want to stay. I want to go with you."

She didn't want to get out of the car, and I refused to pull further into the driveway. I said, "You need to get out of the car now!"

77

I tried to leave, but her mom jumped in front of the car and her dad in the back to block me from moving. *Strange, Joey is in the back seat, not saying a word.*

I told the girl, "Get out of the car! Your mom has a gun, and she's upset."

She wanted to leave with me. "Hey Joey, tell her to get out of the car." Joey was in the back seat, afraid to say anything.

I said to her, "Are you kidding? Your mom has a gun in her hand, and she's going to kill me! What's going on? Why does she want to shoot me? Did you run away from home?"

She wouldn't answer me.

Then I started thinking about it and asked her, "How old are you?"

"I'm 13," she admitted.

"What? Please get out of my car!"

Joey finally yelled, "Get out of the car now!"

The girl's mom screamed louder, waving the gun above her head, "Boy, you get out of that car now!"

I hesitated and then heard a loud gunshot. I panicked and screamed, "Don't shoot me." I slowly opened the car door and

78

jumped out. I raised my hands and handed the car keys over to the girl's dad, Big Clarence. I quickly noticed that Big Clarence was about 6'5" in height, no hair on his head, and weighed 350 pounds.

Little Judy shouted, "Boy, get into the house now!"

Big Clarence shouted, "You heard her boy. Get into the house!"

I yelled at Joey, "The big guy is really angry."

When Big Clarence started walking toward me, I ran, jumped up onto the front porch, over the doorsteps, and entered the living room. I saw Joey sitting alone on a red couch, not saying a word. I didn't even notice him get out of the car. *Boy, Joey was fast.*

I was followed closely into the house by the girl with her mom and dad. I sat on the red couch next to the front door and watched Little Judy pistol-whip her daughter, hitting her on the head. Joey was still quiet. I asked myself; *If she starts to shoot me, is Joey going to run out the front door or out the window to get help?*

Then Little Judy turned to me and pointed her gun at my face, "Boy, did you rape my 13-year old daughter?"

Little Judy didn't say anything to Joey.

79

Big Clarence shouted, "Yep, you did my daughter, boy."

I yelled out, "No, I did not!"

Again, Joey didn't say anything and didn't try to defend me. I immediately thought; *Joey is getting ready to jump up and run like a buck deer.*

Little Judy yelled at me, "Boy, you're going to die tonight!"

She pointed her handgun, which looked like a small .22 automatic, at my face. I knew from my country boy experience in hunting that a small-caliber bullet might bounce off the couch pillow and miss my face. So, I raised the small couch pillow slowly in my arms and held it near my chest, praying I made the right decision.

Little Judy turned and told Joey, "It's time for you to leave. Get out of here, now."

Joey moved quickly out the front door, like a rabbit about to be shot in the butt. He left without saying goodbye or anything.

Finally, Little Judy told her husband, "Take this one outside and beat the shit out of him."

I looked up at Big Clarence and said with excitement, "Yes sir, let's go outside!"

80

I knew I had a better chance outside to run from Big Clarence. I already knew Joey wasn't going to help. He was probably hiding behind a tree or running to his home several miles away.

I immediately jumped off the couch and hit the front door like a fox squirrel jumping into a tree hole, followed closely by Big Clarence. I would have to run to my car, hopefully outrunning Big Clarence, except he had my car keys.

When I got outside, I waited for Big Clarence to pummel me. Instead, he threw my car keys on the ground and yelled, "Get the hell out of here, boy!"

I grabbed the keys off the ground, jumped into the car, gave Big Clarence my middle finger, and never looked back.

I suddenly heard something moving in the back seat of my car. I was thinking to myself; *Please, it can't be that girl running away from her mom.* I looked in the back seat and saw that Joey was lying down, hiding on the floor in the back of my car.

I almost got killed for not getting a kiss from that girl! She had the body of an older woman, but not the mind. I thanked God for saving me again.

Suddenly I remembered; A time to be born and a time to die. (Ecclesiastics 3:2 New International Version).

Wow, I am still alive

.

He Would Kill Me

On one occasion, my two sisters, Debbie Jean and Linda Lou were playing in the all-girls church softball game at the old High School ballpark in Taylorsville. I was at the softball game with my latest girlfriend, Bobbie Lee. Bobbie Lee was very pretty with a great figure. Bobbie Lee had long beautiful black hair down to her butt. She had dark brown skin and big brown eyes.

I asked Bobbie Lee, "Do you want to get naked and run across the ballpark with me?" I was wishing and thinking; *I really want to see Bobbie Lee naked.*

She laughed and said, "Are you serious? My dad is the Taylorsville town cop, and he would kill me if he saw me naked with you. Dad knows you're a Hardin boy. My dad says he stops you a lot in town for having beer and moonshine in your car."

I told her, "Your dad is one of the cops that takes my beer and moonshine. Does your dad drink alcohol?"

82

"Yes."

"Do you still want to get naked?"

"No!" she said.

"How about later in the car?"

She smiled and hugged me.

I really wanted to run naked across the ballpark with Bobbie Lee. I just wanted to do it as a prank. I saw a tall, skinny guy with a long mustache drooping down over the corners of his lips, and blond hair down to his shoulders standing next to me. He is smiling at me, and I was thinking, *That long-haired guy heard me talking to Bobbie Lee about running across the ballpark naked.*

I asked him, "What are you smiling at, buddy?"

He said, "I'm watching your sister Linda Lou playing softball."

"Hey, do you want to get naked and run across the ballpark with me?"

He laughed and said, "Yea! Let's do it."

I asked, "What is your name, buddy?"

"Jimmy Curtsinger."

Two days later, Bobbie Lee's dad and another cop arrested me at home. The cops told Momma, "Your son Larry Ray needs to come with us to Taylorville. Larry is being arrested for running naked at a girl's church softball game. The judge is charging Larry with indecent behavior."

Momma asked, "Are you sure it's not my other son Jeffrey?"

"No," the cops said.

Wow, I thought; My first arrest for running naked at a girls' softball game.

Later that day, Daddy talked to Taylorsville Judge Keiling about my arrest. He told Daddy, "Junior, I didn't know he was your son. Go get your son out of jail."

A few days later, at the County Court House, Judge Keiling said, "Hardin, why did you and the other boy run naked at the girl's church softball game?"

"I'm sorry, Judge Keiling. I didn't know it was a church softball game. I just wanted my girlfriend and me to have some fun."

The judge said, "Who is your girlfriend."

I said, "I don't remember her name.

84

The judge dropped the charge for indecent behavior but fined me $60. I paid in cash. Jimmy stayed in jail for two days because the cops found some marijuana hidden under his car seat.

Jimmy later married Linda Lou. I always wondered if Linda Lou married Jimmy because she saw him run naked across the park. Jimmy died a few years later at age 23 from an accident at work. Daddy was with him at work when Jimmy got hurt. Linda Lou was left to raise their two girls alone.

There is a Rat in the Ceiling

I decided to quit the farm life after shoveling too much cow, hog, chicken, and horse poop for Mr. Pops and Carrol Ray. All that horse poop had a smell worse than a three-day-old dead animal. I told Carrol Ray's son, Peanuts, "No more cleaning horse poop. I'm out of here!"

I dropped the pitchfork and never looked back to shoveling poop again. I guess. Peanuts kept on cleaning the horse poop.

Later, my Uncle, Larry Dale Hardin, found me a job at a Texaco gas station off Interstate 245 near Louisville, Kentucky. Larry Dale was married to Daddy's sister Sara Lee. I always

thought of Aunt Sara Lee as a gentle and kind person that loved her husband, children, and grandchildren. She was one of my favorite aunts.

Mr. Phillips, the manager of the gas station, didn't want to hire me

Long hair and a smile

because my hair was down to the crack of my butt, and I looked like a hippie who smoked a lot of marijuana. He needed someone to start working now, so he hired me. I was never able to assure Mr. Phillips that I wasn't a hippie, but I didn't smoke weed.

I started my short career at the Texaco gas station – pumping gas, changing oil, repairing tires, and cleaning windshields for customers. I wore my new green uniform with a big red star on the front of my shirt. I'll always remember the Texaco gas station's motto, "Trust the man who wears the red star."

I also remembered all the marijuana and sex that was available from customers while pumping gas. Mostly older married

86

women wanted to have sex at the gas station or the motel behind the station. The younger girls sometimes would offer to have sex in exchange for gas. Some of the girls were married with small children inside the car.

I told Daddy I would have felt guilty if I'd had sex with a married woman because I was concerned for her husband. I pledged to myself, not to have sex with married women, only single women at the gas station. Maybe it was my long hair and smile that attracted the women, or maybe it was the free gas. Heck, I had gay men trying to pick me up for free gas, but I stayed away from them.

One day, one of my gas station co-workers drilled a hole the size of a penny in the ceiling of the women's bathroom. He liked to watch the women through the peephole as they sat on the toilet seat to clean their butt. How sick!

When I was working alone one day, a slim young girl with black hair asked me to fill up her car with gas. She asked, "Where is the restroom?"

I pointed to it near the office.

Something evil popped into my mind. I decided to go to the attic and crawl over to take a look through the peephole. I wanted

87

to see why the co-worker enjoyed watching women pee or take a poop. Wow! I saw the young girl sitting there on the toilet seat. Suddenly, I moved my leg because of a muscle cramp and made a noise. The girl slowly looked up at the ceiling. She stared up at the small hole in the ceiling. Without a doubt, she was focusing like a bird dog on the hole. I slowly pulled my eyeball back away from the peephole and immediately thought, *Did she see my huge blue eyeball looking through the small hole?*

As the girl quickly reached for the toilet paper, I panicked and crawled out of the attic and ran through the office and out to the gas pump as if nothing happened. When the girl was walking quickly to her car, she was freaking out. She nervously said, "I heard something in the ceiling in the women's bathroom! There is a small hole in the ceiling."

I asked her, "Did you see anything?"

She said, "No."

I told her, "There are rats in the ceiling. I'll tell my boss about it."

After paying for the gas, the young girl jumped into her car and left.

88

That was lucky for me. Mr. Phillips eventually caught the employee who drilled the peephole. No one ever knew I once took a look through the peephole, except God.

"If we confess our sins, God is faithful and just and will forgive us our sins and purify us from all unrighteousness" (1 John 1:9).

They're Going to Shoot me in the Back

After a few months of pumping gas, I was working alone at the Texaco gas station on the night shift for the first time. Before leaving the gas station, Mr. Phillips told me, "If someone tries to rob you tonight or any other night, don't go into the back office. If you do, the robber will kill you. Stay out in the open area where the gas pumps are so other customers can see you being robbed, especially if law enforcement is driving by the station. The robber won't shoot you out in the open."

It was a hot summer night, and I was busy pumping gas for a lot of customers. I didn't have time to put the cash away in the office safe. Also, I was repairing a flat tire for a customer inside the garage.

89

Suddenly an inner voice told me to take the cash out of my right pocket and hide it in my sock. Without thinking any more about it, I put the money in my left sock.

I was relaxed and thinking; Now it's getting late, and I can repair the customer's flat tire before closing.

Within minutes, a gray four-door Mercury with two young scruffy-looking men pulled up next to the gas pump. As I quickly walked out toward the car, I watched the driver get out of the car and look around. Without saying a word to me, he walked right into the front office. Then he went into the garage and saw the customer standing next to the flat tire. The customer was clueless about what was happening. He was only concerned for me to return to repair his flat tire.

The passenger suddenly poked me in the back and whispered in my right ear, "Don't move, or I will kill you mother f----."

I said, "What are you doing?"

He poked me again and said, "Just shut up!"

Then he slapped me in the face and told me to go into the office where the driver was waiting.

90

I remembered what my boss told me earlier that day; They will kill you once you are in the back office.

I suddenly told the passenger, "No! There are cops everywhere driving around here."

He slapped me again hard on the face and moved his hands quickly down my legs where he found the cash hidden inside my left sock. I was surprised and thinking; *How did he know the money was in my sock?*

The driver then came out of the station. He and the passenger both grabbed my waist and arms, forcing me to go with them inside the office.

I yelled at them again, "Man! Some cops and customers might see you guys robbing me."

The driver let go of my arm and walked over to shut the hood of the car. He then jumped in behind the wheel. At that moment, I was in a dream-like state and thought; *He is going to shoot me in the back and leave me crawling on the ground, fighting for my life.*

The passenger let go of my other arm and turned around with his small black revolver in his right hand. I was angrily

91

thinking; *Here's a chance to wallop this guy on the head and maybe get his gun. But I couldn't move my body. It felt as if someone was helping me not to fight back.*

The passenger pushed the black revolver into the front waist of his pants and hopped into the passenger seat. The robbers took off and left me standing there, watching them driving slowly down the road. The customer inside the gas station yelled, "Are you okay."

I said, "Yep, I'm okay. Thanks."

I was freaking out. I was still alive and not shot in the back!

Immediately, I called the police, and within minutes, two state troopers arrived at the station. I gave them a description of the robbers and their car. I told the cops, "Two young scruffy-looking men took the money I had hidden in my sock. One of the robbers had a gun pointed in my back and was hitting me in the face with his hand. I thought I was going to get shot in the back. But I was not going to die."

The state trooper said, "These are the same robbers who raped a woman inside her car tonight at the shopping mall where she worked. Those guys stole the woman's car and then came over here to the gas station to rob you. She's lucky to be alive! So, are you!"

As I was talking to the state trooper, the customer fixed his own flat tire and drove slowly away from the station without saying goodbye and paying for the service.

I'm so glad I put the money in my sock! God knew this was not the time for me to die. I needed to listen and trust in the Lord. Again, I thought; *A time to be born and a time to die. Today I didn't die. But when and how?*

I quit my job at the gas station. That was the end of my gas-pumping career and wearing my green uniform with the red star.

"Jesus replied: 'Love the LORD your God with all your heart and with all your soul and with all your mind.' This is the first and greatest commandment. And the second is: 'Love your neighbor as yourself." All the Law and the Prophets hang on these two commandments'" (Matthew 22:37-40, New American Version).

Watch Her with Other Men Around

After leaving the gas station career, I found a job at the local hospital working as a surgical orderly and later in the maintenance department. Once again, I saw so much marijuana and sex from the women at the hospital that was readily available during and after work.

I was confused about why some of my co-workers would smoke weed in the hospital. Sex was not a problem with some of the nurses and me, but some of the girls were smoking weed. It was crazy!

I had five nurses and nurses' aides to date at any one time. When I wanted a date, I would call one of them to find out who was available to go dancing and drinking beer after work. I couldn't handle more than five women. I wasn't able to save any money after all that partying.

My favorite girlfriend was a redhead named Rose. She had long red hair. She was a little fat but had a beautiful smile and laughed about everything I said. Rose loved drinking beer and eating catfish. Rose was engaged to get married, but that never

94

stopped her going out with me when her fiancée was traveling out of town on business.

After a couple of years working in the hospital, I found a girl named Sue. She was attractive and had a good heart. On our first date, she told me, "I am waiting for marriage to have sex." Sue gave me the impression she was a virgin.

Sue played the piano at a Southern Baptist church, where her parents were very active members. I thought; *Sue is a virgin, goes to church, and is a nurse. I have found my true love.*

Wow! A few days later, I was sitting on a brown sofa with Sue while at her parents were in the kitchen. She laid down on the couch and pulled up her dress. She was not wearing any panties. Immediately, I jumped on her like a red fox entering a big hole. We were alone making out on the couch. Incredible, Sue was talking to her mom and dad, who were in the kitchen while I was making a lot of noises on the couch. Later, I was upset and thought; *Sue wanted to wait for marriage to have sex. She has done this before. Wow. I was wrong to think she was a virgin.*

After Daddy and Momma met Sue, Daddy told me, "The girl is no good for you. She's not ready for marriage."

95

Momma didn't like Sue either.

Daddy told me, "Watch her with other men around. When you drop her off at her parents' house, go back and see what happens."

I asked myself; Why would Daddy and Momma say that about Sue? They don't even know her.

I refused to listen to the wisdom of my parents until one hot summer night, my future wife wanted to go home early. After we had sex at the ballpark behind a tree, and later in the back seat of my white Chevy car, Sue said, "I am a little tired. I want to go home."

I dropped her off at her parents' home. Then I drove away from her house. After driving for several miles, I started thinking; *She was acting a little strange tonight. She didn't look sick. What was it Daddy said a few days ago about Sue?*

I suddenly turned my car around and returned to her parents' house. Before I pulled up into her parents' driveway, I saw my future bride, hugging and kissing a guy on the front porch. I said to myself; *That guy goes to the same church where Sue and her parents go. The guy must have been waiting inside her parents'*

96

house when I dropped Sue off. Where did he park his car? I couldn't believe what Sue was doing with that guy on the front porch.

It was already dark, and the front porch lights were on. I could see Sue clearly. How stupid they were! I was disappointed and thinking; *This is not the first time she cheated on me. Daddy and Momma were right about Sue not being faithful.*

I drove up into the driveway and slowly got out of my car and walked to the front porch. As I approached the front porch, I was about to step up on the porch to slap the guy in the face, but instead, I almost hit Sue in the mouth. She jumped off the porch into my arms and bit me on the chest. I stared into her big brown eyes while she was biting hard on my chest. I felt no pain from her biting me.

Sue finally stopped biting me, and I pushed her away. I turned around and walked back to my car. Without looking back at Sue, I got in the car and drove away. As I was driving home, I started crying and swearing to myself that I would never let other women make a fool of me again. I had given up all my girlfriends at the hospital for Sue. I was sadly thinking; *I was ready to settle down and have a family with Sue. I should have listened to Daddy*

and Momma.

I never saw Sue again.

Right then, I gave up on ever finding my true love.

I drove down to the property on Big Plum Creek Road that I purchased from Mr. Pops. I had planned to build a home with Sue and raise our two children. I sat in my car and cried all night until the next day. Early the next morning, Daddy came to the property in his Chevy pickup truck looking for me. I said, "Daddy, you were right about Sue. She made me feel like a fool last night."

Daddy said, "Come on home when you're ready."

I questioned myself; What am I going to do now?

"Trust in the LORD with all your heart and lean not on your own understanding; in all your ways acknowledge him, and he will make your paths straight" (Proverbs 3:5-6)

The Dying Man's Face

After a few months, I was lying in bed at home, thinking about what I wanted to do with the rest of my life. I wanted to travel and see the world. My little brother joined the Navy at seventeen

98

and traveled a lot. *Maybe I'll join the Navy and travel the world like my little brother.*

Suddenly, I found myself walking up a rocky hill. There were no trees and bushes. It felt like daytime, yet I looked up, and the sky was almost dark. In front of me, I saw a square wooden pole with the feet of someone nailed to it.

Then, I saw what appeared to be three men dressed in strange clothes with swords and one with a spear. *This is a dream;* I was thinking. The legs of the man hanging on the wooden pole had deep cuts, but the blood was dried. *These three men are killing someone.*

Immediately, I glanced around, and a lady and young man were standing near the pole. They looked at me with sadness in their faces. The young man is holding the lady, and they were not crying. I noticed they had dark eyes and brown skin. They were wearing dark robes, and the lady had a dark scarf over her head.

I turned around and faced the wooden pole and reached up to touch it. I wasn't sure, but I saw one of the three men quickly raise his spear. Something terrible just happened. Standing next to the wooden pole, I saw reddish water running down onto my arm.

99

Then some of the water splattered on my head and face. The reddish water was coming from the man on the wooden pole. I screamed, "Please, someone help him."

Then I looked at the man's feet, his legs, and body. His body was marked with dried red bloody strips. I wanted to see the man's face.

When I looked up towards his face on the wooden pole, a bright light blinded me. Immediately, the intense light from the man's face knocked me to the ground, and I ended up on my knees. I was confused and thinking; *The man's face is like the sun, but brighter. The light from his face is bright and peaceful.*

Who is this man on the wooden pole?

After a few seconds with my knees on the ground, I got up slowly and walked away. I felt so ashamed to look back at the man on the wooden pole. As I walked down the hill, *I heard the man's voice from the wooden pole telling me what I need to do for the rest of my life. In a gentle voice, Jesus said, "Be my disciple."*

I walked away without helping Jesus. But, I realized Jesus was not dead; Jesus is alive, and HE was helping me not to walk the path of the devil but believe in HIM.

100

Suddenly I said out loud: "Is this a dream?"

After several days, I went down to Little Plum Creek Baptist Church to tell the Preacher about my dream and seeing Jesus Christ alive on the cross. The Preacher was our family spiritual guide as we struggled with our faith after losing Jimmy and Doodle Bug.

I said to the Preacher, "Jesus did not die on a wooden pole. Jesus is alive. Our Lord Jesus said, "I am the light of the world; he that follows me should not walk in darkness but should have the light of life."

The Preacher told me, "It's not a dream. You had a vision."

I asked him, "Can you baptize me in the creek under the Waterford Creek bridge?"

On a Sunday afternoon, I was baptized, dipped into the

Plum Creek

Little Plum Creek water by the Preacher, and witnessed by some of the members of Little Plum Creek Baptist Church. I was age 23.

After a few months, I quit my job at the hospital and enlisted in the Navy. I needed a change in my life, a different direction to travel. I needed to trust in the Lord and fight my greatest enemy: Myself.

After Daddy died on February 4, 2018, my cousin, Glenn, said, "When you were in the military, your dad was baptized at Little Plum Creek Baptist Church." Daddy never told me he had been baptized.

Little Plum Creek Baptist Church

"When I was a child, I used to speak like a child, think like a child, reasoned like a child; when I became a man, I did away with childish things" (1 Corinthians 13:11 New American Standard Version).

My Career

I Will Find You and Cut your Throat

I joined the Navy at age 25. It was difficult to leave Daddy and Momma. Before leaving home, Daddy said, "There will be a

lot of water under Big Plum Creek Road bridge until you come home again."

I said, "Daddy, it's only four years in the Navy."

In the Navy, I worked as a Religious Program Specialist assigned to the Chaplain's Office with the Seabees, Battalion 5.

While stationed in Rota, Spain, with the Seabees, I met a beautiful Spanish woman with dark skin and olive eyes. Her name was Kathy.

Later, I met Kathy's father at her oldest sister's (Toni) home in Puerto Real, Cadiz. At the dining table, Toni gave me a bowl of garbanzo beans with a large long round piece of dark red meat. I was thinking out loud; *That is a big piece of red meat.* Kathy's dad was sitting at the table, watching me very closely. I guess this was her dad's first-time eating garbanzo beans with an American. Kathy's dad was Senior Pedro, a retired Guardia Civil, and served in Franco's military Spanish war. Kathy's mom died before I met Kathy.

I started to eat the garbanzo beans when her nephew, George (Jorge), speaking good English, said to me, "The meat in the bowl is a bull Picha."

"What is a Picha?" I asked politely.

Then George whispered to me in English what his Grandpa (Senior Pedro) was saying in Spanish, "It's a bull's dick." I said to myself, *I remembered hearing something during military training about the culture and customs of Spain, and when the bull is killed in the bullring, the Spanish people would eat it. Also, if you get invited to a Spanish family home to eat, be sure to eat everything on your plate. Okay. I am going to eat Picha.*

Senior Pedro kept looking at me, not saying a word while I was chewing the massive long round dark red meat.

Everyone was watching me at the dining table as I finished eating. Well, I ate all the meat and garbanzo. It was delicious, even knowing that the meat was a bull's dick. After eating the Picha, George said, "It's chorizo (a dark red sausage), not a bull's Picha."

Senior Pedro had a good laugh about it.

Kathy and I became good friends after six months of just talking about life and family, and most of the time, Kathy's sisters were hanging out with us. At one point, I asked her, "Do you want to walk on the beach?"

Kathy said, "Yes, laughing."

Wow, for the first time after six months, Kathy and I finally are walking on the beach alone in Rota, Spain, and holding hands. I was excited and thinking; *I am on the beach without Kathy's sisters or nephews watching. This is great.*

Later, at a nice restaurant, I told Kathy to close her eyes, I had a surprise for her. When she closed her eyes, I softly kissed her for the first time. Kathy quickly opened her eyes and didn't say a word.

Three months later, I asked her, "Do you want to get married?"

She started laughing.

I said, "What is so funny?"

105

Then, she said, "Yes."

Riding Pepper the Spanish
Bull in Rota, Spain

While on the military base in Rota, I joined the Rodeo to ride the bulls; sometimes, the bulls would ride me. These were the bulls who never made it to the big Spanish Bull Ring; instead, some of them went to the Rodeo. After a few bad rides and getting the horn in my butt, I promised Kathy I would stop pretending to be a Kentucky cowboy. Back home on Big Plum Creek Road, it was easier for me to ride hogs.

Pepper almost riding Larry Ray

Before Kathy and I got married, I was selected to attend training for six weeks with the Marine Corps at Camp Lejeune.

With the marines, I felt like I was back home on Big Plum Creek Road, walking up and down the hills, crossing the creeks, camping all night in the woods, carrying my gun, and looking for

106

targets to shoot. I became an expert rifleman. After finishing the Marine Corps training, I returned to Rota to get married.

Later, when I met with her father, Senior Pedro, again, I gave Senior Pedro an American smoked ham, a case of American Budweiser beer, and grey boxer underwear as a gift from his future son-in-law. I don't think Senior Pedro liked the boxer underwear.

I tried to tell Senior Pedro, in Spanish, that I wanted to marry his daughter. I think Senior Pedro already knew that because of the gifts.

After the wedding, Senior Pedro walked up and looked me in the eyes and smiled. *Wow!* I remembered his eyes were so black. Senior Pedro pointed his finger at his head and made a circular motion several times while speaking Spanish. Of course, I could understand some Spanish, but not Andalusia.

"What is Senior Pedro trying to say?" I asked George, my future wife's nephew.

My Grandpa is asking you, "Why did you want to marry Kathy?"

Then, her father moved very close within inches from my face and looked directly into my blue eyes for a few long seconds without saying a word. He then moved his finger slowly across his throat. Senior Pedro was no longer smiling. He was saying something else to George, while he still looked directly at me.

George immediately translated for me, "If you ever hurt or mistreat Kathy, my Grandpa will find you and cut your throat."

I was wondering; Senior Pedro is going to be my father-in-law? What am I getting into?

Then, Senior Pedro asked me for his box of Cuban cigars. *Wow, I forgot to get the cigars.*

George said, "It's too late; you can't run from my Grandpa."

I slowly moved away from Senior Pedro.

Within a few minutes, Kathy's aunts Concha, Nena, and Antonia were trying to say something to me about how to treat Kathy on our honeymoon night.

Once again, George translated, "Her aunts are telling you to be gentle and not be a wolf with their niece on your wedding night. Don't hurt Kathy."

I said, "Okay," and the aunts all smiled.

Dancing the Spanish Flamenco
Larry Ray and Kathy,
San Fernando, Spain

In Puerto Real, Spain, I married a Spanish woman, a flamenco dancer, and a great cook. I also married her family. I always had girlfriends but not a woman friend. Kathy is my best friend and true love. My Spanish woman.

"Man shall leave his father and his mother and be joined to his wife; and they shall become one flesh." (Geneses 2:24 New American Standard Version).

You Need to Become a U.S. Citizen

After we got married, I was transferred to the Marine Corps Air Station (MCAS) in Yuma, Arizona. Once I arrived in Yuma, we decided not to have any children right away. I was not sure if she wanted to live so far away from her family in Spain and in America. I sure didn't want children if we got a divorce.

Also, Momma always told me, "Larry Ray, you might not be able to have children. You had the mumps as a child. The mumps

109

could have affected your 'Marbles' (testicles). It makes your sperm lazy."

Later, I told a Doctor in Yuma what my Momma said about mumps. The Doctor explained that mumps could cause the sperm to become weak, unable to travel up to the home sweet home. The sperm needed a little help to push it to reach the *target* to get a woman pregnant. I didn't mention to her about the mumps until years later.

I told Kathy to focus on her dream of getting a college degree. Kathy wanted to start working and go to college. About two years later, she received her college degree as an honor student with a 4.0-grade average.

She said, "Now I want to be an Officer in the U.S. Navy."

I told her, "You will need to become a U.S. citizen. Then, you might have a chance to be a Naval Officer someday."

Before I was honorably discharged from the U.S. Navy, I received a college degree and two Masters' degrees while in the military at MCAS in Yuma; an AA, BS, and two MAs. I served six years and four months, mostly in the Marine Corps, receiving several Navy and Marine Corps medals and awards.

Kathy and I moved to San Diego to stay with her sister, Toni, while we looked for a job in California. This was when Kathy got her U.S. citizenship in Phoenix, Arizona.

After She Became a U.S. Citizen

After Kathy became a U.S. citizen, she got a job with the Department of Defense as a Special Agent in San Diego, conducting background security clearances for the military and defense contractors that required a clearance. Later, she was accepted into the United States Navy Reserve as a Line Officer, Ensign. Less than five years later, she became a U.S citizen and a Naval Officer.

Throughout Kathy's Naval Reserve career, she was assigned most of her time to the Naval Base in Rota, Spain, at the Naval Criminal Investigations Service (NCIS) as an Intelligence Officer.

Kathy's first criminal case with NCIS was a rape investigation in Rota, Spain. NCIS had information from the local Spanish cops that an American enlisted sailor was raping Spanish girls in Rota. NCIS agents were unable to get the raped victims to testify against the American Sailor. The victims wanted not to be known in the Spanish communities where an enlisted American sailor raped the girls.

NCIS agents knew that Kathy was from Spain, and she had worked with the Spanish military in Rota. The NCIS agents asked Kathy to interview the raped victims and their families. After she talked to the victims and their families, the girls agreed to identify the rapist. The rapist, an American sailor, was convicted and sentenced to the military prison in the United States. Kathy was so pleased that she was able to help get a rapist convicted and justice for the Spanish girls in her first NCIS criminal case.

After 27 years of service, she retired as a Naval Officer Lieutenant Commander.

I am a Cherokee Indian from Kentucky

When I left the military, there were no cell phones, pagers, or the Internet. Cities had telephone books with white pages that listed names and businesses alphabetically, and the yellow pages had the businesses listed by category. Because of my previous employment with the military, I decided to look through the San Diego county telephone yellow pages for law enforcement telephone numbers. I called the Secret Service in San Diego to see if they were hiring.

Within the next several weeks, I met with a Secret Service agent at his office downtown San Diego at the Federal Building. I explained to the Secret Service agent my education degrees and work experience while in the Navy and Marine Corps. I told the agent, "My wife is from Spain; she has a college degree and is a U.S. citizen."

The agent said, "Is your wife looking for a job in the Federal Government."

I nodded, then the agent told me, "Look! Your education and military experience make you qualified for the Secret Service job, but you need to change your last name to your wife's."

For a moment, I thought the agent was joking. I asked him, "My wife's last name is Gomez. Why should I use her last name?"

"Congress wants Secret Service and other federal agencies to hire minorities," said the agent.

113

"I am an American by birth, served with honors in the military, and have two Masters' degrees. What should I do? Do you think I should change my last name from Hardin to Gomez? Are you saying I have to change my last name to Spanish to get a job with the Secret Service and in the Federal Government? This is wrong," I said angrily.

"I'm sorry," said the agent. "I can take your application and see what happens."

I left the Secret Service office disappointed that the U.S. Congress was putting pressure on federal law enforcement agencies to hire only minorities. As I walked by the Federal Bureau of Investigation (FBI) office, I noticed on the front door a poster saying the FBI was hiring.

Now, I was upset and thinking; *FBI probably wants minorities, too.* Then, I remembered Momma telling me her great-grandfather was a full-blooded Cherokee Indian from Kentucky. *Wow, I might be a minority.*

I went into the FBI office and filled out an employee application. The application wanted to know my race and color. I marked in the box that I am white and wrote in the space I am American Indian from the Cherokee Nation.

Within two weeks, I received a letter from the FBI to report to the San Diego office for a job interview. *Wow. I have an interview with the FBI because I am a Cherokee Indian, and that makes me a minority.*

Several days later, I walked into the FBI office dressed in a grey suit I had bought for $5 at the Salvation Army store in Oceanside, California. The FBI lady sitting behind the desk asked, "Yes, can I help you?"

I gave her my FBI letter and said, "I'm here for a job interview."

The lady looked at me somewhat confused, then she said, "You need to go into the waiting room and wait for instructions."

As I entered the waiting room, I immediately saw only black and brown people sitting in the chairs. I was the only white minority in the room. I did notice two men in dark suits standing in front of the room. Someone said, "The two men are FBI instructors."

I sat down happily, thinking, The FBI application where I check-marked American Indian worked. I have an interview with the FBI because I am Cherokee.

Within minutes one of the instructors in front of the room looked at me and said, "What is your name?"

"Larry Ray Hardin."

"Where are you from?"

"Taylorsville, Kentucky."

"Did you mark you are an American Indian on the application?"

I said, "Yes, sir."

"What kind of an Indian are you?" asked the FBI instructor.

I told the instructor, "Cherokee Indian. Momma always said I have Cherokee blood because her great-grandfather was a full-blooded Cherokee Indian."

Both instructors smiled, and one of them asked, "Do you have Indian tribal papers with you?"

"What are tribal papers?" I asked.

Then the instructor said, "Can you speak Spanish?"

116

I thought; Why does the FBI think I can speak Spanish? Do Cherokee Indians speak Spanish? Kathy is from Spain, and she speaks Spanish to me. But she is not an Indian.

I looked at both FBI instructors and said, "Yes, I can speak Spanish."

Then, one of the FBI instructors escorted me to another room. The room was very small with no windows, and a Hispanic male was sitting there alone at a tiny square metal table. The instructor said, "You both will need to listen to the tape recorder on the table for instructions in Spanish. After you listen to the Spanish tape, write down the answers in Spanish on the papers I am giving you. You have one hour for the exam." Then he said, "Is everything okay?" Then he left the room.

Within a few seconds, I started listening to the recorder in Spanish. I was disappointed; *I can't understand the Spanish words on the recorder.*

I looked over at the Hispanic guy and asked, "How are you doing with the Spanish exam?"

He said, "Man, this is difficult. I can't understand some of this Spanish on the tape recorder."

117

"Where are you from?" I asked.

"I live in San Diego, but my family is from TJ,"

I said, "What! Tijuana, Mexico?"

After about an hour, the FBI instructor entered the room and said, "The Spanish exam is finished. Within a few weeks, you will hear from the FBI about your results of the Spanish exam."

Later, I received a letter in the mail from the FBI. The letter said I did not pass the FBI Spanish exam. *What a surprise!*

Anyone in Your Family Ever Been Arrested

After the FBI Spanish exam, I looked in the telephone and saw the Drug Enforcement Administration (DEA) listed. I didn't know what DEA was; so, I called the phone number and spoke with a recruiter. The DEA recruiter told me his story about being shot in the neck and hip, wounded, and almost killed during an undercover narcotics case in Chicago.

I thought about what the DEA recruiter said when he was almost killed, but what he said didn't deter me. The recruiter's story drew me closer to thinking that I might want to be a DEA agent. I told him, "I have two master's degrees and just got out of the military. Can we meet?"

A few days later, I met the recruiter, a guy by the name of Gus, at the DEA office in National City, California. Gus was wearing tight blue jeans, a big gold color belt buckle, brown cowboy boots, and a beige cowboy hat.

Gus said, "Hi, let me show you my office and meet some of the agents who are working the Kiki Camarena case."

I was extremely impressed with Gus and the other DEA agents I met at the office, how they were dressed, how they carried their guns, and how they acted. I thought, *Wow, if you're going to do criminal work on the streets, this is what it's all about.*

I suddenly felt an inner voice telling me this is what I am going to do.

Gus asked, "I want you to review some recruitment paperwork and to understand what the mission of DEA is."

Then, he asked me to come back for an interview.

"I look forward to seeing you again. Is next week okay?" I told him.

119

After about a week, I called Gus about the interview. He told me, "Can you meet tomorrow at my office?"

The next day I was in Gus's office for the interview. He asked, "Has anyone in your family ever been arrested?"

I told him, "Yes. Grandpa Johnson. My Momma said cops arrested Grandpa. He was making moonshine whiskey inside a cave somewhere in New Haven, Kentucky, when the cops arrested him. He needed to make some money to buy food and clothes for my Momma's brothers and sisters. Momma said her dad went to prison for five years for making moonshine."

Gus asked, "Anyone else arrested in your Mom's family?"

"Well, Momma said her brother went to prison for armed robbery. Momma said her younger brother really never robbed a bank; only drove the car for his buddies when they came out from the bank.' He served five years in prison for the bank robbery he said he never committed."

"Is there anybody else who was arrested and went to jail on your Mom's side of the family?"

"No. I don't think so."

Gus says, "How about your dad's family. Has your dad ever been arrested?"

"My Daddy was arrested and went to jail several times when he was a young boy for drinking and fighting in public, reckless driving, and drag racing his car in Taylorsville, Kentucky.

"How about your dad's brothers and sisters," Gus says.

I said, "No. But if my uncles and aunts did something wrong, they never got caught."

Gus laughed.

"How about you, were you ever arrested?" asked Gus.

"Yes. I was arrested for running naked at an all-girls church softball game in Taylorsville. I went to Taylorsville jail for a few hours and later paid the town judge a fine for indecent behavior. I paid for several tickets in cash to town cops for speeding and reckless driving in Taylorsville, but never went to jail. Sometimes the cops would stop me and search my car. If the cops found any moonshine or beer under my car seat, the town cops took it without charging me."

Then Gus said, "I'm going to call your Mom about you being arrested and what happened at the church softball game.

121

Don't say anything to your Mom while I'm talking to her on the phone."

When he got Momma on the phone, he said. "Hello, Mrs. Hardin?"

After Gus introduced himself and explained why he was calling about my past misbehavior with the law, Momma immediately told him, "Larry Ray is a good son. His Daddy and I never had any problems with him. We are proud of Larry Ray. My other son Jeffrey is the one having problems with the cops in Taylorsville. Jeffrey was arrested for growing marijuana and went to jail for a few days."

Gus said, "Okay, Mrs. Hardin. Thank you for your time."

Gus hung up the phone and smiled at me, "We are done with this interview."

I called Momma later that day about her talking with Gus. She told me, "I was so nervous, wondering why the DEA recruiter wanted to talk to me about you and not Jeffrey."

I said, "Momma, you did okay, but why did you mention Jeffrey?"

"It's the truth Larry Ray, about Jeffrey."

122

I told Kathy about the interview with Gus. She told me,
"You'll never get a job with DEA because of you and your family's
criminal past."

"I told the truth. I am not ashamed of it."

I met with Gus over the next several months, and we
became good friends.

Moving on to DEA

Dope Trafficking and Prostitution

While waiting to join DEA, I got a job as a correctional officer with the Federal Bureau of Prisons in San Diego, California. Then with the Immigration & Naturalization Service. About a year later, I received a phone call from Gus, offering me a job with DEA. Kathy was shocked, and so was I.

I was very excited to be able to work with DEA. I went to the DEA Academy in Quantico, Virginia, for 13 weeks. I had a lot of training in firearms, working undercover, how to develop informants, self-defense, tactical driving, and understanding the legal side of due process. I was happily thinking; *What a blessing to work with DEA!*

After completing DEA training at the Academy in Quantico, I returned to National City as a Special Agent. I was assigned to the Organized Crime Drug Enforcement Task Force (OCDETF) group. After one day on the job, my Group Supervisor (GS) told me, "Don't get caught drinking or having sex with women in your government car, especially informants." The GS only talked about women and drinking, not what I learned at the DEA academy.

125

I was excited; I'm ready to "hit the streets running" and develop my first Confidential Informant (CI) to buy cocaine, heroin, and meth.

I worked for about one week at the San Diego DEA office with other agents and cops. I conducted interviews to determine who was selling drugs. I developed informants and watched bad guys sell their drugs on street corners, at bus stations, train stations, and church parking lots; anywhere the dopers could sell their poison to the public throughout the San Diego county area.

After several weeks working on the streets, I started to realize I was given a lot of power by DEA to arrest people for committing crimes. I worked primarily targeting narcotics traffickers but could detain and arrest anyone for just about anything – drugs, bank robbery, spitting on a public sidewalk, or whatever. It was a little intimidating because the power and authority I had were so broad.

One year later, I transferred to the Narcotics Task Force (NTF) and started working with the narcotics street team in San

126

Diego county. Within a few days, I finally bought methamphetamine (meth) and made my first arrest.

My NTF partners (agents and cops) observed me meeting a skinny young white girl standing on a street corner near a bus stop on El Cajon Blvd. This street corner was known among local police officers for dope trafficking and prostitution.

I walked up to the skinny girl, "I'm a police officer. Federal Agent Narcotics," I stated as I quickly opened my left hand, showing my DEA badge.

The girl smiled nervously and asked, "Are you going to arrest me for standing on the corner?"

I said, "Why should I arrest you? Are you underage? Are you a prostitute?"

I explained to her how dangerous it was for her to be alone on the streets because she was so young. I asked the girl her age, and she said, "I'm eighteen."

"Do you have any ID?" I asked.

She said, "No!"

Then, I asked her, "Are you on dope?"

The girl replied, "Not really."

127

"Where did you get the dope?" I asked her.

As she started to cry, she pointed to a house across the street and said, "I got my meth at that old house. Please don't arrest me."

I gave her my work number in case she needed to talk to me later. I also gave her my last five dollars to buy something to eat.

Then, I walked to the dope house where she got her meth, followed by my NTF partners. It was a single-story stucco house. I knocked on the front door, and within a few minutes, an old white man opened the door. I observed sores on the old man's face, and his teeth looked rotten, the signs a meth user. I asked him, "Hey, man, I want to buy some dope."

The old man said, "What?"

I showed the old man my DEA badge in my left hand and said, "I'm a narcotics agent."

He looked at the badge and tried hard to spit out his words, "What? Who are you?"

I immediately pulled my gun from the front waistband under my shirt and pointed it at the old man's chest and yelled, "Don't you move, or I'll kill you right now."

128

It was too late; the old man suddenly ran down the hallway like a three-legged dog.

For officer safety, not knowing if the old man might be getting a gun or running out the back door, I carefully followed behind him down the hallway until he disappeared into a dark area. The other NTF agents and officers were inside the house, behind me searching the other rooms. I continued to walk slowly down the hallway, looking for the old man.

As I entered a bedroom, alone, I saw a small white girl lying naked on the bed, screaming and trying to get up from the bed. Not knowing where the old man went or who else might be in the house, I immediately jumped on the bed, landing on top of her.

I pointed my 9mm automatic Sig Sauer handgun between the girl's eyes and told her, "I'm a narcotics agent," and yelled, "Stop screaming. Where is the dope? Where is the gun? Where is the old man?"

Suddenly, she moved her hands down toward her vagina.

I immediately grabbed one hand while her other hand tried to get something or hide something near her vagina.

129

It is stupid, and I was thinking; Is this girl reaching for a weapon? Her nasty hairless thing stinks like rotten fish.

I pointed my 9mm gun in her face and yelled again, "Don't move or I'll kill you. Where is the gun? Where is the dope?"

I started squeezing slowly on the trigger of my gun. The girl screamed at me, "The meth is under my butt."

I moved her hands away from her butt and found a clear plastic bindle with white powder that she was trying to hide inside her butt hole. Then, I grabbed her throat, and as I squeezed it, she stopped breathing. Her brown eyes started bugging out, her lips were turning blue, and her eyes were turning dark black. I immediately let go of her throat.

It scared the hell out of me to know that I could kill her so quickly.

The other officers detained the old man. No other dope was found in the house.

While the officers watched the old man, I told the girl, "Put on your clothes."

She had no identification (ID). I was sure she was underage but didn't have time to prove she was a minor. I said, "I won't arrest you if you help me find where the meth was made."

She said, "Yes, I can help you."

I let her go after she decided to work as a Source of Information (SOI) for the Narcotics Task Force (NTF).

Later, at the local cop bar, my partners asked me, "Hey Blue, you chased that old man down the hallway like your Grandpa's dog running after a coon. You jumped in bed and on top of that little naked girl like you really enjoy it."

Previously, I was at a local bar with the officers. After drinking too much beer and talking about my Grandpa Hardin's dog, old Blue, I told some of the NTF officers, "Blue was a blue-eyed dog that would chase coons (raccoons) all night, up and down the hills and hollers on Grandpa's farm back home in Taylorsville, Kentucky.

The NTF officers laughed and immediately nicknamed me "Blue" after hearing that story.

The officer said, "What do you think, Blue? Did you have probable cause (PC) to enter that suspected dope house without a

131

search warrant? Was the meth legally seized as evidence from inside the girl's butt? Can you arrest the girl? You know Blue, that little girl was probably 12 to 14 years old."

Wow! Am I glad I let the girl go!

Another time when I was working with NTF, one of the officers took custody of money and several pounds of meth from a Border Patrol agent at a U.S. Checkpoint in California.

The NTF officer didn't want me to count the money with him, but he gave me the meth. He said, "I'll count the money at the NTF office."

I took the meth and placed it into evidence storage at the NTF office.

After a few days, a Border Patrol agent from the checkpoint called me and said, "I arrested a Mexican drug trafficker with meth and seized a lot of cash hidden inside the Mexican's car. I counted $75,000. The NTF officer reported that he only took custody of half that amount."

I knew what the Border Patrol agent was getting at.

Before the Border Patrol agent could go on, I stopped the Border Patrol agent and said, "Don't say anything to me about missing money. I took the meth for evidence and storage at the NTF office. I didn't take any money from you. You'll need to talk to the NTF officer!"

I wanted to make it clear to the Border Patrol agent; I am not getting mixed up in any corruption. It's unbelievable, and I was angrily thinking; *If the Border Patrol agent or the NTF officer took some of the money, what could I do? I didn't want any part of working with that NTF officer alone again.*

Later that year, on Thanksgiving Day, the same NTF officer called me, "Larry Ray, I need your help. A DEA fugitive wanted for narcotics trafficking is picking up some money at a stash house in Oceanside, California. I have a CI watching where the fugitive is."

The officer wanted me to come with him to arrest the DEA fugitive. *Why me again?*

I went with the NTF officer to the location where the fugitive was to pick up the dope money. After spotting the fugitive in his car, the officer contacted the local police department to help stop the fugitive's car for a traffic violation. I observed a police officer driving a marked unit stopped the fugitive's car. When the

133

fugitive got out of his car, I approached him with my handgun pointed at his chest and yelled, "Don't move. If you try to run, I will kill you. You are under arrest."

After the fugitive was handcuffed, I asked him, "Do you have any guns or money inside the car?" He said, "I don't have any guns, but I have money in the trunk." The NTF officer searched inside the car for weapons, drugs, and cash. The officer then opened the trunk!"

Wow, there's a big pile of money dumped in this trunk.

I asked the fugitive, "How much money do you think you have here in the truck?"

He said, "About $245,000."

The NTF officer said to me without hesitation, "You go ahead and take the fugitive back to the police department, and I'll take the fugitive's car back and count the money.

The next day when the story came out in the local newspaper, it said the car was seized with $37,000 in it. I was upset and thinking; *That was not the amount the fugitive said he had in the trunk.* I didn't say anything about it to my NTF supervisor or anyone else at NTF.

134

I learned quickly after one year on the job with NTF; you don't ask questions or say anything to your supervisor about another NTF officer's integrity.

I didn't know that was the norm for some of the officers working for NTF taking money without counting it in front of other witnesses. Not for all officers, but there were definitely some. It was hard to ignore how someone might be suspected of stealing, and it shook my belief in working with some of the NTF officers.

I heard from some agents and CIs about drugs and money taken from "corrupt cops" would go missing. I never got involved with the hearsay if I thought the agent or officer was corrupt.

Several weeks later, at the San Diego county courthouse, an NTF officer who was riding with me picked up two young married law clerks. The officer invited the law clerks for lunch. I was disappointed and thinking; *Why did he invite these married women to have lunch with us?*

As I sat in the driver's seat talking with one of the women, the NTF officer was trying to have sex with the other woman in the backseat. As much as I wanted to tune it out, I couldn't help hear what was going on back there.

135

After dropping the women off at the courthouse, I asked the officer, "How can you crawl in the backseat with a married woman and try to have sex? You have a beautiful wife and two little boys."

The NTF officer just laughed it off and asked why I didn't try to have sex with the other woman.

I said, "I am married, and the woman is married."

I was disappointed with the officer's behavior, but he didn't care what I thought.

I watched a few NTF officers take advantage of their position with women. I refused to participate in sex with the women on the streets, from the courthouses, SOIs, CIs, or the women I worked with, but I was willing to join in the drinking.

A few NTF agents and officers got drunk after work. I did too. There was one time I once stopped by the bar after working on the streets. After drinking several beers and eating cheese hotdogs with the officers, I decided to go home. As I was driving home drunk on Interstate 5, traveling north to Oceanside, I almost hit a car with children inside. I considered myself very lucky I did not hurt or kill any of the children. I thanked God for helping me to get home safe. That was the last time I drove home drunk.

136

I remembered once when I was drinking with other NTF agents and officers in a bar before going home, and a well-dressed young woman sat next to me. I started talking with her and asked, "What kind of work do you do?"

She said, "I'm a schoolteacher."

NTF Officer Paul whispered something in the woman's ear. I figured he must know her. Suddenly the schoolteacher pulled up her dress with no panties on and showed her vagina.

I said out loud, "Is she crazy? She is showing me her hairless thing."

Officer Paul whispered and said, "No, she's not a teacher. She's a prostitute."

I quickly moved away from the woman while the others laughed.

I believed that once an agent or an officer got involved with sex, drugs, and dirty money, they crossed over to the "dark battle" of corruption. Self-control is the only way around it. Sex and dirty money were always available to any agent or officer who wanted to take advantage of it.

We all have faults, and I saw a lot of crazy stuff working with NTF. It was up to me to just say, "No." I wasn't tempted to have sex with other women or take a bad guy's money. I stayed away from the corruption.

A few months later, at the firearm range, one of the NTF officers mentioned that Officer Paul had shot himself accidentally in the butt on the range when he quickly pulled his weapon from his holster.

The other NFT officer said, "Don't stand next to Paul. He might shoot you in the butt." I looked at Paul standing next to me and asked, "Are you going to accidentally put a bullet in my butt."

I returned to the NTF office after shooting at the firearm range with other officers and agents. I noticed Paul was cleaning his handgun at his desk.

Wow. I had a firecracker inside my desk drawer. Suddenly, I remembered the time my brother, Jeffrey, threw a firecracker under Mr. McGee's seat on the old yellow school bus. With the firecracker in my hand, I thought, *Paul was the one who whispered in the prostitute's ear at the bar. Then she raised up her dress and showed me her hairless thing. I'm going to throw the firecracker*

under Paul's chair while he's cleaning his gun. Why not!

I lit the fuse and quickly threw it under Paul's chair. A loud noise was heard throughout the Narcotics Task Force building. The secretaries screamed, agents and officers jumped with guns in their hands, looking for where the shot came from. But Paul, he didn't move; he was frozen to his chair. Everyone is looking at Paul. Paul stopped cleaning his gun and looked up slowly from his desk, then looked at his handgun. Another officer yelled, "Hardin threw a firecracker under Paul's desk."

Paul or any other NTF officer never set me up with a prostitute again.

While serving in the military, I learned people are different all over the United States and the world with varying levels of integrity. When I talk about the "dark battle" of my work, I'm referring to the few agents and officers I knew who were involved in the misconduct.

For me, I pray to God to stay strong in character, integrity, faith, loyalty, honesty, truth, and family. Most of the DEA agents shared my values. And most of the NTF officers I worked with had the same upstanding character, as well.

I thanked God. Trust in the Lord with all my heart and reminded myself that I need to stay off the Path of Devil and continue to fight my greatest enemy: Myself.

Move to Yuma, AZ

In 1990, Kathy had the opportunity to be transferred to the Department of Defense Investigative Service (DIS) in Yuma, Arizona. DEA has a small office in Yuma with only three agents and one secretary.

Kathy and I had lived in Yuma for a few years when I was assigned to the Marine Corps Air Station (MCAS). Yuma was a small desert town community just ten miles north of the Mexican border, easy to get around in town without a lot of traffic.

We decided to move to Yuma if our agencies agreed.

I thought it would be a great place to live as a DEA agent.

I was happily thinking; I can relax and not work long hours chasing drug traffickers. I can spend more time at home with Kathy.

140

Kathy was the first to move to Yuma. Then I asked my supervisor for a transfer to Yuma as well.

Don't Move or I'll Blow Your Head Off

Before transferring to Yuma, I decided to go home and see my family in Kentucky. I was going back as a Special Agent with the Drug Enforcement Administration.

After a few days of fishing with Daddy and working in his vegetable garden, I decided to spend some time with Momma. It was late in the evening, and Momma would be in bed before the sun disappeared into the night.

I was sitting on the couch with Momma. Daddy was lying back on his worn-out recliner, chewing his last piece of tobacco for the day. Daddy hadn't taken off his "sugar shoes" yet, but when he did, he would follow Momma to bed.

I was listening to Momma talking about some of her aunts, uncles, and cousins dying from kidney and heart disease. Then Momma said, "Larry Ray, life is going by us all so quickly. Your job is so dangerous. How do you stop someone from hurting you?"

141

Before Momma could say anything else, I jumped up, pointed my finger at her, and yelled, "Don't move or I'll blow your fucking head off."

I sat down and said, "Momma, that's how I stop the bad guys from hurting me. It's not like what you see on TV."

Momma stared at me like she was in shock. Then she said, "Oh my God."

I glanced at Daddy. He was not moving from his recliner, and he was no longer chewing his tobacco.

Momma started to cry, saying, "Larry Ray, you scare me. I'm going to bed."

I immediately hugged Momma and told her, "I'm sorry, Momma for scaring you." I said, "Momma, it's violent and filthy working on the streets. The streets are very dangerous, and its trash talk. You can't be gentle and kind to the bad guys. The bad guys will hurt and kill you if they can."

Momma slowly got up off the couch and said, "I'm going to bed." She walked towards the bedroom with her head looking down at the floor. Then, suddenly, she turned around and said, "Your

Daddy and I are so worried about you. Why that job, Larry Ray?"

I couldn't give Momma an answer to why I chose DEA.

I told her, "I love you, Momma. I'm sorry I scared you and Daddy." As Daddy was taking his shoes off, then his socks and looked at me and said, "I am going to bed. I love you. I'll see you in the morning."

Later that night, I went into their bedroom and sat in Momma's rocking chair next to the big window, watching Momma and Daddy sleep. I whispered to God, "I have to leave soon to get back to my job on the streets. I love Momma and Daddy so much. God, please take care of them." I then kissed Momma and Daddy on their foreheads like I did every night when I was home.

It was our Last Dance Together

Several days later, we had a family reunion picnic at My Old Kentucky Home Park. Daddy and I arrived early to set up the picnic tables and cooking equipment. Within minutes Daddy's brother, Joe Luis, and his wife Helen arrived. Immediately, Uncle Joe Luis started to fry fish and some turtle meat for family and friends who arrived later that morning for breakfast.

143

Then Uncle Charlie showed up grinning like a possum ready to eat some fried fish. Daddy and Charlie caught the fish and the turtles at Charlie's lake.

Joe Luis was the first to taste the fried fish to see if it was well-cooked. After Joe Luis tasted it, he smiled from ear to ear like a baby ready to full up his stomach, a signal that the fish and turtle meat were ready to eat.

I yelled first before Daddy could, "Breakfast is ready."

Daddy, Uncle Charlie, and I joined Uncle Joe Luis and Aunt Helen for an early hot fried fish breakfast. Sometimes Daddy's uncles Jessie Lee and Edison Lee Hardin (Grandpa's brothers) would join us, too.

I finally saw that the karaoke music arrived at the picnic. Daddy and Joe Luis continued to fry fish and turtle meat, while Charlie continued to entertain the family and friends. I was excited and thinking; Wow. *Our family and friends will be eating, singing, and dancing throughout the day* when we *are all together again.*

Later after eating, Momma's brother, Ernie Johnson, walked up to the karaoke to sing some of his favorite country songs. As Uncle Ernie started singing some of his favorite country songs,

I asked Momma to dance with me. Strangely, I felt like this might be the last dance Momma and I would ever have together today.

I grabbed Momma's hands as she reached out towards me. I was sad and thinking; *All the washing, sewing, cooking, and cleaning made Momma's hands rough and callous.*

Our last dance together
Uncle Ernie Johnson singing
Mom's song

As we slow danced, I looked in Momma's blue eyes and told her how much I loved her and Daddy.

Momma responded, "We love you, too."

I looked around to see who else was dancing. "Momma, nobody is dancing, except us. The family, relatives, and friends are sitting at the tables, watching us." Momma smiled and laughed as we continued to dance.

After we danced, Momma said, "I love you, Lawrence Raymond. Your Daddy and I are proud of you."

It was our last dance together.

146

As a DEA Agent in Yuma, Arizona

The Mexican Brothers

In 1975, DEA special agents Don Ware and Roy Stevenson were in the thick of a Mexican heroin investigation. The two agents had been making progress targeting a heroin trafficker when things took a turn for the worse, as they often do in drug-related situations. The Mexican cartel targeted the agents for murder.

The DEA Yuma agents focused on three Mexican Garcia brothers, Jaime, Javier, and Joselito. The brothers were members of a cartel known as much for the excessive drugs they sold to the American public as their coldhearted killings. Don, Roy, and their Confidential Informant (CI) were poised and ready to make a heroin buy from one of Garcia's traffickers. Don, Roy, and the rest of their DEA street team agents anticipated something might go wrong as they set up surveillance in the center of the Mexican desert town of San Luis to watch their CI make a heroin deal from the Garcia trafficker.

Don and Roy jumped in their '74 Chevy pickup truck and took off for the northern part of town to observe the deal with the CI and heroin trafficker. Minutes into Don and Roy's journey, they

147

realized they were being followed by a black car and a red car racing toward them. The black car accelerated ahead and cut the agents off in front. Don and Roy were highly experienced and well-trained narcotics agents, but this was serious business. The agents knew they were in trouble, and their hearts raced uncontrollably.

The two occupants exited their black car and pointed guns at Don and Roy. The red car full of Mexicans pulled up behind the agents, and the gunmen pointed their guns and forced the agents out of the pickup truck. Don and Roy had no choice but to comply.

Wordlessly, the two agents exited and left the safety of their pickup truck. The Mexican assassins (sicarios) wasted no time getting to work and sending a message to the other DEA agents working nearby that Don and Roy were not welcome there. The gunmen beat the two agents with their guns, pistol-whipped the agents in the face, and slammed their weapons into the sides of their heads until both agents were incapacitated. Once on the ground, the agents were stomped and kicked until Don and Roy were severely injured.

The Mexican gunmen lifted the injured agents and tossed them into the open bed of Don's Chevy pickup. One of the Mexican hitmen jumped into the driver's side of Don's pickup truck and sped away with the two agents lying helplessly in the back.

Don and Roy knew they were about to die. Don said, "We have to do something, or we're going to end up in the desert."

The agents both knew what that meant. You don't come back alive from the desert in Mexico. Don was critically injured, but he was able to tell Roy, "Don't worry, my snub nose .38 special fell to my crotch."

The sicarios failed to search Don below the waistband while he was lying on the ground and being kicked in the ribs. Many law enforcement agents carry their guns in their pants below the waistband because attackers will avoid touching the crotch area.

Don couldn't reach the snub nose .38 caliber; his body was too broken. Roy was also injured, but able to move around some. The agents both rose up from lying down in the truck to see where they were headed and discussed how they might escape from their captors. Don and Roy noticed the same black car following close behind with two of the Mexicans watching them. The agents never noticed that the red car had stopped following them. They were focused on the two bad guys in the black car.

149

The Chevy pickup truck had only gone about a block when Don noticed a public bus ahead of them. Don said to Roy, "Get my gun, and as soon as the truck stops, I want you to end this. Make the driver stop, and then we're both getting out."

The agents didn't have much to work with, only Don's snub nose handgun. The two men in the black car following had eyes on the agents. Don and Roy's options were few, but their instincts were sharp. Although Don and Roy knew it was looking like they wouldn't make it out alive, and if there was any chance in hell of making it, they were going for it.

When the pickup truck stopped behind the public bus, Roy was able to climb out with the snub noise .38. Roy walked up to the Mexican driver of the Chevy pickup truck and pointed it directly into the driver's face. Since Roy spoke Spanish fluently, he was able to tell the driver to let them go. The driver tried to reach out and punch Roy. Roy had neither the time nor the inclination to fight, so he shot the driver in the face, and the driver collapsed onto the steering wheel.

Roy planned to return to the back of the pickup truck and lift Don out, but he saw his partner had already rolled out and was limping to the side of the road. Don didn't look like he knew what he was doing or where he was going, but he was moving away from the truck.

Roy caught up with Don and quickly grabbed him by the arm to guide Don to an old car junkyard on the side of the road to wait for the other DEA agents to arrive. The two Mexicans who had been watching from the black car behind got out and started shooting. Both Don and Roy took several hits. Roy shot back at the two sicarios.

Don and Roy lay bleeding in the middle of the road. When the shooters ran out of bullets, Roy pretended to be dead and told Don to do the same. The strategy worked, and the shooters disappeared from the scene moments later in their car.

Don was shot four times, and as he lay face down in the street, he was sure his life was over. People walked by, but no one would stop to help him. Don asked people walking by for a priest, but the people of the town knew better than to help gringos who'd been messing with the Mexican cartel, especially the Garcia brothers.

Roy was shot once in the leg and once in the back. Roy pulled himself up and managed to hobble over to the Chevy pickup truck. Roy was able to move the driver over on the passenger seat. Then he slid into the driver's seat and grabbed the hand-held radio to call for help. Roy put the pickup truck in drive and almost hit Don before realizing his right leg wasn't working correctly.

Help arrived from the other DEA agents working in San Luis. The agents took Roy to a hospital in Yuma, Arizona. Don was in worse shape, and it was feared he wouldn't make the drive to Yuma. So, the agents immediately took Don to the town's hospital in Mexico that was a lot closer.

Don was lucky to survive the brutal attack by the sicarios and suffered from severe pain for many years. Don died in 2004 in surgery due to complications from his injuries in Mexico.

The Mexican Federal Attorney in San Luis, Mexico, initiated federal arrest warrants against the Garcia brothers and their associates for involvement in the attempted murders to the two DEA agents.

The youngest brother, Joselito, bragged, telling a corrupt Mexican police officer and a DEA CI, "I'm unhappy that the DEA

152

agents were not killed in San Luis. We did intend to murder them."

The brothers were arrested in San Luis, Mexico, in 1975. Later, the

Mexican Federal Judicial charged Joselito for being responsible for

the kidnapping and shooting.

Arizona/Mexican border

Usually, there were only two agents in the office at any

given time. My job was to work "dope" investigations, primarily at

the Arizona/ Mexican border. The DEA Yuma office took care of all the drugs

DEA & IRS on the 2nd floor.
1st Floor was Bureau of Land Management

seized from

Mexico at the Border Patrol checkpoints surrounding Yuma,

Interstate Highways, including San Luis Port-of-Entry (POE).

The secretary told me, "Yuma is a hot, dry desert but humid

in the summer with an average temperature of 117 F° in the early

afternoon. Be sure you drink lots of water and have water bottles in

your car. You don't want to have a heat stroke in the desert."

153

Within a week, I seized several pounds of marijuana, a ten-pound brick from Mexican traffickers near the border of San Luis, Arizona and Mexico.

A 10 lbs. brick of marijuana in Yuma desert

I was not able to arrest the dope traffickers because they ran back across from the Port of Entry (POE) into Mexico. My SOI's said, "It's the Garcia brothers' marijuana."

That made me curious about who these Garcia brothers were because I kept hearing their name in the Yuma law enforcement community. *I need to learn more about these brothers.*

I wanted to find out how drugs were entering into the U.S. through the POE at San Luis, Arizona, from Mexico.

My collateral duties were burning marijuana (weed) weekly that was left in the desert by Mexican smugglers and found by Border Patrol Agents.

I remembered once on a hot day in Yuma when I had about 4,000 pounds of marijuana to burn somewhere in the desert.

Burned over 4,000 lbs. of marijuana in Yuma desert

Agent Saul Morales filled up the red plastic gasoline container and bought matches from the gas station clerk. I bought a 12-pack of cold beer to drink and later use the empty bottles as targets to shoot at while the weed was burning.

I told Saul, "You got the gasoline and matches. I got the beer. Let's go and burn the weed next to the Arizona State Prison down near the Mexican border."

"Let's go," he said.

It took Saul and me a few hours to open the marijuana packages and dumped them into a large pile on the desert sand. I looked at him and said, "Okay brother, put the gas on the weed and

155

light it. I'm ready for target practice with some of the empty beer bottles."

Saul dumped the gasoline on the weed. Suddenly, he looked at me and said, "Wow. I lost the matches."

I told him, "Don't worry, let's do it like the actors do in the movies; when the actor shoots into a car gas tank or gas station pumps."

I said, "Okay, who is the fastest to draw their guns and shoot into the pile of weed?"

Saul and I both quickly pulled our guns and shot the weed until we had no more bullets.

The gasoline in the weed did not explode like in the movies. Saul said, "What are we going to do with all that weed?"

Within minutes, two Border Patrol agents arrived to see who was shooting. They quickly recognized Saul and I were DEA agents. Who else could it be out in the desert firing their guns into a pile of weed?

I asked them, "Do you guys want a beer? I have some tortilla chips but no hot salsa."

156

After drinking another beer, I looked at Saul and the agents. I smiled, got up, and slowly walked over to my SUV. I reached in the back and pulled out an emergency road flare stick.

The Mexican weed had a burning sweet smell that I enjoyed inhaling while I was drinking my last cold beer. I was wondering; *Are the Border Patrol agents inhaling the smell from the weed like I am?*

We finished drinking the beer then shot at the empty bottles. I was laughing and thinking; I wonder if the prisoners at the state prison are enjoying the sweet smell blowing towards the prison?

After a day of burning weed and working in the hot desert near the border, I'd be wet and sticky from the heat and humidity. All I wanted was to get home and hop in the shower. I had to peel the clothes off my body before washing the sand off.

Sometimes, I wasn't sure I'd made the right decision to relocate to Yuma. The work was getting so demanding, and I heard from other DEA agents about corruption in the local law enforcement community in Yuma and at San Luis POE.

It was even worse for a DEA agent's career because you could be stuck in Yuma for years. That's a long time to spend near

157

the border of Mexico in the turbulent, wild, wild, west of Southern Arizona.

After about four months in Yuma, I asked DEA Phoenix management if I could be transferred to Puerto Rico. But my request was strongly denied.

Mexican Traffickers Moving Drugs

Within a few days after arriving in Yuma, I was at a safe house playing poker with a DEA agent and three local law enforcement officers. DEA had a *safe house* near the Mexican border used as a base for the agents and officers to work all-night surveillance for major dope cases.

An officer was in the kitchen, making hot dogs and spicy Mexican chili. Other officers were just lying around on the couches and floor, waiting to hear that a vehicle loaded with drugs was traveling from a targeted residence in Yuma or entering from the Mexican border.

One of the poker players, DEA agent Pete, mentioned three Garcia brothers; Jaime, Javier, and Joselito Garcia. Pete said,

"Larry, you are a new agent to Yuma. I'm going to explain to you who the brothers are and their connection with corrupt officers."

Pete explained that no drugs came across the POE into the U.S. from Mexico that wasn't arranged without the Garcia brothers' approval.

That night at the safe house, Pete got a phone call from a DEA CI that one of the traffickers was moving cocaine to a residence in Yuma. Some of the officers took off to investigate. I kept playing poker with Pete. I wanted to stick around and hear more stories about the brothers.

After hearing about the Garcia brothers at the safe house, I began looking for everything I could find and asked a lot of questions to get more information about these three brothers. I made notes about dope trafficking and other crimes the brothers committed from what I heard from my SOIs and interviews with cops who targeted the organization.

I was surprised; There were so many narcotics criminal cases in Yuma County that are related to the brothers.

I discovered a lot about the Garcia brothers' family - how the brothers were entrenched in the Yuma community, and their

159

strong ties at San Luis POE and Algodones POE, a Baja California border checkpoint. I continued hearing rumors from other DEA agents, Customs agents, and local PD (Police Department). I was curiously thinking; *Wow, I'm going to look into this. Why doesn't anyone want to work on getting the brothers?*

I learned there had initially been four brothers in the Garcia family. One had been killed earlier somewhere in Mexico. It was not known how it happened. The other three brothers were still living in San Luis, Mexico, and Yuma, Arizona.

Joselito was the youngest and most dangerous because he often reacted without thinking. He was involved with cocaine and heroin crossing at the POE and trying to kill the cops in Mexico or others who attempted to stop them.

Javier, the second oldest brother, was probably the smartest. Javier inherited a shrimp company in El Golfo, Mexico, from a drug cartel associate who was known to DEA as a Mexican drug kingpin. Javier owned a grocery store in San Luis, Mexico, and a restaurant in El Golfo, Mexico. He was always very polite and well-dressed when meeting with the public in the Yuma business community. His wife was involved in Yuma community charity groups, and very active in the Catholic church; organizing help to feed the poor and with under-nourished children.

Confidential Informants and SOIs said Javier was transporting Mexican and Asian Heroin in his shrimp trucks into the U.S.

Javier's son, Leonardo, was selected and endorsed by an Arizona Senator to go to an Air Force Academy in Colorado Springs, Colorado, for a career as an officer. Later, Leonardo was arrested and released the same day by Immigration Inspectors at San Luis POE for smuggling marijuana into Arizona. It wasn't known why he was released the same day at the POE. Later, Leonardo dropped out of the Airforce academy.

According to CIs, SOIs, and Private Investigators (PI), Javier knew an Arizona Senator Ed Pastor very well. Senator Pastor was Hispanic-American and supported the agricultural trade in Mexico. He was familiar with Jaime's agriculture business in Mexico.

Jaime, the oldest, was an agriculture produce grower in Mexico and a well-known criminal working with the cartels in Mexico and Colombia. The dope traffickers called Jaime "Lobo."

CIs and SOIs said Jaime was extremely dangerous when he was upset, especially when DEA seized his cocaine and Mexican heroin.

According to Mexican officials and CIs, the Garcia brothers were very wealthy. But the brothers had a weakness for dope and girls. They were always partying – snorting cocaine and having sex with young Mexican girls brought to Jaime's home for entertainment.

The Mexican cartel and drug traffickers would often send young girls over to Garcia brothers' home for them to enjoy. This was another reason I was committed to seeing them all in the United States prison.

A DEA CI, well connected to the Garcia brothers said, "When one of the traffickers lost some *dope* at San Luis POE, they made the trafficker pay for the lost dope. Recently a trafficker had to give up his daughter in exchange for the missing drugs."

The trafficker's daughter was only 12-years old and was used by the Garcia brothers for their sexual pleasure.

The CI asked me to help the little girl escape from the Garcia brothers. I did my best to try to help her. I didn't have much

162

luck with my Group Supervisor (GS), Juan Antonio Moreno and the Assistant U.S. Attorney's (AUSA) office in Phoenix.

Although former DEA agents in Yuma continuously tried to penetrate the Garcia brothers' organization, the agents and their CIs continually failed. The brothers had strong ties in the law enforcement community who were very active in Yuma and at San Luis POE, Arizona. The brothers operated with impunity for more than 20 years. I learned from former agents, CIs, and SOIs about law enforcement officers at San Luis POE were tragically corrupt.

"The Lord is my light and my salvation; whom shall I fear? The Lord is the strength of my life; of whom shall I be afraid?" (Psalm 27:1 King James Version).

Leaked to the Press

By the Reagan-Bush Administration

According to U.S. law enforcement in the 1980s, the Garcia brothers' drug smuggling organization was probably the third-largest drug cartel in Mexico. On March 16, 1986, President Ronald Reagan spoke on national television with a plea for restoring congressional aide to the Nicaraguan Contras. Later, the United

163

States supplied weapons to the Contras. Weapons were transported across the Arizona POE through Mexico to Nicaragua. Barry Seal was one of the pilots who transported weapons in exchange for drugs.[5]

Seal worked with the CIA in the 1980s when he was a pilot in the U.S. Army's Special Forces. He was busted by U.S. Customs while working as a commercial pilot for Trans World Airlines for attempting to smuggle explosives into Mexico for a group of Cubans against Castro. He lost his job with the airlines but was protected by his connections with the CIA.[6]

Seal began flying his private planes. He was known as one of the top drug smugglers and dealers for Pablo Escobar's Medellin Colombia cartel. He started his operations in Louisiana, smuggling cocaine and marijuana. In 1982 with the CIA's help, He moved his airstrip and operations to Mena, Arkansas.[7]

DEA caught Seal in the early '80s and flipped him to work for them. They allowed him to continue flying drugs and money, just to see where everything was going and from where it was coming. Seal became known as "the most important witness in the history of the U.S. Drug Enforcement Administration (DEA)."[8]

This was one of the ways DEA caught on to Manuel Noriega's drug running. Oliver North's big claim to fame in his career was the Iran Contra Affair that involved Noriega in Panama. DEA was in a unique position to see where many pieces of the puzzle were coming together. The DEA agents were able to connect a lot but didn't put it all together.

In the 1980s, Seal "became one of the most important and daring undercover operatives, infiltrating the top Colombian drug operations...Seal was scheduled to be the key witness against...Jaime Ochoa, the top Colombian drug boss...in jail in Spain, [who was] about to be extradited to the United States."[9] Seal was then relieved from his connections with the DEA.

Seal flew his private planes from Mena to cartel airstrips in Colombia and Venezuela with supplies and guns for CIA operations. On the return trip to Mena, he would refuel in Panama and Honduras. While flying over farms on Seal's property, he would drop parachutes attached to bags of cocaine for Colombian cartel distributors in the U.S.[10]

Two of the cartel members he worked with were Jaime Ochoa and Frederico Vaughn, who were close associates of the

165

Sandinistas violent drug cartel in Colombia. Vaughn's cousin, Barney Vaughn, worked for the Popular Bank and Trust Company. This was the bank used by the CIA and Oliver North when they were working with the Contras.[11]

Barry Seal lived on a property in Arkansas, which was managed by the Rose Law Firm, where Hilary Clinton worked. It was Bill Clinton who called someone at the County courthouse to get Seal released from jail. According to the local cops, Clinton's brother, Roger, was a known dope-user and was involved with Tyson Chicken, also in Arkansas.[12] Former defendants and Informants provided to the law enforcement community that Roger and some of the employees at Tyson chicken were suspected in smuggling drugs for the Colombians.

U.S. officials arrested Seal and sentenced him to five years in a Florida prison.

In 1986, after serving only three years, Seal was moved to a halfway house in Baton Rouge, Louisiana. "He'd been told by his friends that the Medellin cartel, run by Colombian drug lords and Pablo Escobar, had put a $500,000 bounty on his head after his status as an informant for the U.S. government had been leaked to the press by the Reagan-Bush administration."[13]

Seal was murdered in 1986 by five men with machine-guns, ordered by Jaime Ochoa and Pablo Escobar when he was waiting to testify for the government. Seal was in the witness protection program and sitting in his car outside the house when he was murdered.[14]

Seal "was a victim of suspected Oliver North's press leaks."[15] Seal was well-connected with the CIA, and they used him. Seal's the one who paid the price with his life, not the CIA or others involved. The CIA agents went on with their careers.

Facts were limited by CIs and SOIs that the Garcia brothers were helping the Nicaragua government smuggle weapons across at San Luis POE into Mexico. The brothers were using corrupt Customs and Immigration officers at the POE. Once the smuggled weapons were in Mexico, corrupt Mexican officials moved the weapons further south until the weapons were delivered in Nicaragua.

DEA Agent Murdered in Mexico

Enrique (Kiki) Camarena was a highly decorated Marine, a Vietnam vet, and a DEA agent working and living in Guadalajara with his wife and three children. Kiki was born in Mexico and became a U.S. citizen at a young age.

"Kiki started hitting big people hard, and they couldn't understand where he was getting his intel," recalled former DEA agent and Kiki's friend.[16] "He brought a lot of attention to himself" and was murdered at the age of 37.[17]

Kiki had discovered a large marijuana field, approximately 2,500 acres, on property owned by a Mexican drug cartel. The Mexican cartel used other Mexican criminal organizations to move marijuana from the southwest border into Arizona and California.[18]

Kiki and his CI were kidnapped in Guadalajara. The CI was killed immediately. Kiki was not as fortunate. He was skinned alive. A cartel doctor gave him drugs to keep him alive so that the kidnappers could torture him even longer. The cartel made an audiotape of the vicious murder. DEA agents heard Kiki screaming and crying before dying in unspeakable pain.[19]

The cartel wanted to know what the U.S. government knew. When Mexican law enforcement wouldn't help locate Kiki, the United States temporarily closed the border. That's the only time in U.S. history when that happened.

DEA discovered from informants that a close relative of the Garcia brothers in San Luis, Sonora, Mexico; an unidentified woman, was on hand for the Kiki's torture and recorded the whole event. DEA agents recovered the tape, which proved to be a valuable piece of evidence during the trial.

It was a Mexican cartel organization that kidnapped and tortured Kiki. Garcia brothers' organization was part of that group. A cousin of the brothers was a shrimp importer in Mexicali who used San Luis POE. Javier Garcia's cousin was arrested in the Kiki case. Javier then took over his cousin's shrimp business after he was arrested for the death of Kiki.

Many of those involved in the kidnapping and torture were brought to trial. Three men were convicted, but none of them were from the Garcia brothers' organization. However, some cartel members who were arrested for Kiki's death were connected to the brothers.

169

The trial records included so many files and tapes that it took Private Investigator, Randy Torgerson, three months, eight hours a day, five days a week to go through them in the archives at the downtown Los Angeles Court House. "There were five to seven stacks of files that went from floor to ceiling. That's how big this case's files were, innumerable pages! It was crazy! There were phone records, notes, and surveillance reviews tying people to those in the Garcia brothers' case in the 1990s."[20]

Through telephone records from January 1986, it was discovered in Kiki's case that two of the murder defendants had made calls to one of the brothers' homes in San Luis, Mexico.

One of the gatekeepers for the most powerful drug cartel in Guadalajara was sentenced to 40 years in prison, according to *Huffington Post*[21] (30 years according to *LA Times*).[22] Others were also arrested in connection with the Kiki Camarena case.

According to a reporter in the *Los Angeles Times* and a reporter of the *Huffington Post*, we would later learn that Kiki's case was also connected to the Iran Contra scandal. One of Kiki's Mexican cop friends who ordered the kidnapping and torture was released after serving only 28 years because of a technicality.[23] [24]

170

Thinking about the Garcia brothers' involvement in the shooting of Don and Roy as well as the kidnapping, torture, and murder of DEA Agent, Kiki Camarena made me even more determined.

Through my research targeting the Garcia brothers, I continued to learn details about how the brothers were involved in Kiki's death in Mexico on February 9, 1985.

A former DEA Group Supervisor (GS) was awarded the prestigious DEA Administrator's Award for his work in handling and solving the Kiki case. The former supervisor said, "Twenty-seven years ago, the kidnap, torture, and murder of a U.S. Drug Enforcement Administration agent by Mexican drug traffickers sparked one of the biggest manhunts the United States government has ever launched in North America. It also offered an ominous warning of things to come."[25]

A Former Presidential Staffer and a Professor

At the DEA Yuma office, U.S. Customs Agent Billy Winter of the Arizona Southwest Border Narcotics Task Force (NTF) asked me to work with him on a joint investigation targeting a
171

corrupt former Political Official involved in marijuana cultivation in Arizona, California, and Hawaii. According to Agent Billy Winter, his SOI had information on marijuana cultivation and the distribution organization operating in the area of Yuma, Arizona and Bard, California.

I told Agent Winter, "You know I am swamped targeting the Garcia brothers' drug trafficking organization in San Luis, Mexico."

He said, "If you work with me on this case, I will help you out on the brothers' case."

"Agent Winter, I am busy with other cases, too. I want to focus on the brothers," I told him.

Then he told me he didn't want to work with any other DEA agent at the Yuma office. He said, "One of the bad guys was a former Reagan Presidential Staff. The other is a Professor from the University of California in Berkeley."

"Wow. Okay, Agent Winter, let's meet with your SOI."

Within the next few days, I met with Agent Winter and his SOI, Freddy Lost, in Yuma.

According to Freddy, Earl Lick was a former White House employee for President Ronald Reagan. In 1987, while providing security for the President in Bonn, Germany. Lick went to Amsterdam and other European countries to purchase marijuana seeds. Because of his U.S. State Department's diplomatic status, Lick was able to smuggle the seeds into the United States and to Arizona. Freddy told me he later learned Earl Lick was concealing marijuana in his own cotton fields and worked in partnership with Pat Weed.

Pat Weed was a professor at the University of California in Berkeley. Freddy provided his cotton crop field to conceal the marijuana and the facilities to harvest and process it for Earl Lick and Pat Weed. Freddy said Lick and Weed continued to grow marijuana using cotton fields and citrus groves in Yuma, Arizona and Bard, California. Bard was a small town at the southern tip of California, along the Arizona border with Mexico. Freddy told DEA the agents could find Earl Lick in Yuma or Bard, on a cotton field or citrus grove. Also, the agents could find Pat Weed at the University of California in Berkley.

Agent Winter asked Freddy, "What is your relationship to Earl Lick?"

"Earl Lick was a legitimate salesman that helped with distribution of my cotton."

Freddy told me Lick knew a lot about the agrichemical business. Lick lost a large sum of money in an earlier investment. To recoup his loss from the bad investment, Lick enlisted help from Weed. Earl Lick was providing the seeds from Amsterdam, and Pat Weed provided the labor from Northern California to harvest and distribute the marijuana.

Agent Winter asked Freddy, "Explain to Agent Hardin and I, who is Pat Weed?"

"Pat Weed is a professor who teaches mathematics at the University of California in Berkeley. He has land in Mendocino and Humboldt Counties and a home in Captain Cook, Hawaii."

"Weed provides his marijuana cultivation expertise and labor force from his properties in Mendocino and Humboldt Counties. His labor force consisted of old 'hippies' to harvest and trim the marijuana." Freddy said he might be able to identify 36 of Pat Weed's associates for marijuana and distribution.

"Can you show Agent Hardin and I the cotton fields in Yuma and Bard where Earl Lick and Pat Weed grow their marijuana plants?" Agent Winter asked.

The following week Freddy showed Agent Winter the location of the cotton fields. Freddy said, "Earl Lick supplies the citrus farms, cotton crop, vehicles, and water irrigation for Pat Weed to cultivate the marijuana in the cotton fields and citrus groves."

Later, the Amsterdam marijuana seeds were cultivated inside cotton fields and citrus groves.

He Squealed like a Pig

When Earl Lick later learned that his friend Freddy was talking to DEA and Customs agents, he decided he would speak to DEA if he got caught. When he finally did get caught by the Yuma NTF officers while standing in his cotton field, he began telling the officers about Pat Weed. Earl Lick squealed like a pig to Customs and DEA agents about his criminal business. Lick said, "I wanted to talk to the guys at DEA in Yuma before Pat Weed had the opportunity."

175

Earl Lick provided information to Customs Agent Winter and me about Pat Weed and his labor force. Pat Weed's employees did the marijuana harvesting and distribution throughout the United States.

Earl Lick said Pat Weed paid his children, the trimmers, and for the cultivation expenses. Then, Weed divided the remainder of the money with him (Lick). Lick remembered Weed giving him $750,000 from their first crop of marijuana grown on a cotton farm near El Centro, California.

Agents asked Earl Lick, "How can you grow marijuana in cotton fields without law enforcement aircraft seeing the plants?"

Lick explained that he could have the marijuana plants grow flat on the ground, below the cotton. This method was less risky for exposure to DEA and other aircraft surveillance. Without DEA seeing the plants lying on the ground, he was able to produce more substantial profits.

With the information from Earl Lick, Agent Winter and I corroborated the evidence from search warrants and interviewed cooperating defendants that worked for Pat Weed. Later, after Weed was arrested, I coordinated DEA agents to identify residences and farms in Arizona, California, New Jersey, Pennsylvania, and Hawaii. In Kona, Hawaii, Agent Winter and I identified three residences belonging to Pat Weed that were worth approximately 1 million dollars and found $170,000 hidden inside an underground volcanic cave.

With Earl Lick's cooperation, Customs and DEA successfully prosecuted at the Arizona State Court and Federal District Court in Phoenix, thirty-six cultivators and distributors working with Pat Weed. I later identified 20 additional members of Weed's organization in California for possible prosecution. After the 37-month investigation ended, I was now back on track to focus on the Garcia brothers and the corruption at San Luis POE.

I was happily thinking, Wow. I went to Hawaii twice for two weeks. I had a great time in Hawaii with the local cops, and with Pat Weed's help, I located several properties and a large sum of money for the taxpayers.

The Mafia and Hells Angels

Group Supervisor Juan Antonio Moreno told me, "I know you're busy with the Garcia brothers' investigation and working with Customs Agent Billy Winter's marijuana case. I need you to work with the Arizona Southwest Border Narcotics Task Force (NTF) Officer Daniel Blackman. Officer Blackman is targeting the mafia and Hells Angels methamphetamine (meth) trafficking organization. He has requested you and no one else from the DEA office."

I explained to GS Juan Antonio that working with Customs Agent Billy Winter on the marijuana case demanded a lot of travel away from the office and home.

GS Juan Antonio said, "I need you to help with Officer Blackman's Arizona state investigation. Officer Blackman needs a Federal DEA agent, and he wants to work with you and no one else from the DEA Yuma office."

Officer Blackman and I had worked together on other drug cases - so, I trusted him, and he trusted me. I told my GS, "Juan, I am so busy, but let me think about it."

178

GS Juan Antonio said, "The Garcia brothers are also involved with Officer Blackman's case."

Later, Officer Blackman confirmed that the Garcia brothers were involved with Joe Cactus. Joe Cactus was connected with the mafia and Hells Angels in his meth manufacturing and criminal distribution organization. I also learned the DEA and Arizona Southwest Border Narcotics Task Force (NTF) targeted Joe Cactus and his traffickers since 1977. Cactus was known to the FBI and other law enforcement as a suspected mentor of the Las Vegas criminal underworld and the Hells Angels in California. Cactus was also connected to the Garcia brothers' drug smuggling organization at San Luis POE.

I asked FBI Agent Stone if he wanted to help out on Officer Blackman's NTF case, but he told me, "No."

Agent Stone made it very clear that he didn't want to work with Officer Blackman or the local NTF Officers because of corruption. I suddenly thought, *What does the FBI know that I don't know about corruption at NTF.*

I initiated another federal case on a major methamphetamine trafficker named Joe Cactus and his partner

179

Nick Star, in Yuma, Arizona. Officer Blackman said he would focus on getting an Arizona state electronic interception on Cactus' residence in Yuma.

I was the only DEA agent working with Officer Blackman in Yuma. I had the responsibility, as a Federal Agent, for coordinating and directing DEA and Arizona State surveillance teams. There were several times I followed Joe Cactus and Nick Star's traffickers, leaving Arizona, traveling to California.

I had the DEA Phoenix office technicians install listening and recording devices inside Cactus and Star's homes. After placing the devices inside the houses, Officer Blackman and I surveilled Joe Cactus and Nick Star's activities for three months in Yuma, San Luis POE, and throughout the U.S.

We identified Joe Cactus' and Nick Star's criminal network where Cactus and Star distributed over 50 pounds of methamphetamine (meth) each month to the mafia and Hells Angels. I also learned from CIs and SOIs about Star's agriculture produce cooling business in San Luis and his relationship with the Garcia brothers.

I reviewed several financial banks and personal income statements listing transactions between Star and the Garcia agriculture business. Cactus's financial records linked him to the Hells Angels operating in San Francisco, California.

On one occasion, Officer Blackman and I went to New York to collect information on Joe Cactus' criminal associates. We were able to reveal valuable information from electronic interceptions and state search warrants on Joe Cactus' home in Yuma and Nick Star's produce cooling business in San Luis POE. I learned that the brothers and their criminal organization in Mexico were providing Cactus and Star with cocaine and sometimes methamphetamine to distribute in the United States. According to the CIs and SOIs, the brothers were using corrupt law enforcement officers at the POE.

Later, a CI told Officer Blackman and me that Jaime Garcia and his brothers were shipping large amounts of cocaine through San Luis POE to Nick Star's agriculture produce cooling business near the border.

181

The CI told us, "There are corrupt Customs and Immigration officers at San Luis POE working for the Garcia brothers."

Finally, when Joe Cactus and Nick Star's case ended, Arizona Southwest Border NTF officers and I arrested Cactus and Star at their residences in Yuma. We also arrested 11 of Cactus and Star's close criminal associates on Arizona State narcotics charges. Cactus and Star were later released from the Yuma county jail on a $140,000 bond that was initially posted by Jaime Garcia.

Throughout the Cactus and Star investigation, I worked an average of 16 hours a day for over 60 days conducting surveillance on Cactus and Star's case. I remained focused on the Garcia brothers and the corruption at San Luis POE.

The Garcia brothers were not charged for their suspected criminal activities with Joe Cactus and Nick Star. Officer Blackman and I agreed that there was not enough direct evidence with the brothers; only a lot of hearsay. Without a doubt, I believed that the brothers were involved in Cactus and Star's meth investigation.

I asked Officer Blackman, "Do you think the Garcia brothers are connected with the Spooks (CIA)?"

"Yes. The brothers are connected with the *Spooks*."

I was upset and thinking; I need to be careful if the brothers are working with the CIA. I am going to focus on the Garcia brothers and the law enforcement corruption at the Southwest POEs. I will arrest the brothers and end the corruption at the U.S. and Mexican POEs.

539 Pounds of Cocaine

Soon after the Pat Weed and Joe Cactus investigations were prosecuted on Federal and State narcotics violations in Arizona, I focused, again on the Garcia brothers and the corrupt officers and inspectors at San Luis POE.

Several days later, I received word early in the morning from an SOI that cocaine hidden inside a car seat was going to enter San Luis POE later today. The SOI told me the Garcia brothers had someone working at the POE to let the car, with the cocaine, enter the U.S. without an inspection.

183

Later that day, I arrived in the area and parked on a small hill overlooking San Luis POE. I wanted to be sure Customs and Immigration officers working at the POE would not see me watching from close by.

With a description of the car smuggling the cocaine and the SOI's information, I was able to see with my binoculars the suspected dope car entering the POE and traveling into the U.S. I called the DEA Yuma office for help to follow the *loaded dope* car. I saw the car drive into a public parking lot next to the POE. The male driver of the car parked and suddenly got out and walked away from the car. He disappeared quickly in the public parking lot.

I was confused and thinking; Why did the driver walk away from his car? Could he have entered one of the local stores? Did the driver see someone following him? Did a corrupt officer at the POE tell the driver I was watching him from the hill?

Once I arrived inside the parking lot, I wasn't able to look for the driver on foot because I was alone. I needed to stay where I could see the abandoned car with the cocaine. I waited for help from the DEA office and a Border Patrol narcotics dog sniffer.

184

Hopefully, the narcotics dog would alert to the presence of drugs in the dope car.

After a few minutes, a Border Patrol dog handler arrived at the parking lot. I noticed the narcotics dog was excited, jumping, and pulling his handler before they started to walk around the abandoned car. The dog

Seized 539 lbs. cocaine near San Luis POE

immediately alerted to drugs inside the car. Later, I found 539 pounds of cocaine inside the abandoned car's back seat. Help from the DEA office finally arrived at the parking lot.

I waited for the driver to return to his abandoned car because I wanted him to tell the Garcia brothers that DEA took their cocaine. I also wanted the driver to let the Garcia brothers know that I knew who the corrupt Immigration officer was at the POE. *It was incredible; the driver never returned for his car. I guess he walked back into Mexico.*

The Garcia brothers' organization had connections like tentacles of an octopus, reaching out and grabbing people in the

185

Yuma community to help smuggle their dope across the POE. The brothers appeared to be untouchable by law enforcement. But I had a sense of what I needed to do to get them prosecuted.

Everything started coming together. It was all there – marijuana, cocaine, heroin, corruption, and money laundering coming into the States from the POE. It seemed like every time an agent or an officer in law enforcement got close to the brothers' organization; the Garcia's case would shut down before federal and state prosecutions were final.

Spanish Priests called the Mountain

"El Camino del Diablo"

I didn't get the opportunity to meet with Don Ware, personally, when he was living in Las Vegas, Nevada. I knew he could provide a lot of information on the Garcia brothers' involvement in his kidnapping and attempted murder. I called Don and introduced myself. "I'm going to get the Garcia brothers in San Luis, Mexico, for what they tried to do to you and Roy."

"That would be great!" Don replied.

He said he was living in Las Vegas and still working for DEA. He had been through several surgeries and was in constant pain.

Don filled me in on details of what went down in San Luis, Mexico. Some of what I learned from Don was never in the reports that I had read.

There was no one I could trust at the Yuma office or in the Arizona Southwest Border Narcotics Task Force (NTF) without risking the Garcia brothers finding out that I was targeting them for what they did to Don and Roy. I didn't want some corrupt cop knowing I spoke with Don about the brothers. Not even my GS knew I talked to Don.

With Don and Roy always on my mind, I pushed myself to focus on the Garcia brothers' organization. I'd never met Don or Roy throughout the investigation, but they were part of my DEA family. This drove my determination to arrest the brothers, even though I was working other good criminal narcotics cases at the same time. The brothers' case was one I needed to solve as I kept Fighting my Greatest Enemy: Myself.

I decided to go after the three Garcia brothers slowly and cautiously. I needed to be careful and keep it very quiet within my office and in the Yuma law enforcement community. Even though I worked with both good and bad cops, I never forgot that I had to be careful. Yuma was a small hot desert border town located near the border of Mexico, and I wasn't sure who I could trust in law enforcement. I truly felt like I was on my own.

I found information from a variety of sources on the Garcia brother's organization. I discovered years of phone records from the *Sicarios* behind the attempted murder of Don and Roy. Calls were going to one of the Garcia brothers' homes in San Luis, Mexico. This occurred in 1985, during the time Kiki and his CI were tortured and killed.

I often did surveillance of the Arizona and Mexican border in San Luis from the Rocky Mountains overlooking Yuma. One day I went to San Luis POE with a Border Patrol agent that was assigned to the DEA office. As we returned to Yuma, driving North back from the POE, I looked toward the mountains on the east side of Yuma. I asked the Border Patrol agent, "How far do those mountains over there go down to Mexico from Arizona?"

188

El Camino del Diablo/Path of the Devil
the mountain in Yuma, AZ

"That mountain range runs from the Sonora Mexico region up through Yuma County," the Border Patrol agent told me. "In the early 18th century, Franciscan missionaries from Spain named the mountain range the El Camino del Diablo."

The Spanish missionaries used the base of the mountain range to guide them from Northern Mexico to Arizona and then on to the missionary churches in Southern California. The missionaries and other travelers talked about the trail up along the mountain being deadlier than going through Death Valley at that time. The Border Patrol agent said, "There are many unmarked graves along El Camino del Diablo mountain."

I thought the Garcia brothers' investigation was like El Camino del Diablo mountain and decided to name the brothers' criminal case "Camino del Diablo: Path of the Devil." The brothers and their *Sicarios* traveled the Path of the Devil, and now I was traveling alone on the same path, trying to catch them and their

189

Sicarios. But I needed to fight my greatest enemy: Myself, if I was going to succeed to end the corruption.

As the investigation into the brothers' narcotics smuggling operation progressed, several federal and state interagency and jurisdictional considerations came up. These considerations required my coordination with the Federal U.S. Attorney in the District of Arizona, DEA offices outside the area of Yuma County and Mexico.

Suspects in the Attempted Murder of DEA Agents

One of the agents in the DEA office, Agent Saul Morales, a Hispanic guy, received a call from the prosecutor in San Luis, Sonora, Mexico. The Mexican prosecutor had some information about suspects in the kidnapping and attempted murder of Don and Roy.

Later that day, I went with Saul to meet with the Mexican Prosecutor at his office in San Luis, Mexico. I asked the Prosecutor about the Garcia brothers' organization. He told me, "I'm working on several other ongoing criminal cases involving the brothers and their family."

As the Prosecutor said that, he pointed to four brown boxes stacked on the floor in his office. Without mentioning the Garcia brothers, he explained, "Those boxes contain criminal investigative reports written by FBI, DEA, Customs, and INS."

I said, "Can I look at the criminal documents in the boxes?"

He let me look at the reports written by U.S. law enforcement officials. I was shocked to see nothing redacted in the investigative reports, like the names of DEA agents, FBI agents, Customs agents, Immigration officers, and local law enforcement officers involved in ongoing investigative cases in the U.S and Mexico.

The investigative reports also included the methods of how DEA and other law enforcement agencies learned about the dope and who smuggled it into the U.S. by Mexican defendants who were trafficking for the Garcia brothers. I even saw DEA identification numbers for CIs and the names of witnesses on the reports.

I asked the Prosecutor if I could take the boxes. He told me, "Those boxes belong to someone else."

"Who is someone else, and how did you get them?" I asked.

191

"I received them from the U.S. Attorney's offices in the United States when I was checking on cases related to Mexican citizens arrested in the States. I think you Americans call it discovery."

I looked over at Saul and said, "The drug cartels will read the written *discovery* reports to learn how our agency, FBI, and other law enforcement operate in the United States, Mexico, Colombia, and many other counties in Central America, South America, Europe, and Asia. The cartels and the brothers are using our *discovery* to move their drugs and hide their money. DEA can never win the war on drugs. Our Justice Department knows that."

So, the drug cartels know the names of our agents, CIs, and witnesses from the released discovery investigative reports. It's incredible. No wonder DEA and cops can't win the war on drugs. The criminals are always one step ahead of us.

Driving back to the DEA Yuma office, I thought to myself; How could the boxes of law enforcement investigative reports and the Mexican prosecutors overlook the strenuous efforts made by the Garcia brothers to cover up the ambush of the two DEA agents. Don and Roy were kidnapped, beaten, shot, and left for dead near

192

the brothers' home because DEA had traced the major drug operations in San Luis to the brothers as written in the investigative reports.

Once we returned to Yuma, I reported to my GS and DEA Chief Legal counsel in Washington, D.C, what I saw in the boxes at the Mexican prosecutor's office in San Luis, Mexico.

Several days later, I drove up to Phoenix to meet with Assistant U.S. Attorney, AUSA Jonah Goodwill and presented him with what I knew, so far, about the organization and the boxes of investigative reports at the Mexican prosecutor's office. AUSA Goodwill had already learned from his prosecution reports that the three Garcia brothers were behind the attempted murder of the DEA agents in 1975, and there were U.S. warrants for the brothers' arrest in Mexico. Somehow, the brothers were never arrested in Mexico.

I explained to Goodwill about the meeting with the San Luis, Sonora, Mexican Federal Prosecutor. The Mexican Federal Prosecutor told me that Mexico was very interested in pursuing the arrest of the Garcia brothers. He was anxious to get them for the attempted murder of DEA agents Don Ware and Roy Stevenson.

He encouraged me and said, "DEA needs to pursue this again!"

Then he added, "Larry, let's go ahead and open up a criminal investigation on the brothers."

We negotiated the venue, extradition, and prosecution to obtain evidence from a foreign country (Mexico). He explained that the U.S Attorney's Office in Phoenix would coordinate any legality issues with San Luis, Sonora, Mexican Federal Prosecutor's office regarding the extradition of the brothers to the U.S. and the released discovery reports.

I said again, "The discovery reports related to drug offenses released to the defendants in Mexico and throughout the world have to stop. DEA can never win this war on drugs."

Shaking his head in disgust, He said, "I'll look into it."

Like me, he was upset with the corruption of law enforcement in Yuma and advised me to be careful with the investigation. He knew the Arizona and Mexican border was a very dangerous place to work because of the corruption. I told him, "I am more worried about getting shot by a Customs or Immigration officer, than the Mexican police or one of the Garcia brothers."

I'm from Bogota, Colombia

Drug cartel leaders would never talk drugs with undercover cops or informants, only to close family members and relatives. I needed a way into the Garcia brothers' organization, starting at the top. An undercover agent or a CI can't just walk into an organization and ask for drugs from the brothers. An undercover agent or a CI could do that at the *street level*, but it's no way to penetrate the top of a drug organization.

I knew it was all about the money for the brothers and for the corrupt Customs and Immigration officers. Money played a role on both sides of the U.S. and Mexican border, and someone in law enforcement or maybe our government was keeping the brothers out of jail in Mexico and the United States.

I decided to find a CI that was not from Yuma, Arizona or San Luis, Mexico. I needed a CI who was not Mexican but could speak Spanish. He needed to be a business type of informant to help me uncover what was going on with the brothers' drug organization and to help identify law enforcement corruption at San Luis POE.

195

I called the main DEA office in Phoenix and told the agent, "I need to develop a CI who doesn't live in Yuma or in Mexico. Most local and federal cops and their sources know everyone in the Yuma County area. I need to bring in a CI with his or her own legitimate agriculture produce business or any other business, hopefully outside of Arizona."

"What kind of Confidential Informant (CI) do you need?"

"Someone classy and well-dressed who doesn't look like a doper. The CI needs to have his own business. Preferably in the U.S."

While waiting for a CI from Phoenix, I started meeting with the PIs and SOIs, regularly when the PIs were in Yuma. They provided me with a lot of information about the Garcia brothers' operation moving drugs on agriculture produce trucks and corrupt law enforcement, helping the brothers smuggle their dope across San Luis POE.

Several weeks later, I got a call from an agent at DEA Phoenix. The agent in Phoenix said, "I found a CI who owns a shrimp business in Hermosillo, Mexico. The CI was arrested by DEA for cocaine trafficking in the United States and served five years in federal prison. After five years, he was released from federal prison and has a felony record for trafficking drugs. This guy is a reliable source who's helped DEA with some good cocaine cases in the U.S. and south of the border. However, he has a cocaine problem and a weakness for women. He sniffs cocaine and screws anything that looks like a girl."

The agent said, "The CI is from Colombia."

I told him, "Okay, that's perfect! The CI is what I want. I want to meet him. Have him call me."

I was thinking; It takes a crook to do a crook. Wow! Now, I can have a reliable CI who owns a shrimp business in Mexico operating in the Garcia brothers' own backyard.

The CI contacted me a few days later, and I invited him to Yuma so that we could meet in person. I wanted to see what the CI looked like and the way he dressed. It was also crucial for me to let him talk about who he was and what he did for DEA. This was my way of learning how truthful he was and if I could trust him.

When the CI and I met for the first time in Yuma, he drove up to the restaurant in a very nice gray Lexus. He was wearing black slacks and a red polo shirt. His hair was black, cut above the ears,

197

and his face was clean-shaven; very classy and spoke English well with a heavy accent. I could tell he was educated and came from a good background from Colombia.

I said, "You don't look like a Mexican."

"I'm not, I'm Colombian."

"You're Colombian?"

"Yes, I'm from Bogota, Colombia."

Everything was going great, and I was trying not to get too excited. This CI is very polite and easy-going, and everything the CI told me was validated by what I already knew about him.

"What's your background? Why do you want to work for me?"

"I snorted a lot of cocaine and made a lot of money several years ago from selling the stuff. One time I made a phone call to a DEA agent who was working undercover. DEA arrested me, and I went to federal prison for five years for conspiracy and trafficking cocaine," said the CI.

He told me, "I live in Phoenix, but I have my own shrimp business in Mexico. I have to travel back and forth to check on my shrimp business."

I suddenly thought, *Yeah, there's more involved here*, but I kept my suspicions to myself.

I told him, "But you're out of prison now and working for DEA. Look, this is what I want you to do. I want you to work for me, and I want to see what you can do."

Then, I told him, "There's this other guy you might know who lives in Mexico and owns a shrimp business. Have you heard of Javier Garcia?"

The CI didn't know the guy.

I said, "Okay, if you want to work for me, I'll pay you, but you come under my direction and nobody else. While working for me, you don't snort cocaine or screw women, especially young girls. Do you know the difference between a woman and a girl? If you get hurt while working for me, you'll get disability for the rest of your life. In other words, you're a part of the DEA family. I am very serious about that. I'm going to call you Santo. Are you okay with that name?"

"Sure."

"This is what we've got going on, Santo."

Fighting for Our Lives

I was working with Yuma Internal Revenue Service (IRS), Agent Tony Cash, and targeting the Garcia brothers' agriculture farm and shrimp business financial records in the United States. Agent Cash established that the brothers were making millions of U.S. dollars selling produce and shrimp in the U.S. Because of my close working relationship with Agent Cash, I trusted him. I decided to move into his IRS office next door to the DEA office. Both offices were located in the same building on the second floor with the FBI.

Tony told me he found out from his sources the brothers' produce warehouse in San Luis, Mexico, was severely damaged in a fire early in the morning.

I said, "Hey Tony, let's go take a look at the warehouse. I'll drive into Mexico."

Within a few minutes after crossing into Mexico from San Luis POE, we arrived at the burned produce warehouse. As we exited the car and started walking into what was a warehouse structure, I looked on the damaged floor for any criminal evidence.

I noticed several black honeybees flying near hundreds of broken and burned honeycombs.

I remembered once when I was cutting tobacco on Carol Ray's farm, and I got into a fight with big black Bumblebees. The Bumblebees stung me in the butt several times, and I realized I was losing the battle. I started to walk away from the Bumblebees, but they kept following me until I ran home. Within minutes I had red hives on my skin and could hardly breathe. Momma immediately took me to Doctor Skaggs's office in Taylorsville. At the doctor's office, I learned that I was allergic to bee stings.

I immediately yelled, "Hey Tony, be careful stepping on the broken honeycombs. Whatever you do, don't fight the bees if they try to sting you." From my farm boy experience fighting Bumblebees, I thought to myself; *These bees are really mad that a fire destroyed their honeycombs inside the warehouse. I am also allergic to bee stings.*

I was too late. When I looked at Tony, he was already waving both hands, trying to hit the bees. I screamed, "Tony, stop fighting the bees."

201

Suddenly, I saw thousands of black bees attacking Tony's head. He was screaming, "Help me! Help me!"

Knowing I'm allergic to bee stings, I quickly walked away from Tony and the broken honeycombs. I was going to get inside the car, but I heard him still yelling, "Help me!"

Without thinking, I turned around and slowly walked up to Tony. I reached for his hair and grabbed a handful of bees in my left hand, squeezing them to death. I could feel the bees stinging my hand. Then I grabbed his hand with my right hand, and we moved quickly into a vacant building.

After the bees flew away, Tony and I immediately went to my car. "We have to get to Yuma Hospital now. I am allergic to bee stings," I told him.

He was not saying a word.

After entering San Luis POE into Arizona, I drove at high speed to the Yuma hospital emergency room. In the emergency room, the Doctor told us, "You were both stung several times all over your bodies. You were lucky these were not the deadly brown bees."

The next day, Tony told me he was in trouble with his IRS Supervisor for not getting approval to leave the United States and enter Mexico. "I needed an IRS supervisor's approval to enter a foreign country (Mexico)."

I told him, "I don't understand, Tony. I don't need DEA's approval to work across the Mexican border. I just let someone at the Yuma office know I am going down to Mexico. Once I'm in Mexico, I drink a few corona beers and get something barbequed to eat. Sometimes, I looked at the bad guys' residences and wrote down license plates numbers, especially U.S. license plates."

"Larry, you are DEA. You can go anywhere you want, but me, I am in trouble with IRS," he told me.

An Explosion Inside the IRS Office

Several days later, I found some firecrackers in my desk that my nephew, George, gave me. Some of the firecrackers were very small, but they made a loud bang, like a gunshot sound.

George, a California Highway Patrol (CHP) officer in San Diego, California, had confiscated several boxes of firecrackers and bottle rockets during a traffic stop near the San Ysidro border.

203

When he came to Yuma to visit, he had the firecrackers and bottle rockets with him.

I said, "George, let's buy a case of beer and pick up our friend, Ramon. We'll drive out to the open desert and have some fun with the firecrackers and bottle rockets."

Driving Kathy's little green Mazda, we all went out to the desert at night to lite the firecrackers and bottle rockets. I remembered Ramon had a huge bottle rocket in his left hand and a bottle of beer in his right hand. George lit the fuse on the rocket and told Ramon in Spanish to let it fly up into the dark sky.

Suddenly, Ramon dropped his beer to the ground. He reached down to get his beer, and the bottle rocket flew off his left hand and entered the open rear window of the little green Mazda. The Mazda's back seat exploded in sparkles and white smoke.

I screamed, "The boxes with the firecrackers are going to explode. Run."

I was lucky the boxes didn't burn and explode.

With one of the firecrackers in my hand, I recalled the time when my brother Jeffrey threw a firecracker under Mr. McGee's seat on the school bus. Also, the time I put a firecracker under a narcotics officer's chair while he was cleaning his gun at his desk.

At Agent Cash's office, I was wondering; Is this firecracker going to make a sound like a gunshot when I set it off inside the IRS building?

Wow. Did it make a big bang! Some of the IRS employees thought I shot my gun off accidentally.

I told Agent Cash later that it was a firecracker, but he didn't laugh.

After that incident, I moved back to the DEA office. I guess Agent Cash and his supervisor didn't like the firecracker incident inside their IRS office.

Leaks and Corruption in Law Enforcement

DEA developed an Organized Crime Drug Enforcement Task Force (OCDETF) in 1982 to create "a comprehensive attack against organized drug traffickers" and money laundering. DEA agents ran the local OCDETF, and all the agents became cross-sworn Deputy Sheriffs with credentials to arrest people on state charges.[26]

205

The local OCDETF members were from regional offices of DEA, Customs Service, FBI, IRS, United States Attorney's Office, Yuma County Attorney's office, Yuma County Sheriff's Department, Yuma Police Department, San Luis Police Department, Indian Tribal Police, Border Patrol, Arizona Southwest Border Narcotics Task Force, and several other law enforcement agencies in the Yuma County area.

With the approval of AUSA Goodwill in Phoenix, I initiated an elaborate conspiracy against the brothers. I was able to build a specialized law enforcement local group in Yuma to work with me to focus solely on the investigation of the Garcia brothers' organization.

The investigation was unique because it incorporated the Garcia brothers and their family relatives' drug trafficking organization with Mexico, Colombia, Spain, Southeast Asia, and the United States. The brothers had a conspiracy to smuggle large quantities of narcotics into the U.S. and launder vast amounts of U.S. currency back into Mexico.

According to my CIs and SOIs, the brothers were all-powerful drug traffickers. They had been targets in the United

206

States and Mexico for various federal, state, and local law enforcement investigations since the mid-70s.

The brothers were principal organizers and participants in the importation and distribution of large quantities of drugs into the U.S. using agriculture and shrimp trucks with the help of corrupt law enforcement officials at San Luis POE.

According to CIs, SOIs, and local law enforcement, the brothers' organization transported marijuana, cocaine, meth, and heroin into the U.S. They used other relatives working with corrupt U.S. Customs and Immigration officers, Border Patrol agents, local law enforcement officers, and politicians. Previous DEA investigative cases had been shut down before ever getting to prosecute the brothers because of internal leaks in law enforcement agencies.

Law enforcement corruption at San Luis POE created many roadblocks for me to seize narcotics from the brothers. Most of the federal agents and the local law enforcement officers knew how to avoid corruption at San Luis POE. They stayed away from working with me, targeting the Garcia brothers.

207

Corrupt law enforcement at San Luis POE allowed the Garcia organization to smuggle drugs through their tunnels, cars, trucks, and semi-tractor trailers trucks into the U.S.

I didn't mention corruption at this time to any other agents or officers in the OCDETF, only to GS Moreno. I was still not sure who I could trust or where the leaks might be coming from.

The brothers were well protected and insulated by the "family" and corrupt law enforcement at the POE.

The SOIs and CIs continued to provide me information that the Garcia organization was controlling other Border Patrol checkpoints along the U.S. and Mexican border.

I didn't see how an investigative case was dismissed by the AUSA office in Phoenix every time an agent or cop got close to the brothers' criminal activities. It may have been possible there was someone corrupt higher up in the law enforcement community. I became even more determined to get the brothers and anyone in the law enforcement connected to their drug trafficking operation.

Only a very few unidentified law enforcement officers on the U.S. side of the border knew about the brothers' tunnels, and they were the corrupt few.

208

I was disappointed and wondering; How is it possible that law enforcement didn't know about the tunnels?

I felt like I was never going to be successful because of corruption. I learned the CIs and SOIs provided information to other DEA agents on corrupt officials in Mexico, and the U.S. who furnished protection and cooperation with the Garcia organization. I established that the alleged corrupt officials at San Luis POE were, most likely, the overriding factor in the brothers' trafficking success.

I worked alone but sometimes with the PIs, CIs, and SOIs. To avoid leaks and corruption, I only communicated with AUSA Goodwill in Phoenix and the DEA Chief Legal Counsel Department in Washington, D.C.

I didn't want to get involved with corruption at the border or in Yuma, so I didn't push to target the corrupt agents and cops. Life is too short, and there was only so much I was willing to risk of not getting shot by a corrupt agent or officer.

I'm Not Stopping

I received a phone call from a CI in San Diego who needed to meet with me regarding the Garcia brothers. Kathy told me, "I want to go and see my sister in San Diego."

I said, "Okay, but we are not stopping for you to pee or poop until I am in San Diego. I don't want to be late for the meeting with the CI."

After driving about two hours traveling west on Interstate-8, Kathy said, "I have to pee."

"What! We will be in San Diego in less than one hour."

She said again, "I have to go."

"Here is my empty coke cup, because I'm not stopping for you to pee."

Kathy grabbed the cup.

After finishing, she said, "How do I get rid of the pee?"

"I am not going to stop the car, but I will slow down. Throw it out the window."

She threw the pee out the window but not the cup. The wind outside pushed the pee back into the car, hitting me on the face and lips.

I yelled, "You were supposed to throw the cup out the window with the pee!"

With my face and lips wet from Kathy's pee, I was angrily telling myself; *Next time she has to pee, I am stopping, especially if she has to poop.*

"Be on the alert; stand firm in the faith, act like men, be strong" (1 Corinthians 16:13 New American Standard Version).

Little Sweet-Pea .38-Revolver

I was following the Garcia brothers' family members throughout the hot day in San Luis, Arizona, and across the border in Mexico. I got a phone call from my GS Juan Antonio Moreno for help to locate a felony. He told me there was a Federal felony arrest warrant for Poncho Gato, a suspected murderer. According to a sister of the felon, Poncho, was staying at their parents' home in Yuma.

GS Juan Antonio said, "Poncho Cato is armed and extremely dangerous. The sister does not want DEA agents to go to the house and arrest Poncho because her parents are old and sick.

211

She said, 'Poncho is leaving tomorrow morning early. She wants DEA agents to wait until Poncho leaves their parent's house tomorrow morning."

On the way back to Yuma from San Luis, Mexico, the new Agent, Carlos Lopez was driving his car. I was sitting in the passenger seat, thinking about calling Kathy to tell her I want to be home tonight. I noticed there were about a dozen white sheep in front of us walking out of the lemon grove slowly across the road, followed by a young Mexican boy.

I yelled at Agent Lopez, "Slow down; you're going to run over the sheep and the boy."

I yelled again at him, "You're going to kill the sheep and the boy!"

He skidded the car right into the sheep.

It was too late. Some of the sheep were jumping around everywhere, even on top of the car hood. Agent Lopez quickly jerked the car off the road. After traveling up along the water canal and missing several lemon trees, he finally drove the car back onto the highway.

I told him, "I don't think you killed any sheep. I saw the boy in the canal. Speed it up! I need to get to the office now, so I can get out to Poncho Cato parent's house to arrest Poncho before he decides to leave Yuma."

When I got back to Yuma, with the information from GS Juan Antonio, I had Agent Saul Morales and Agent Lopez go with me to Poncho's parent's house. Agents Morales, Lopez, and I went in separate cars. Agent Lopez had been on the job for less than a year. We arrived in our three unmarked cars and set up undercover surveillance near Poncho Cato parent's house.

Later that evening, I found out from my office that, according to GS Juan Antonio, the sister of the felon, was staying the night inside with her parents. She would contact DEA early in the morning when Poncho is ready to leave the house.

Without a doubt, this was going to be a typical long night. I couldn't let Poncho Cato leave the house, armed, and was thinking, *If I don't arrest this guy, Poncho might hurt a cop during a traffic stop. Poncho's an armed murderer with a DEA Federal warrant for his arrest. This 'bad guy' is a danger to the public and the law enforcement community.*

213

I had asked Agent Lopez to park next to Agent Morales and me for our safety and told him, "I don't want Poncho to sneak up on me while I am relaxed or sleeping. If he does, you are going to regret it. I want you to focus on Poncho's house like a night owl that just found his first rat."

I told Agent Lopez to watch the front door of the house and Poncho's car and not to worry. "I will get a call from the office if Poncho leaves the house."

I was wondering; Can I trust Agent Lopez not to fall asleep while Agent Morales and I are sleeping?

He told me, "I'll watch the house, and if there is any movement, I'll wake you up."

I closed my eyes for a few minutes. Suddenly, I opened one eye and looked over at Agent Lopez's car. I could see his head on the car steering wheel. *Wow, the new agent is sleeping.*

It was between 2:00 am and 3:00 am., I got out of my car and jumped in the passenger seat with Agent Morales and touched him on the arm.

He woke up and asked me, "What happened?"

214

"That damn new agent is sleeping! But don't worry, Poncho's car is still at the residence. I haven't received any information from GS Juan Antonio about Poncho leaving his parent's house."

I slowly rolled down the passenger window and pulled out my little sweet-pee .38-revolver snub nose midnight special from inside my pants.

Agent Morales said, "What are you going to do with your gun."

I told him, "Watch Agent Lopez jump screaming for help."

Agent Morales could see I was aiming towards Agent Lopez's car. He was surprised I was going to shoot my Sweet-Pea over Agent Lopez's head.

Little Sweet-Pea .38

I pointed my *little sweet-pee .38* out the window in the air and squeezed one bullet round into the darkness.

Agent Lopez jumped up from his car seat with his gun in his right hand, screaming, "What happened? What happened?"

215

I yelled at Agent Lopez, "You are supposed to watch the house."

He didn't say a word.

It seems like the sound of the bullet round from the *.38* echoed in the early morning darkness for several seconds. Within minutes, a Yuma County Sheriff's marked car arrived in the area, driving slowly, with his patrol car's spotlight shining on our undercover cars.

The Sheriff officer soon recognized that DEA agents were up to something in the neighborhood. He immediately turned off his spotlight and left the area. Shortly after the loud noise of my *Sweet-Pea*, the sister called GS Juan Antonio from inside the house. She told him, "Poncho and I heard a gunshot, and Poncho sees a police car going by our house. My brother is leaving the house now."

Poncho came out the front door, running to his car barefoot and no shirt. Agent Morales and I were already in position standing next to Poncho's car with our guns pointed directly at him. I shouted, "Hey Poncho, DEA. Don't move, or I'll shoot you between the eyes."

216

Poncho almost ran over me, trying to get to his car.

Within seconds, Agent Lopez had Poncho on the ground, eating dirt and handcuffed him. I thought; *Agent Lopez is doing a good job, but the new agent can do a lot better by staying awake.*

Undercover Los Angles Narcotics Officers

I told my Group Supervisor (GS), Juan Antonio Moreno, "I got a call from a Private Investigator (PI) working with two Los Angeles Police Department (LAPD) Narcotics officers. LAPD and PI want to talk to me about the Garcia brothers and law enforcement corruption in Yuma. I'm going to meet with the PI and the two LAPD Narcotics officers in San Diego to find out what they can tell me about the brothers and who the corrupt officials are at the POE."

GS Juan Antonio gave me his okay.

While I was getting things ready to leave for San Diego, I got a call from GS Juan Antonio. He told me, "I had a meeting with the Customs supervisor and mentioned your work with the Garcia brothers' case. I told the Customs supervisor you are meeting with reliable LAPD narcotics officers and a PI in San Diego to get more information about the brothers' criminal connections at the POE."

Why would GS Juan Antonio do that?

He told me the Customs supervisor asked if I could take one of his new Customs agent with me to San Diego. The Customs supervisor's office was also looking at the drug activities of the brothers at the POE. I was devastated.

Then I thought, I remember once at a barbeque at the NTF parking lot in Yuma that the Customs supervisor introduced his wife to me. After I drank a few beers with Customs agents, the wife told me she was her husband's Informant. Wow! A Customs supervisor married his Informant.

I couldn't believe what I was hearing. I had worked so hard to keep a low profile in Yuma, and now my efforts were for nothing. I asked GS Juan Antonio, "You're telling me I have to take a Customs agent with me to San Diego?"

"Yeah, because Customs is targeting the brothers, too."

"But Customs is not working the Garcia's case with me. I don't work well with Customs agents, and I typically don't share information with Customs, especially anything on the brothers."

218

"But Larry, Customs is working on the Garcia brothers' narcotics trafficking organization. This new Customs agent is out of Florida, and she doesn't know anything about the brothers. She is just going to go with you to the meeting in San Diego to see what DEA has already learned so she can tell her Customs supervisor."

I wondered; Why would the Customs supervisor assign a young Customs female agent to go with me to San Diego. She had less than a year on the job and no experience working in this kind of case. There was nothing wrong with her, but if you're going to give me an agent, provide me someone with experience, especially with the severity of what's going on out here with the corruption at the POE.

I had no choice. I accepted my new *temporary partner, a Customs agent.*

The new Customs agent and I showed up in San Diego. I noticed a man dressed in a black suit walking between two white guys who looked like they were homeless. I was curiously thinking; *Without a doubt, he is the PI walking towards me between two typical-looking LAPD (Los Angeles Police Department) undercover narcotics officers.*

219

The LAPD officers looked like they lived on the beach! One wore baggy shorts, a Bermuda shirt, and worn-out tennis shoes. The other wore blue jeans, an open-collared shirt, and white tennis shoes. The narcotics officers were both smiling as they walked up to me.

The PI first introduced himself as Private Investigator Harry Fresno. I then looked at the LAPD narcotics guys. I immediately trusted the officers, and when I'm comfortable with someone in the law enforcement community, they're part of my family. I take care of my family.

"Hi, I'm Larry Ray Hardin."

I shook hands with the Narcotics officers and PI Fresno. The PI nodded to the girl and asked, "Who's this?"

"She's a Customs agent out of Yuma," I said.

"No, I don't want to talk to you. I want to talk to Agent Hardin," said PI Fresno.

"What?" I asked, "Why don't you want to talk to her?"

"I don't want to talk to the Customs agent," PI Fresno said, "I am not sharing information with Customs about anything in Yuma or at the POE." Then he turned to walk away.

220

The two LAPD Narcotics officers grabbed PI Fresno by his arms. They told him, "Look, you came down here to San Diego. Go ahead and talk to Larry." The officers finally convinced him to come back and talk to me.

We all went into a coffee shop and sat down and started talking about the Garcia brothers. I noticed the PI kept looking over at the Narcotics officers. The next thing I knew, one of the officers, with the baggy shorts and the Bermuda shirt, began flirting with the Customs agent.

Then he said to her, "Let me buy you an ice cream cone! Come on! Let's go." And she followed him out of the coffee shop!

I couldn't believe that she would be that naïve to follow the Narcotics officer! I questioned myself; She may think he's just going to buy you ice cream, but he plans to take you to his car. Who knows what he is going to do to you?

I could tell PI Fresno was just happy to have the Customs agent out of earshot.

PI Fresno said, "My client, who is the owner, heard from one of his managers at his maquiladora furniture company in San Luis, Mexico, about the use of his trucks for drug trafficking. He

221

wants to put a stop to it immediately! The manager at the maquiladora company also told him it was an agent from DEA searching the furniture trucks. This was not something he wants to be associated with his furniture company."

I asked him, "Did your client mention the DEA agent's name that was searching his trucks?"

PI Fresno told me, "He said, the DEA agent's last name was Hardin."

I was wondering; Who told the manager at the maquiladora company my last name? Did someone in my office or at the POE leak my name to the brothers?

PI Fresno explained, "A Customs agent in Las Vegas told me, 'Don't deal with the Customs agents in Yuma. But this DEA Hardin guy seems like he has good integrity. You may be able to talk to Hardin. He has an active case going on with all of the Garcia brothers. Don't talk with Customs agents or anyone else in the law enforcement community in Yuma; only with Hardin."

I explained to him, "One thing about my job is that I don't talk about my case with any civilian or PIs. You give me the information on the Garcia brothers' drug activities and any law enforcement corruption. If you give me information, I'll check it out. If it's for real, I'll come back and tell you that your information is right on. I'll let you know if it gets too dangerous. If I feel anything is wrong or you're getting too close, I'll tell you."

"I'm not here to give you information about what I'm doing, but tell me what you have," I told PI Fresno.

I added, "Be very careful because when you are in Yuma and asking questions about the brothers. You need to understand that there are bad people on both sides of the fence in Yuma and San Luis, Mexico."

I then listened to what he and the LAPD Narcotics officer knew about the brothers' involvement with corrupt cops in the Yuma and San Luis POE. I did not offer anything in return.

They talked about how the furniture trucks were used for the Garcia brothers' criminal activities.

PI Fresno said, "I know the Garcia brothers are using the owner's furniture trucks to transport narcotics into the United States at San Luis POE. I believe someone in law enforcement is protecting the brothers."

223

PI Fresno couldn't speak for long, because the other Narcotics officer and the Customs agent came back to the meeting. After that, PI Fresno didn't want to continue talking in front of the Customs agent.

I said to the PI, "I'll tell you what, you come out to Yuma, and I'll meet with you at one of the hotels. There you can talk more about the Garcia brothers and what you know about the corruption in Yuma."

I was thinking, PI Harry Fresno already knew of corruption inside the law enforcement community in Yuma. He had done his homework, too. He knew the brothers were involved in smuggling narcotics, and that something was taking place at the owner's furniture business in Mexico.

Driving back from San Diego to Yuma, the Customs agent started crying.

I said, "What happened with you and the LAPD officer?"

She said, "I don't like the way the PI treated me at the meeting. He wouldn't let me be part of the discussion about the brothers."

224

She knew the PI intentionally did not want her at the meeting.

"Look, I'm not here to protect you. You're a United States Customs agent. You have a badge and a gun, and you're assigned to the Arizona Southwest Border Narcotics Task Force in Yuma. You could've stopped that bullshit right away with the PI. You're in control; you are a federal agent."

I asked her, "Why did you leave with the officer? Did he buy you ice cream, or did he take you to his car? You know what, you're a woman, a lot of cops are going to try to get into your panties, deal with it. You're young, and the way you're acting, people will hit on you, especially guys in law enforcement."

I felt like I gave her some good advice about cops.

She started to cry again, so I ask her, "What happened now?"

She finally stopped crying and didn't say anything more.

Regardless of the drama with the Customs agent, I was impressed with PI Harry Fresno. He was very smart and forthright, and I felt like I could trust him, even though he was a PI and an

225

SOI. He had been a lieutenant at the Los Angeles Sheriff's Department for many years. I just had a good feeling about him.

He told me at the meeting about Joselito Garcia. Joselito was using his client's furniture trucks to smuggle drugs into the U.S. from Mexico at San Luis POE. Joselito was very dangerous. I warned him to be careful dealing with Joselito.

There were a lot of different trucks coming across the border at San Luis POE into the U.S. that I knew were being used by the Garcia brothers. I just wanted to get one truck with the dope.

In less than two weeks, a meeting was set up in Yuma with PI Harry Fresno and me.

The Mexico White House

PI Harry Fresno flew his private plane to Yuma to meet with me in Yuma. He told me he was staying at the Shiloh Inn, a very nice hotel outside of Yuma. I asked DEA Agent Saul Morales to go with me because I didn't want to see the PI and his employees alone. That was something I didn't do.

We met in PI Fresno's room. He had two of his PI employees with him; PI Jeff Pearce was the lead investigator.

226

I explained, "What you're giving me can help with my case on the brothers' drug activities."

PI Fresno said, "I have information that my client's furniture business in San Luis, Mexico is being used by the Garcia brothers and their family members to smuggle drugs into the United States."

He was giving me all the intel on the brothers, their relatives, and law enforcement corruption in Yuma and San Luis POE.

He said, "The owner in Los Angeles doesn't want their top managers indicted by DEA. That is why he wants me to work with you and DEA."

After some discussion, I agreed that PI Fresno had some of the same information on the Garcia brothers' organization. He also told me about a lot of law enforcement corruption in Yuma.

It was unbelievable how PI Fresno and his two PIs got their information from the brothers' criminal associates. PI Jeff Pearce gave me the name of Garcia's brother-in-law, Flaco El Pulpo. El Pulpo was one of the employees at the furniture business in San Luis, Mexico. According to PI Pearce, El Pulpo was the brother-in-law of Javier Garcia. Then PI Pearce provided me El Pulpo's phone number in Mexico.

When we ended the meeting, I offered to take PI Fresno's two PIs across the border to see the Garcia brothers' homes in Mexico.

The next morning Agent Morales and I met at the DEA office and drove an undercover reddish-brown, beat up, ugly Mercury G-car over to the hotel to pick up PI Fresno's two PIs. Everything was very professional. "Come on, you two. Come with us." PI Pearce and the other PI got into the back seat.

Before taking off, Agent Morales put a Mexican plate on our DEA undercover car. I told the PIs, "We do it all the time before entering Mexico. The DEA agents and I change the Arizona license plates to Mexican plates for our safety when doing undercover surveillance in Mexico and entering San Luis POE."

At San Luis POE, U.S. Customs and Immigration officers knew Agent Morales and I were DEA agents, but Mexican Customs didn't. The windows on DEA undercover cars are blackened out, so no one could see inside the cars. The Yuma agents and I drove our

DEA cars and pickup trucks across the border from Arizona into Mexico, with Mexican license plates.

Within a few minutes, I told the PIs, "Okay, we're coming up on it."

"Coming up on what?" PI Pearce asked.

"The Garcia brothers' homes."

The two homes looked like miniature versions of the White House, sitting catty-corner from each other. PI Pearce yelled, "I can see the gun turrets on top of the homes."

I pointed out Jaime Garcia's house, right next to the warehouse. "It's called the Conqeladora (*Ice House*). PI Pearce said, "My sources told me the brothers have underground tunnels connecting all their homes and the Icehouse."

Miniature White House

The other PI in the back seat had his camera and was ready to take pictures. I told them, "You need to be very careful here in San Luis, Mexico. The local Mexican town cops are protecting the brothers and their family

229

members. You don't want the Mexican cops to see you taking pictures of the brothers' homes."

It was highly unusual to see two large homes like that in San Luis, Mexico. There was no way the brothers would have those homes just from their produce and shrimp businesses.

American Business in Mexico – The Maquiladora

The PIs, SOIs, and CIs often reminded me of the work they were doing at the border and in Mexico targeting the brothers' drug activities. I knew one day I was going to find drugs on Jaime's produce truck or Javier's shrimp truck. The only explanation was the brothers were getting help from corrupt law enforcement, employees at a maquiladora business, and their relatives working as U.S. officers at the POE.

When an American business had a location in Mexico, it was known as the maquiladora. Mexican law required a president of the maquiladora business to be a Mexican citizen. If I could only connect the drugs with a maquiladora business, I could show how the Garcia brothers were smuggling some of their dope into the U.S.

230

The PIs, SOIs, CIs, and I knew some of the maquiladora companies in Mexico were terrible. Many of the companies working conditions were unpleasant and unsafe, and some of their employees were only getting 50¢ an hour. The Garcia brothers used some of the maquiladora employees earning lower wages to transport their drugs into the United States.

The United States and the Mexican government were making money from the legitimate maquiladora companies operating in Mexico. The brothers also were taking advantage of the maquiladoras for drug distribution in the U.S. I believed the Garcia brothers were paying off the corrupt managers of the maquiladora companies and officials on both sides of the border to move their dope in the company trucks into the U.S.

I thought; The brothers are Mexicans, but when they lived in the United States and ran their dope business using the maquiladora companies in Mexico, they never worried about law enforcement at the POE.

Almost Shot by a California Highway Patrol Officer

I received information from the PIs that a load of "dope" with furniture was on an 18-wheel semi-truck left Yuma traveling west on Interest 8 (I-8). With the description of the furniture truck and the driver, I jumped into my old grey Mercury car with Agent Saul Morales in the passenger seat.

I pushed the old Mercury up to about 95 to 120 miles an hour traveling towards El Centro, California, going west on I-8 highway. Agent Morales said to me, "California Highway Patrol (CHP) and Border Patrol agents are going to chase us down."

I yelled, "Don't worry, buddy, the CHP and the agent's cars are not fast enough for this old Mercury."

I was only thinking; I want that furniture truck, the driver, and the Garcia brothers' dope.

Well, I was wrong. My old Mercury car was not fast enough to outrun the CHP and Border Patrol cars.

In my rear-view mirror, I could see a CHP marked car and Border Patrol cars and pickup trucks approaching quickly behind me. I said to Agent Morales, "I have to stop. If not, the cops might spike the tires up the road."

232

I decided to slow down and pulled over to the side of the road. Suddenly, I could see in my rear-view mirror several Border Patrol agents and CHP officers, pointing their handguns and rifles toward my car. I heard a female voice say, "Driver exit your vehicle with your hands up and over your head."

I said to Agent Morales, "Hey brother, stay cool, don't move. I'll take care of it. Just watched how I handle this."

I put my DEA credentials in my left hand and slowly got out of my car. I saw that the CHP was a female officer. She looked very pretty, standing behind her driver's side car door, pointing her gun at my face. I yelled at her, "I am DEA, credentials in my hand."

She continued to point her gun at me, saying, "Don't you face me. Turn around and walk backward slowly until I tell you to stop."

As I walked back to the officer, I noticed Agent Morales inside the old Mercury was yelling at me, "Larry, hurry up! We're going to lose the truck!"

I was thinking, Wow, there are a lot of guns pointed at me. Agent Morales needs to stop yelling.

233

Finally, the CHP officer said, "Stop and turn around slowly with your hands in the air."

I told her, "I am a DEA agent," as I turned around to walk back to where she and the Border Patrol agents were waiting.

The CHP officer took my credentials from my hand. Then she said, "I am sorry, I didn't know you were DEA. Your license plate on the Mercury is Mexican."

Wow!

I smiled and said to the CHP officer and the Border Patrol agents, "I am following a load of dope. I forgot to take off the Mexican license plate. I am sorry I scared you guys."

Once I was in the driver seat of my old Mercury, Agent Morales asked, "What happened?"

"Nothing much. The female CHP officer was doing her job. You know that the furniture truck is too far away for me to find it. It is hot out here in the desert. Are you ready to drink some cold Corona beers and get something to eat before we go back to Yuma?"

He said, "Okay."

I was happily thinking; Another great day on the job.

234

Young Girls and Cops

Even though the Garcia brothers lived across the border in Mexico, their families were very active in Yuma and with the church community. The brothers owned homes in Yuma. Jaime Garcia taught his young daughters how to spy on law enforcement officers. The young Garcia girls learned quickly from friends at church, school, parties, and corrupt relatives in the law enforcement, the local bars where the good cops hung out in Yuma.

Once Jaime's daughters targeted a cop or an agent, the girls would use sex to develop a close relationship with them. The girls didn't care if the cop was old enough to be their dad or grandpa. They wanted to help dad find a weak link to help him and his brothers with their drug business.

Working Alone Across the Border in Mexico

Because of corruption in law enforcement at the POE, I was forced to work without support from Customs and Immigration officers. At first, I trusted the agents in my office. Later, I learned from the PIs that one of the DEA agents would go out and talk to other law enforcement agents and officers at NTF or the POE.

I also learned from Officer Blackman; a DEA agent from the Yuma office told some people in the local law enforcement community about my contact with the PIs and CIs who worked in Mexico investigating the Garcia brothers. According to them, the information was getting back to the brothers' family members at San Luis POE.

I could not rely on any cooperation from other agents or officers in Yuma or the Phoenix AUSA. I had to work mainly alone with the PIs and CIs.

There were some agents and cops I could trust and count on in Yuma. The only one I could trust in my office was the secretary, Mrs. Tucker. She kept me squared away with my paperwork and made sure everything I wrote was completed and read smoothly for the AUSA office in Phoenix. She watched over me and protected me from agent gossip about why I worked alone on the streets and in Mexico. The only other people I trusted outside of the office were my CIs, PIs, and SOIs.

Other DEA agents in the office focused on their drug cases, their careers, and the possibility to become group supervisors and move up in the organization. Later, all of the Yuma DEA agents became supervisors, but I never made it to that level. I wasn't thinking that way about my career. Sure, I was ambitious, but it wasn't something I chose for my focus. I never thought about the paycheck or my status within DEA. I only focused on the brothers trying to kill Don and Roy.

At times, I'd work alone across the border in Mexico, checking on the brothers' residences and businesses. I wrote down several U.S. license plates, especially those parked at the brothers' businesses. A lot of these license plates were registered to known drug traffickers in the U.S.

When employees got off work at Jaime's produce business or Javier's shrimp business in Mexico, I would follow some of them back into the U.S. They lived in very nice homes in Yuma. But a lot of the brothers' employees in Mexico lived in houses made of plywood. The employees living in plywood homes were not involved in drug trafficking.

237

I searched many produce and furniture trucks, most of them 18-wheelers, coming across at San Luis POE. When I got information from the PIs, CIs, and SOIs that there might be drugs on a truck, I'd stop and search it. I wanted the brothers in Mexico to know that I, DEA Agent Larry Ray Hardin, was going to seize their drugs and trucks at San Luis POE. And yet, the Garcia brothers and their family members were making millions off their dope.

I learned from the PIs, CIs, and SOIs that the brothers and their family members were behind shipments of drugs coming across the border on produce, shrimp and furniture trucks to warehouses somewhere in Yuma county.

I got a call from the PI's client, the owner of a furniture company out of Los Angeles and in San Luis, Mexico. "Agent Hardin, I heard from PI Harry Fresno you're stopping some

Algodones POE in California near the San Luis Arizona POE

of my trucks coming across at San Luis POE and sometimes at

Algodones POE. I hope PI Fresno and his PIs can help you to find drugs on my trucks."

I didn't say much to the owner, only that PI Fresno was providing all the information I needed.

As it turned out, I learned from PI Fresno; the owner was not aware of the situation in Mexico until he heard that I was stopping his furniture trucks when the trucks entered the U.S.

The owner and PI Fresno knew if I could seize one of these trucks used by the brothers to traffic drugs, I might be able to put a stop to their smuggling activities at San Luis POE.

Be Careful with that Young Girl

After I was entrenched in the DEA Yuma office, DEA Phoenix management increased our personnel numbers up to four agents. Usually, there were only two agents in the office at one time, while the other two were on vacation or training. Later, DEA hired a part-time student aide to help out with the paperwork.

Within a few months after hiring her, Mrs. Tucker told me, "One of the agents was standing very close to the student aide in the file room. I think he was rubbing her breasts."

239

When I heard that, I immediately told the agents, "Be careful what you do in the office with that student aide." They just laughed.

A few days later, she told me again, "I believe the girl might be having a sexual relationship with one of the agents."

I told her, "I'll talk to the agents."

Mrs. Tucker said, "If you don't tell him to stop, the girl is going to lose her job."

After working for about 12 to 16 hours that day on the Garcia brothers and other investigation cases, I decided to go home. It was late in the evening, and I told the agents, "Lockup the office and turn on the security alarm when you guys leave."

I went out the front door, then realized I had to return to pick up some paperwork. I decided to enter through the back door of the file room. As I came into the office, I saw the agents flirting with the student aide.

I yelled emphatically, "Knock that off!"

The girl looked at me.

I walked past the agents and the aide, over to my desk, picked up the papers I needed, turned, and got ready to walk out.

240

"This type of activity upsets me," I told them, "Don't do that in the office anymore!"

Shortly after, the student aide quit working for DEA.

There was nothing new about agents having sex with co-workers, attorneys, law clerks, informants, married women, church-going women, or prostitutes. It was part of the job for a few of the agents and NTF officers. I couldn't understand how the agents and the officers loved their wives and children yet to have sex with any woman who dropped her panties.

Corruption at the Mexico Border

The PIs, CIs, and SOIs later informed me that the Garcia brothers had a partner, Franco Finca. Finca owned an agricultural outlet, less than 100 yards from the border in San Luis, Mexico. He had been in the agriculture produce business in San Luis, Arizona, for many years.

Later, I introduced myself to Franco Finca at his produce outlet company at the border and asked him about his agriculture business dealings with the Garcia brothers and their family members. I asked Finca if he was the United States contact for the

241

brothers' narcotics activities in Arizona. He nervously denied any involvement but admitted he was aware of the drug operations in Mexico.

I explained to Finca, "DEA can seize properties from associates of the Garcia brothers because of their involvement with narcotics trafficking. If needed, Finca, I can seize your company."

Finca immediately replied, "I am not involved with the brothers' dope business." He then turned around and quickly walked into his produce company.

I was convinced that Finca was involved with the brothers' dope business, but how? I also was convinced that there were some corrupt American and Mexican law enforcement officials at San Luis POE. Information provided from my CIs and SOIs confirmed it. The brothers later confirmed and bragged to a DEA CI that their niece worked at the POE as an Immigration officer. She could furnish protection and cooperation from some of her co-workers, U.S. officials, and dirty Mexican cops to help move her uncle's dope across the border into the U.S.

They Drank and Did Some Dope

PI Jeff Pearce had provided me with the name, Flaco el Pulpo, at the first meeting with his boss, PI Harry Fresno. PI Pearce said, "el Pulpo is a manager at our client's furniture business in San Luis, Mexico. El Pulpo might be related to the Garcia brothers."

I later explained to my CI, Santo, that I required his loyalty and outlined some things about the trucks I was watching at the Arizona and Mexico border. I told Santo, "I have the name and telephone number of Flaco el Pulpo. El Falco works at a maquiladora furniture processing factory in San Luis, Sonora, Mexico. I want you to give el Pulpo a call and see if he'll meet with you in Yuma or somewhere in San Luis, Mexico. You and el Falco have something in common. Women!"

I added firmly, "Santo, you can't use drugs working with DEA. Got it?"

I gave Santo the telephone number to contact el Pulpo. "Tell him you met him at El Tigre Bar. The bar is a popular place where dopers meet in Tijuana, Mexico."

243

I didn't mention the Garcia brothers' names to Santo because I wasn't sure how el Pulpo was helping with the brothers in the drug trafficking organization.

I didn't want Santo to commit crimes or do anything that might jeopardize the case. Under normal circumstances, Santo could get away with some things in Mexico but not in the United States. But this was not a typical case! I knew what it took for Santo to get information on the brothers and stay alive.

Santo called Flaco el Pulpo. Speaking in Spanish, Santo said, "Hey Flaco, you and I met down at the bar in Tijuana, at El Tigre Bar. I was there several weeks ago and got to talking to you about women. I also talked about my shrimp business, and you mentioned you know someone else who has a shrimp business in Mexico."

El Pulpo told Santo, "Come on down to San Luis; I'd like to meet with you again."

After el Pulpo and Santo talked on the phone, Santo called me and said, "I had a nice conversation with el Pulpo about the time I met him at El Tigre. I talked about my shrimp business and told him I'd like to meet his friend, who also has a shrimp business."

"He gave me the address for his business in San Luis Rio Colorado, Mexico."

"Okay, Santo. Good job. Go and meet him in Mexico, but be careful. Call me when you return to the U.S. after you meet with him."

I was thinking; *This is too good to be true!* I knew from PI Pearce and other SOIs that el Pulpo might know the Garcia brothers.

Under my instruction, Santo went to San Luis, Mexico, to meet el Pulpo. They drank two shots of tequila and snorted some cocaine. Although I didn't know until later, Santo was snorting cocaine with el Pulpo. After a few minutes, el Pulpo told Santo, "I want to introduce you to my friend, Javier Garcia, who owns a shrimp business in El Golfo."

Santo asked him, "Okay. When can I meet Javier?"

"I'll get back to you on that," said el Pulpo.

When Santo called me later that evening, I asked, "Where did you meet with el Pulpo?"

"I met him at a maquiladora company that makes furniture in San Luis, Mexico. He told me that he is one of the general

245

managers at the business who coordinates with Customs and Immigration officers at the POE to ship furniture in the company's trucks into the U.S."

Santo said, "He snorted a few lines inside his office. Then, he told me that Javier Garcia transported a lot of shrimp, even cocaine and heroin to Los Angeles, California."

I made it very clear to Santo, "Don't do drugs while working for DEA."

Santo didn't say anything.

I was extremely excited and thinking; *This is incredible news.*

Stay Focused and Be Safe in Mexico

A few days later, Santo called me. "I met with el Pulpo in San Luis, near his furniture business. He said Javier is moving a lot of shrimp from El Golfo across the U.S border. Javier has two brothers. El Pulpo said Javier's oldest brother's name is Jaime. He wants me to meet at Javier's grocery store in San Luis, Mexico."

I asked Santo, "Why at Javier's grocery store? Why not a bar where there are some beautiful girls."

246

Santo told me, "I believe el Pulpo is living the "Great Life" in Yuma and Mexico as the general manager of a maquiladora furniture business. The more he drinks tequila and snorts cocaine, the more he talks."

I told Santo, "You and Javier can discuss your shrimp business and nothing else."

I couldn't believe Santo was going to meet with Javier Garcia. *This was everything I hoped for.*

I was excited; *El Pulpo wants Santo to go with him to the grocery store that Javier owns in Mexico.* The brothers won't talk dope with just anyone, not even with Santo. You have to be a family member or a very trusted individual before they would even mention their drug activities.

I told Santo, "Okay, let's give it a few days. Then call el Pulpo back and tell him you'd like to meet Javier. You want to talk to him about your shrimp business."

Santo asked, "Who's this guy, Javier? Do you know him?"

I told Santo, "I don't know anything about Javier or his store. You'll learn what kind of a person he is soon. Stay focused and be safe." *I lied to Santo for right now. But he will find out Javier is a major drug trafficker.*

I played my poker face and didn't express any emotion of excitement in my voice on the phone with Santo. Santo didn't know Javier was connected with trying to kill Don and Roy.

I finally found a weak link through Flaco el Pulpo to get into the Garcia brothers' organization. So far, Santo was doing a great job entering slowly into the brothers' criminal world through el Pulpo. My first thought was; *Thank you, PI Jeff Pearce, because you gave me Flaco el Pulpo's name and phone number. It's paying off big time!*

Two weeks later, Santo called el Pulpo about the meeting with Javier at the grocery store in Mexico.

He said, "Javier will see you tomorrow at his store."

Santo said, "I'll see you and Javier in the morning."

The next day, Santo met with them at the grocery store.

Santo called me late in the evening after his meeting with el Pulpo and Javier and said, "The meeting was very short. Javier and I talked about our shrimp business. Javier wants to meet again, but

248

next time, he wants to meet in El Golfo, where he has his shrimp business."

Santo said, "Javier's shrimp business is a two-hour drive south from San Luis. It's in a little fishing village called El Golfo; off the coast."

Santo told me, "I think this could be a good meeting with Javier in El Golfo. I think he wants to discuss drugs with me. He told me that I would meet his brother, Joselito, at this meeting in El Golfo."

"Santo, this could be an opportunity for you to ask Javier and Joselito about helping you move some cocaine from Colombia to Arizona," I said to him.

Illegals Believe Border Patrol Agents Shooting at Them

After another long day of following the *drug traffickers* around Yuma and down into Mexico, Group Supervisor (GS) Juan Antonio Moreno and I decided to go catfishing on the Rio Coronado River canal next to Algodones POE, near the Mexican

249

border. In the past, I caught some big catfish out of the canals and rivers while working.

It was late at night, and GS Juan Antonio and I were not catching any catfish or any other fish. Nearby, I could hear Border Patrol agents yelling at illegal immigrants to stop running back into Mexico. Suddenly, GS Juan Antonio heard a noise behind him in the bush. He screamed, "It is a wild hog."

I quickly whispered to him, "It might be an illegal immigrant hiding in the bush from Border Patrol agents."

It was too late. GS Juan Antonio shot one round from his .38 Smith & Weston five-shot revolver at a big black wild animal running towards him. He screamed again, "Wow, I shot a wild pig!"

I yelled, "What pig? It's a large hairy black beaver. The beaver is not dead. It jumped into the river and disappeared in the darkness."

Within minutes, several illegals were running around us, traveling south to the Mexican border. I guess the gunshot scared them. The illegals were running from U.S. Border Patrol agents. I

Rio Colorado River, San Luis, Arizona

was wondering, *I think the illegals believe Border Patrol agents are shooting at them.*

I said to one of the Border Patrol agents as he ran by me, chasing the illegals, "I am DEA. Do you need any help?"

The Border Patrol agent said, "Nope. Did you catch any fish?"

I told the agent, "No. But I saw a beaver."

I didn't catch any catfish, but GS Juan Antonio Moreno did shoot a beaver.

Have You Ever Killed Someone?

I knew Santo needed protection when he met the Garcia brothers and the brothers' associates in El Golfo, Mexico. Santo was one of the best DEA informants I'd ever had. I had to find another CI to drive and protect Santo when he met with Javier and his brothers in El Golfo. As a shrimp business owner operating in Mexico, it didn't look right that Santo didn't have a bodyguard.

251

It would also be helpful to have another witness to testify against the Garcia brothers. Confidential Informants typically testify in cases they've been involved with, but Informants are not mentioned by name in court to protect their identity and keep them safe.

I told Santo, "Santo, you need to find someone to drive you back and forth from Mexico. Someone to protect you down there in El Golfo, who you can rely on. If something happens to you, I can't help you fast enough to save your life. Please, I don't want to know if you have a gun or whoever is going to protect you carries a gun."

He told me, "Okay, I think I know someone that can protect me in Mexico."

Three or four weeks later, Santo called, "I have someone, he's Colombian. That's where I met my friend in Colombia. I really trust this guy. I think he'll take excellent care of me."

"Ok, bring him out to Yuma and let me meet him."

I met Santo's protector; he was really short, probably about five feet tall, husky build, and didn't talk much; really quiet. He said very little when I asked him questions about his past criminal life.

I asked him, "Have you ever hurt someone?"

"Yes."

I then asked, "Have you ever killed someone?"

He looked at me and said, "Have I shot a bad person?"

If he wasn't a criminal, he fooled me.

I said, "I am going to call you Angelito. In Spanish, it means little Angel. Are you okay with that name?"

Angelito smiled.

Later I asked Santo, "Are you okay with Angelito?"

Santo replied, "Angelito appears to be very humble, yet he can kill quickly if necessary. I believe that if he couldn't kill the bad guy, he would go after the family."

I said, "Angelito, you're going to work with me. You're going to stick with me, and I want you to stay close to Santo. Don't snort drugs or carry a gun. Do you understand me?"

"Yes," Angelito responded with a smile.

Santo trusted Angelito with his life and wanted him to be his bodyguard and driver. Santo and Angelito trusted each other. They were both Colombians dealing with Mexicans, and there was

253

no love lost between Colombian and Mexican drug smugglers. For some reason, Mexicans don't like Colombians, but they want their drugs, especially their cocaine. This was perfect.

I looked at both Santo and Angelito and told them, "Let's go after these brothers!"

I was thinking; Could Angelito be armed every time he went into Mexico? If he weren't, he'd be stupid.

American (Gringa) Women Don't Carry Vaseline

Santo and Angelito didn't know the Garcia brothers were behind the attempted murder of the two DEA agents in 1975, Don and Roy. The brothers' names were never mentioned to Santo and Angelito because I couldn't give my CIs that kind of information.

A few weeks later, in El Golfo, Javier showed Santo and Angelito his shrimp business. After Javier showed them his business, they met with el Pulpo, Marco Oscuro, Jaime's right-hand man, and Joselito at Javier's restaurant for drinks. Santo learned at Javier's restaurant that Oscuro's wife was a schoolteacher and ran the Drug Abuse Resistance Education (DARE) program in Yuma County.

254

Marco Oscuro also had relatives working at San Luis POE. He was extremely connected with corrupt law enforcement at the POE. Javier told Santo not to worry about the border into San Luis, Arizona.

Santo said, "While we were drinking tequila at Javier's restaurant, Joselito shared a lot of stories. He said that when Americans go to Mexico, some of his Mexican police buddies will separate a husband or boyfriend from the woman or girl if she's "hot." The police would then take the woman to the back room and have sex with her."

Joselito said that the Mexican police told the gringa woman not to scream. If she screamed, the police would hurt the ones who were with her. After the police finish with the gringa, they strongly encouraged her not to mention what happened to anyone, or she and her gringo husband or boyfriend will disappear or be charged with a violation.

"In Mexico, this was just a way of life for some women and girls," said Joselito. "It's known that Mexican women sometimes carry a bottle of Vaseline with them for lubrication to their vagina because women never know if they're going to have sex with a police officer or two."

Joselito added, "American gringa women never carry Vaseline. That's why they bleed a lot." Then he laughed and said, "In the United States, it is called *Rape*."

Santo told me later, "I think Javier and Joselito are dangerous people. Javier's shrimp business exports beautiful tiger shrimp to Arizona and California. It appears to be a legitimate business in El Golfo."

Santo said, "I have a feeling from now on that every time Angelito and I meet with Javier, Marco and Joselito will be with him."

I asked Santo, "Who's Joselito?"

"I don't know anything about him, just that Javier told me Joselito is his younger brother."

I was excited and thinking; *Of course, I knew who Joselito was.* DEA and the law enforcement community in Yuma knew Joselito as a very bad dude.

Santo never mentioned to me how he and Angelito snorted cocaine with the brothers until later when I met with AUSA Fly in Phoenix.

Something Isn't Right

When I met with Santo a few days later, he told me, "You know, Agent Hardin, at that POE down there in San Luis, something isn't right. Customs and Immigration officers are asking me and Angelito questions about our visit to Mexico."

I asked, "What kind of questions?"

"The officers asked Angelito and me what's going on in Mexico, why were we going into Arizona, and what we were doing in San Luis, Mexico. I told the officers, Angelito and I live in Phoenix, Arizona." We showed the officers our Colombian passports and our visas. Also, the officers asked us if we knew the Garcia brothers."

I asked Santo, "You didn't slip up, did you?"

"No, I just told them I own a shrimp business in Mexico, and I come back and forth. Angelito is my employee."

257

"Okay, okay. Santo, you and Angelito need to be very cautious with law enforcement at the POE. Especially with some of the Immigration and Customs officers. I'm not talking about the Mexicans; I'm talking about American law enforcement officers when you come into the United States."

Southeast Asian Traffickers

The CIs, PIs, and SOIs also provided me names of alleged associates who were major Mexican, Southeast Asian, and Colombian traffickers connected with the Garcia brothers' organization.

I couldn't let anyone know at the Yuma NTF office which produce or shrimp trucks I would be searching at the San Luis POE because some of them would alert their corrupt buddies at the POE. Then I noticed something important about how the trucks were entering the POE. I started seeing some produce trucks drop off their trailers along the Mexican border before they arrived at the POE. Soon after, another truck would pick up the trailer and bring it across the U.S. border. The Garcia brothers were switching trailers because they assumed, DEA was targeting their trucks.

258

I had the authority from the Department of Justice (DOJ) to seize the trucks carrying drugs. However, someone in the law enforcement community got wind that I was watching the brothers' trucks at the POE. I was trying to figure out a way to catch the drug smugglers of the organization, without involving other law enforcement agencies and the Customs and Immigration officers at the border.

I was sadly thinking, I hope it's not someone in my office.

I also wanted to protect the case from being dismissed by the U.S. Attorney Office in Phoenix for lack of factual evidence. I only had hearsay evidence that the brothers were putting cocaine and heroin into produce trucks and shrimp trucks in Mexico.

I spoke with AUSA Goodwill, and later to the two new AUSAs assigned to the brothers' investigation how to avoid such issues as strategies, venue, extradition to the U.S, and prosecution of the brothers. Then, the second and a third AUSAs refused to prosecute the brothers on conspiracy alone. I had to catch the brothers doing something criminally wrong, not in Mexico, but in the United States.

Corrupt Official and 32 Kilos of Cocaine

An SOI told me that from Mexico, a car with cocaine would be crossing San Luis POE today. He said, "I know the type of car that is carrying cocaine from Mexico across the POE into the U.S. There is a *bad* official at the POE helping to smuggle the cocaine for the Garcia brothers."

With the SOI's information and the description of the car, I was able to seize 32 kilos of cocaine from an abandoned car parked in a public grocery parking lot  in San Luis, AZ. But I was thinking; *Where is the driver?*

The SOI later called and said the driver left the car at a grocery store parking lot. The driver was told by someone to walk away from the car.

I told the SOI, "I was hoping to talk to the driver about the 32 kilos of cocaine in the car and the *bad* officer at the POE. But I missed that opportunity."

Video Camera Inside and Outside

The PIs provided information that a warehouse owned by their client to store furniture in Yuma was being used by the Garcia brothers to unload smuggled drugs from their produce trucks. The brothers' drugs would later be moved into cars and small trucks for distribution throughout the United States.

The warehouse was a vast building with one large room and a high ceiling. I asked the PIs to ask the owner of the warehouse for permission to set up video cameras inside and outside the warehouse. Then, I asked Arizona NTF Officer Daniel Blackman to help install cameras at the warehouse.

I trusted him. He and I worked closely together on the joint Joe Cactus and Nick Star's methamphetamine investigation.

Late one Sunday night, with the help of Officer Blackman, we installed two hidden cameras to watch trucks coming and going from the warehouse. One camera was placed inside the warehouse, and the other was placed up high on the water tower overlooking the outside of the warehouse. I wanted to see if something was being switched at this location from one truck to another truck or a car.

261

The next day, Officer Blackman said, "You need to see the recording from the inside video at the warehouse."

On the recorded video, one of the truck drivers went straight up to the top of the warehouse and put his eyeball up to the video camera.

This information had me wondering if there was a leak in the DEA office or the NTF office. How did the truck driver know about the hidden camera up high in the ceiling of the warehouse? Where was this leak coming from? Could it be from my office or Officer Blackman's office?

The Garcia brothers and their family members were well connected with Yuma area law enforcement and at San Luis POE. Some of the suspected corrupt cops who I knew in the community might be connected to the brothers and corruption at the U.S. border. An agent in my office could have unknowingly been sharing information to a corrupt cop or an officer at the POE that got back to the brothers.

The agents in my office began backing out from helping me on the brothers' investigation because the pressure from the U.S. Attorney's office in Phoenix was coming down so hard on anyone

262

Mexico that someone will be driving a pickup truck with the *produce* in the next few days.

The unknown female couldn't provide anything else to help me, but she had a description of the truck. A day later, I received additional information on the description of the same pickup truck from another unknown source, a male voice, calling about the truck entering San Luis POE with drugs.

Seized 226 lbs. of cocaine near San Luis POE

A few days later, I checked an abandoned pickup truck that met the same description the unknown female and male gave me near San Luis POE in a public parking lot. A Border Patrol agents' narcotics' sniffing dog alerted to drugs inside the pickup. I seized 226 lbs. of cocaine inside the pickup truck.

The unknown female and male never called me back. I was wondering; Is the unidentified female an angry girlfriend with one of the brothers? Maybe the unknown male is a corrupt official who was in the parking lot watching me at the POE?

265

224 Drug Tunnels Discovered Between the United States and Mexico

Mexican cartels are known as the "greatest criminal drug threat" facing America. According to Edwin Mora of Breitbart in 2013, 224 drug tunnels were discovered along the border between the United States and Mexico since 1990. United States authorities and DEA uncovered and destroyed these tunnels that were used to smuggle bulk quantities of illicit drugs along the United States-Mexican border since 1990.[28]

Tunnels for cartels transporting illegal drugs were becoming very sophisticated and continued to threaten United States-Mexico border security. Tunnels were suspected of leading from Mexico to stash houses and produce businesses near the POE in San Luis, Arizona area. I was receiving information from PI, CIs, and SOIs that the Garcia brothers' drugs were going to Yuma into private homes and warehouses.

SOIs and CIs told me the Mexican cartel and the brothers were using underground tunnels to transport large quantities of heroin, cocaine, and marijuana from San Luis, Mexico into San Luis, Arizona. I suspected the brothers were smuggling through tunnels, cocaine and heroin that were cost-effective for concealing and transporting large quantities instead of using produce and shrimp trucks. Heroin was secondary to cocaine because it wasn't always available. Although marijuana was profitable and plentiful, it required additional manpower and more effort to conceal, smuggle, and transport in produce and shrimp trucks.

360 Pounds of Marijuana Packages

After seizing 226 pounds of cocaine from an abandoned pickup truck near San Luis POE, several weeks later, the same unknown female who alerted me before, called about an abandoned car parked near POE. She said in broken

Seized 360 lbs. of Marijuana near San Luis POE

English, "It is the same driver from the pickup truck having the cocaine. The driver works at the brothers' conqueladora warehouse. The car is a white, Ford, and has California license plates. I overheard the driver telling another employee he went through the POE yesterday without any problems with Customs and
267

Immigration officials. The car is parked in the same public parking lot as the last time." Then she ended the phone call.

Later that day, I arrived at the parking lot with another agent from my office. A Border Patrol agent and his narcotics dog were already at the parking lot, waiting for me. After I verified the description of the car, Border Patrol agents' narcotics sniffing dog, immediately alerted to drugs inside the car. When we opened the abandoned car doors and trunk, we found 360 lbs. of packages containing marijuana.

I was upset and thought; I can't believe that someone at San Luis POE didn't check the pickup truck with 226 pounds of cocaine. Now, this car has all this marijuana. Am I being set up by the brothers and corrupt officials at the POE? Why does the unknown female know so much about the driver of the car? Who is she?

Agricultural Produce, Shrimp, and Furniture Trucks

I later learned from the PIs, CIs, and SOIs that the Garcia brothers knew I was planning to stop their produce and shrimp trucks at the POE. Somehow, there was a leak from a corrupt

Customs and Immigration officer informing the brothers. I suspected the leak came from San Luis POE.

The PIs believed the brothers were finding out from corrupt cops that I was going to stop the furniture trucks. The brothers would switch the trucks before they came across the border into the U.S.

Ignoring the leaks from corrupt cops, I continued to search produce, shrimp, and furniture trucks connected to the brothers. I was receiving reliable information from the PIs that the drugs were on the furniture trucks and parked at the border next to the POE.

I was anxious to seize a truck with the Garcia brothers' drugs! As far as I was concerned, I didn't locate the *right* truck. I was stopping and searching a lot of produce, shrimp, and furniture trucks, especially the trucks from Jaime's produce business. I had the trucks searched inside and out with narcotics-sniffing dogs but found no drugs. I was confused not to find drugs hidden inside the boxes of produce or inside the furniture. I had reliable PIs, SOIs, and CIs working inside the brothers' organization in Mexico, providing me information that there were drugs on the trucks.

Where were the drugs I was informed about? I want to know how the brothers are finding out about how I focused on their trucks.

Underground Tunnel near the San Luis POE

As part of the Mexico Sinaloa drug cartel, El Chapo Guzman's first tunnel, built from Agua Prieta, Mexico, to Douglas, Arizona, was 30-feet underground, four-feet wide, five feet high, and about the length of a football field. It had a complete hydraulic system to raise the floor and reveal a ladder into the tunnel at both ends. This one was discovered in 1990 and was used by El Chapo for his second escape from prison. It has become known as "Cocaine Alley" for smuggling drugs into the U.S.[29][30][31][32] and our information connected the Garcia brothers' organization to Sinaloa cartel activities.

I asked the DoD (Department of Defense) Geophysical Survey Team to help locate the possibility of an underground tunnel near the San Luis POE. After flying over the POE twice, DoD personnel revealed there was a 95% chance that a tunnel existed in the area of Franco Finca's outlet agricultural produce warehouse. SOIs in the produce business had said Finca was a close

270

business partner of Jaime. Previously, I mentioned to Finca, if I found dope on his property or in the trucks, I will arrest him and seize his produce warehouse, home, car, and whatever else he owns.

I used two telephone pole cameras and a special recreational vehicle (RV) to monitor the activities near Finca's produce warehouse. The pole cameras and RV were in position where the alleged tunnel existed in San Luis, AZ.

I later executed a federal search warrant on Finca's produce warehouse. Finca was not surprised by the search warrant or to see me again. Finca said, "I told you before that I am not a produce partner with Jaime Garcia.

He declined to say anything else to me. After several hours of searching inside and outside the warehouse, I was unable to locate an underground tunnel.

Finca later told an SOI that he already knew his warehouse was going to be searched by DEA. While I continued to try locating the underground tunnel, I focused on the narcotics trafficking activities at Finca's produce business and law enforcement corruption at the border.

271

How did Franco Finca, an agricultural produce business partner with the brothers, find out I was going to search his business?

Corrupt Mexican Officers and Political Officials in Mexico and the United States

Javier, Jaime, and Joselito Garcia appeared strongly inclined to conduct narcotics trafficking operations with heavy reliance on family members and relatives working at San Luis POE and local law enforcement in the United States. My CIs, PIs, and SOIs stated they were 100% sure that corrupt officials in Mexico and the United States furnished protection and cooperation to the brothers' organization to move dope into the U.S.

With the help of my sources, I identified specific corrupt law enforcement officers and political officials in both Mexico and the United States. The corrupt officials at the POE, were, most likely, the overriding factor in their drug trafficking success.

Catholic Priest is Assassinated

On May 24, 1993, Cardinal Juan Posadas Ocampo, his driver, and five others were shot to death. Ocampo and his driver were sitting in his car at the airport in Guadalajara, Mexico. The murder of Ocampo was one of many violent attacks by drug traffickers during increasing turf wars between smuggling groups.[33] I later learned from CIs, PIs, and SOIs that the shooting and killing in Guadalajara also tied back to the Garcia brothers' organization and with other cartels in Mexico.

Weapons and Narcotics Trade

The PIs provided me with reports showing guerrillas of the Popular Revolutionary Army in Mexico getting weapons from drug cartels in exchange for heroin. The guerrillas were supplying poppy farmers in Mexico with firearms to protect their poppy fields.[34]

Later, I learned that family members of the Garcia brothers' organization were tied to arms smuggled down to Nicaragua through Mexico and weapons traded for narcotics. I heard about trades of firearms and narcotics from the PIs and SOIs. And, it had been happening long before I arrived at the DEA office in Yuma.

273

No Guts to go After Corrupt Cops

One day, I met with Santo and Angelito after they traveled across the San Luis POE into Arizona. They had just come back from meeting with Javier at his grocery store in Mexico.

"Santo, who did Javier have you meet with?" I asked.

"We met with Joselito and Marco Oscuro again."

Santo told me, "At the meeting, Joselito asked me several times about producing coca and smuggling cocaine paste from Colombia into San Luis, Mexico. Joselito said he could sell me a lot of hydrochloric acid and ether for cocaine production. Joselito said he has the right connection at San Luis POE to smuggle anything, even aliens into the U.S! Joselito laughed as he said he is known as the *King of Heroin,* and Jaime is called the *King of Cocaine* in Mexico."

Santo and Angelito said they were going to meet with Javier again at his grocery store in San Luis to discuss their shrimp business. Santo believed that the Garcia brothers were extremely powerful and dangerous in Mexico.

274

According to Santo, Joselito was a punk who gave no mercy when it came to anything – corruption, hurting people, whatever. If Joselito wanted someone, he would go after them and their family in Mexico or the United States.

The other two brothers were known for supplying drugs to their traffickers, not so much for killing. The brothers had professional *sicarios* from the Mexican cartels to do their killing for them. It was always that way with the cartels to supply *sicarios*.

Now, with Santo and Angelito inside the drug trafficking organization, I needed to concentrate on factual evidence and not just hearsay or intelligence evidence from the CIs, PIs, and SOIs. To put the brothers in jail, I had to have the facts.

I was getting excited that Santo and Angelito continued to confirm the involvement of Jaime, Javier, Joselito, and the brothers' connections with corrupt cops moving drugs into the U.S. through San Luis POE. I was learning more about their criminal drug activities with the help of Santo and Angelito.

On one occasion, Joselito told a DEA agent at the American Consulate Office in Hermosillo, Mexico, that his brother, Jaime, was the drug trafficker, not him. The DEA agent in Hermosillo told me Joselito was at the Consulate Office applying for a visa to travel in the United States.

We Will Make Sure They're Dead

Santo told me, "Jaime wants to see us."

I told Santo, "You and Angelito be careful and call me after you meet with Jaime."

Later, Santo and Angelito met with Joselito and Jaime at one of the large white houses in San Luis, Mexico. For two days, I didn't hear from them. When they reported back to me, Santo said, "It looks like the White House, except smaller. There were a lot of guys walking around, armed, and watching us as we met with the brothers."

Santo told me that Javier lived across the street in another large white house that also looked like the U.S. White House.

Santo said, "Jaime boasted about his friends and family working at San Luis POE, and he talked about his connections with CIA. He told us his niece worked at the POE as an Immigration officer."

Santo said, "Jaime bragged about his nephew working at the POE, but never mentioned his name. The more Jaime snorted cocaine, the more he ran his mouth. Just like his brother-in-law el Puplo. He also bragged about how he could never be arrested because of his relationship with the CIA."

Santo said he couldn't contact me because he and Angelito were being watched very carefully by Jaime's employees. Later Jaime pointed an automatic 45-caliber handgun and asked, "Hey, Santo and Angelito. Are you DEA?" Then Jaime started laughing and said, "I'm kidding. DEA can't do drugs or have sex with young girls. They can't have sex at all when they're working."

Now it was Joselito pointing the 45-caliber handgun at the CIs and laughing. Joselito asked Santo and Angelito again, "Are you DEA agents?"

Later, Joselito told Santo and Angelito, his brothers tried to kill two DEA agents (Don and Roy). Joselito said, "There will be no doubt the next time; We will make sure the DEA agents are dead!"

Then he asked Santo and Angelito, "Do you know Tommy Pescado? He owns a car dealership in Yuma. Jaime purchased vehicles from him for $135,000 in exchange for drugs."

Then he laughed and said, "You should buy a car from him."

I later found out that Tommy Pescado was closely connected with the Garcia brothers. He was once the city Mayor of San Luis, Arizona. He was also known as a corrupt used car dealer and a suspected rapist in Yuma.

Santo called me and said, "Angelito and I were locked up in Jaime's house and forced to snort cocaine with him and Joselito. Older women and younger girls come and go from the house."

I didn't ask them for the ages of the girls.

Santo and Angelito were involved in the brothers' criminal world. They started getting free samples of cocaine to snort with the brothers. The CIs were making the connections I needed, and I was building my case against the brothers for how they wanted to kill two DEA agents. I was excited and thinking; *This is it! It's what I've hoped for. Everything's taking shape now!*

278

On several occasions when Santo and Angelito were entering the POE, Customs and Immigration officers continued to ask if they had met with Jaime. Of course, they said nothing to the Customs or the Immigration officers. They had a gut feeling the brothers had protection from corrupt law enforcement at the border.

Santo and Angelito had no idea what made Jaime so important in Mexico. I was excited that they were inside Jaime's home, but I insisted that they don't snort cocaine and not have sex with the younger girls.

Now, I have one more Garcia brother, Jaime. I have all three brothers in my sights, thanks to Santo and Angelito.

"Be anxious for nothing, but in everything by prayer and supplication with thanksgiving, let your requests be known to God. And the peace of God, which surpasses all comprehension, will guard your hearts and your minds in Christ Jesus"(Philippians 4:6-7 New American Standard Version).

U.S. and Mexico Port-of-Entries (POEs)

I continued to develop more information from my CIs, PIs, and SOIs that not only the Garcia brothers' relatives but close friends of the brothers were working at San Luis POE. I suspected these corrupt relatives and friends were officers informing the brothers when DEA was waiting for their produce and shrimp trucks to come across at the POE.

Santo said, "The brothers' organization has bragged about having four different family members working at San Luis POE who help the brothers cross their dope into the U.S."

Santo and Angelito reported to me they remembered a Hispanic female Immigration officer at the POE who would watch them very closely.

Santo said, "The female officer is the one who asked me before a lot of questions about my visit to Mexico."

He continued, "She wore a white shirt, dark blue pants, and a gun attached to her belt. She was a little overweight and wore a badge. The officer was very friendly and mentioned her Uncle Jaime Garcia."

Once again, Santo and Angelito said nothing to the female officer about meeting with her Uncle Jaime Garcia. She smiled and told them to continue into the United States.

Santo said, "I think the female Immigration officer's name tag said, Maria Garcia. The brothers are proud of their niece and nephew working at San Luis POE."

Santo and Angelito were terrified that the brothers would find out from their niece and nephew that they were working with DEA.

The Immigration officer might be the brothers' niece, but the brothers didn't mention the nephew's name who worked there.

At the DEA office, I asked, "Does anyone know a woman named Maria Garcia, an Immigration officer? She works at San Luis POE."

DEA Agent Saul Morales told me, "Yes, I know her. Why?"

"I'd like to meet her. Can you introduce me to her?"

He said, "Sure. Okay."

The next day Agent Morales and I arrived at San Luis POE. I met Immigration officer Maria Garcia face-to-face without her and Agent Morales knowing why I wanted to see her.

Agent Morales gave Officer Garcia a big hug. They both spoke Spanish and then laughed. I noticed they continued to talk in Spanish as they smiled at each other. I had no idea Officer Garcia

281

was a close friend of his, or that she knew he was a DEA agent. She was a very pleasant young lady, nice, short, and heavy; not very attractive.

I confirmed she was the same Immigration officer who worked at the POE described by Santo. Santo and Angelito were right that there might be a leak in the DEA office. I finally identified the niece as Immigration Officer Maria Garcia. I was surprised and thinking; *Does Agent Saul Morales know Immigration Officer Maria Garcia is the niece of the Garcia brothers? Should I tell him?*

I called a trusted friend who worked with the Immigration Office of Professional Responsibility (OPR) in San Diego, California, about a corrupt Immigration officer working at San Luis POE.

I learned from OPR in San Diego that Immigration Officer Maria Garcia had access to U.S. law enforcement databases, including DEA records on computers at San Luis POE. The databases showed who was looking at her family and her uncles' traffickers. She knew when DEA and other law enforcement agents were targeting her uncles' trucks and cars in Mexico and could find out the identities of the CIs and SOIs working for the agents.

Several days later, the OPR from San Diego called and told me to meet a Supervisor at the Yuma Immigration & Naturalize Service (INS) office. I provided to INS at the Yuma office all the details I knew about the Garcia brothers. I also told Border and Immigration Internal Affairs, "You need to help me get the brothers' niece, Immigration Officer Maria Garcia transferred from the border. She and anyone else connected to the brothers need to move away from San Luis POE. I have a lot of information about her."

I later learned from a close friend at the Border Patrol in Yuma Immigration that OPR did nothing to remove Officer Garcia from her border position at the POE. I never went back to the OPR office again. I was happily thinking, *Thank God I didn't mention my CIs to Immigration OPR and the Border Patrol Internal Affairs in San Diego and Yuma.*

There was a leak somewhere in the law enforcement community at the POE; her name was Immigration Officer Maria Garcia. It was becoming more dangerous for Santo and Angelito to meet with the brothers in Mexico. I suspected that there might be another leak at San Luis POE, and it is probably one of the agents or cops I trusted, but I wasn't sure which agent or cop. I was sure Immigration Officer Maria Garcia was one of the leaks. The PIs suspected another leak was from a corrupt agent from within my office.

AUSA Removed from The Case

Suddenly AUSA Goodwill was taken off the Garcia brothers' case. He told me, "I have been reassigned to another federal agency, the CIA. The new AUSA Robin Fly will be assigned to the brothers' investigation. I am sorry, Larry."

I heard from other DEA agents that AUSA Fly was a character that had no *guts* to go after corrupt cops. He never worked drug cases before, only white-collar sex crimes against children. Now, he was assigned to an incredible case. With no experience working drug cases, I had to start all over again to explain to AUSA Fly the Garcia brothers' investigation.

Kilo of Cocaine or a Pound of Heroin

Santo and Angelito met Marco Oscuro and Ana Blanca, close friends and smugglers of the Garcia brothers in El Golfo. The CIs had met Oscuro and Blanca before when they went to El Golfo to see Javier's shrimp business. Ana Blanca liked Santo, and Santo took advantage of the situation.

Ana Blanca became a fountain of information, and Santo immediately developed a sexual relationship with her. Even after he found out that she was one of Javier's girlfriends and a drug smuggler, she told Santo. "Your friend Angelito looks like a very mean person. I feel uneasy with Angelito."

Ana told Santo, "I moved a lot of Jaime's and Javier's drugs from El Golfo to San Luis, Mexico. Jaime always paid me in U.S. dollars to deliver his drugs up to the border. But Javier, he paid very little to me in pesos, not dollars, to move his drugs. I hated Javier but had sex with him when he demanded it. When Javier needs me to smuggle his drugs into the United States from San Luis POE or at the Calexico POE, I do it because I'm afraid to say no."

One day when Ana was with Santo and Angelito at Javier's grocery store in Mexico, Santo asked her, "How does Javier make the easy money from his shrimp business?"

She said, "Javier does not make a lot of money in selling shrimp. He is dealing with the Chinese in the shrimp business. You and Angelito need to be careful who you talk to, especially at Javier's grocery store and San Luis POE. The brothers have family and friends working at the store and at the border."

She added, "I can smuggle a kilo of cocaine or a pound of heroin across San Luis POE for the brothers without any problems from U.S. Customs and Immigration Inspectors."

When Ana was alone with Santo, she asked him, "Do you want me to smuggle a kilo of cocaine or a pound of heroin for you across the border? I won't charge you for bringing the kilo or the heroin across."

After Ana snorted cocaine, she said, "El Golfo is very dangerous, and it isn't safe for you and Angelito to go by yourselves. The Mexican Federal Police are very bad."

Santo told me Ana Blanca is a very attractive woman.

286

The Asian Connection

The PIs provided me information on a Chinese organization in Los Angeles that might be involved with the Garcia brothers. The next thing I knew, the word "Chinese" was popping up from Santo, Angelito, Ana Blanca, and other SOIs about a Chinese organization working with the brothers in San Luis, Mexico.

Santo told me when he met with Javier in El Golfo, Javier was talking about deliveries of shrimp he was preparing and shipping to a Chinese Company in Los Angeles and Phoenix.

At first, I didn't see the connection in the Los Angeles area. I never heard from the law enforcement community that Chinese and Mexicans were working together to move drugs into the United States. When the Chinese trafficked white heroin, they dealt strictly with their own group of people. But for the Chinese to get involved with the Mexicans? This was new for me and DEA.

The Mexican cartel or maybe the Mexican government at the top were allowing the Chinese an opportunity to mix in with the Garcia brothers' drug trafficking network right there in San Luis, Sonora, Mexico.

287

You've got to have the Chinese and Mexican governments working together to make something like that happen!

I was getting more excited, and if I was honest with myself, I was getting a bit nervous. I was overwhelmed. I was just one DEA agent. The Asian connections with the Garcia brothers went way beyond me to understand why the Chinese were involved! I was thinking; *Is it because of the corrupt officials at the San Luis POE?*

I later told Santo and Angelito to focus on whether the connection was real or false between Javier's shrimp business and the Chinese Company in Los Angeles.

I asked the PIs if they had additional information on the Chinese Company's relationship with the brothers.

The PIs said, "No, but we have a connection with DEA Agent Luis Short, who is assigned to the Asian Task Force in Los Angeles, California. We have worked with Agent Short on other PI cases in the past."

I called DEA Agent Luis Short, the Asian Gang NTF case agent in Los Angeles, about the Garcia brothers' connection with the Chinese Seafood Company. I told Agent Short that PI Jeff Pearce had given me his name.

He told me he was working with a DEA Asian Gang NTF in Los Angeles (LA) targeting Chinese drug activities in Chinatown, LA, California.

"Agent Short, you are the right DEA agent I need to talk to about my case connected to a Chinese company in LA."

I explained to him that my CI might be traveling with a known drug trafficker to visit a Chinese Seafood Company in Chinatown or somewhere in the LA area.

His response was, "You're telling me a Mexican dope trafficker is coming over here with your CI to meet the owners of the Chinese Seafood company in Chinatown?"

I said, "Not now. But maybe in the next few months. Wish me luck!"

DEA Agents Ambushed & Killed

After talking with my CIs and the PIs, I remembered that while I was in training at the DEA Academy, three DEA agents were assassinated in Pasadena, California. The Instructors mentioned George Montoya, 37, Paul Seema, 52, and Jose Martinez, 25, were working as undercover members of the Asian

Gang Narcotics Task Force in Los Angeles and were ambushed in Pasadena while purchasing $80,000 worth of white heroin from Asian drug dealers.

The DEA Instructors said that Agents were assassinated, and Agent Martinez was severely injured. Backup DEA agents killed two of the Asian gang members and a third man, Win Wei Wang, known as William Wang, 18, was shot eight times when pursued by agents after the ambush. Su Te Chia, known as Michael Chia, 21, was also involved in planning the DEA agent assassinations.

Wang and Chia were indicted by a Federal Grand July in Los Angeles for two counts of murder and one count each of attempted murder, robbery, and conspiracy to rob federal agents.[35]

California U.S. Attorney Robert Bonner wanted Wang and Chia to face the death penalty. "It's lamentable. Indeed, it is astonishing that it is not possible to obtain the death penalty under federal law for the murder of federal agents. ... Only Congress can remedy this glaring inadequacy in the federal law" Chia's case was overturned because Wang stated Chia was not part of the shooting.[36]

290

You don't Kill a DEA Agent Unless you get Permission

A law enforcement officer knows that when a DEA agent gets hurt or killed by a drug trafficker, all the red flags go up on the Northern and Southern borders. It's like in the old Godfather days with the Mafia. You don't kill a cop or a DEA agent unless you get permission from the Mafia. The Drug cartels throughout Central American and South American know that it's an unwritten rule not to kill a DEA without permission from the organization. Everyone knows in the drug world when you kill a DEA agent, DEA will be coming for you; if needed, with the help of CIA, NSA, and CIs.

Bob Wiedrich of the *Chicago Tribune* stated in 1975, "Any time day or night, DEA agents are risking their lives somewhere in the world, carrying out their duties with professional competence and dedication often far beyond the call of duty. They do not appreciate Jackson's derogatory comments...Neither should the American people who have the greatest stake of all in the deadly serious job of fighting the international drug traffic."[37]

Kiki Camarena trusted the local Mexican cops, and that trust cost him his life. It was corruption, plain and simple. Corrupt

291

law enforcement cops found him and helped torture him to death. His Mexican cop buddies were the ones who knew he'd been tortured.

In 1985, Mexico City suffered a violent earthquake with a magnitude of 8.0. Severe damage affected the greater Mexico City area with deaths of at least 5,000 people. Torture tapes of Kiki Camarena were held in the State Department's office in Mexico City, where, officially, they were destroyed in the quake.

I was seriously thinking about the murders and attempted murders of DEA agents from the past. I told my wife, Kathy, "I'm not afraid of the Garcia brothers and the other criminals in Yuma or in Mexico. But if I'm hurt or killed, it will be a corrupt cop, a Customs officer, or an Immigration officer who pulled the trigger."

I had already lost two co-workers from the Yuma NTF that were assassinated by a corrupt Yuma County Deputy Sheriff officer. The officer was a corrupt cop who was a retired Marine Staff Sergeant working on NTF cases. According to my CIs, the brothers thought that the two NTF officers assassinated were DEA agents.

Traveling Alone Across the Mexican Border

There were so many narcotics cases coming out of Mexico into the U.S. that kept me busy. I would often cross the border into San Luis, Sonora, Mexico, and spent more time there than in Yuma. I would travel alone in Mexico to follow the dope traffickers into pool halls and bars without the DEA office knowing about it. While in Mexico, I watched some of the Garcia's drug traffickers' businesses and their homes to get license plate numbers, especially the U.S. license plates.

After checking on the brothers and dopers' residences and business, I would stop for a beer and something to eat. Corona beer and food were cheap in Mexico. I drank a couple of Corona beers and ate grilled chicken. I preferred eating the chicken because I could see it cooking on the grill. A well-done grilled chicken was always safe to eat in Mexico. But, every time I ate chicken, I wasn't sure if it might be a dog or cat.

Santo told me, "Some of the Garcia brothers' family and relatives in Yuma and San Luis, Mexico always seem to know when you're down in San Luis, Mexico."

Perhaps I was the only white boy hanging out near the brothers' businesses and residences. I guess I had that kind of recognized face and authority. Maybe the brothers found out from the corrupt cops at the POE when I crossed into Mexico.

I never had any problems at the POE until I started to focus on the Garcia brothers and their illegal dope activities in Yuma. I didn't want to deal with the Customs and Immigration officers at the POE. I had learned too much about the corrupt Customs and Immigration officers working along the border. I didn't want anyone suspecting I was in Mexico looking into the Garcia brothers' criminal activities.

I remembered once taking a shortcut around the POE in Calexico, California, through the open desert. When I crossed into the U.S., several Customs and Immigration officers followed me. When I noticed that the officers were following me, I stopped my car. They immediately drew their handguns and rifles on me until I showed them my DEA badge. Then they asked me to return to the POE.

When I went back to the POE with the officers, I was questioned by an Immigration supervisor about my failure to enter the U.S. properly at the POE.

I told the supervisor, "You've got some corrupt Customs and Immigration officers working here at the POE. I didn't want to identify myself to the wrong officer at the POE entry gate."

Then the supervisor said, "You can leave."

After I retired from DEA, I applied for the Customs and Immigration Global Entry card to enter the U.S. without a lot of hassles at Transportation Security Administration (TSA) checkpoints. Within about three weeks, I received a letter from Customs officials stating that I was not qualified for the TSA Global Entry card. I immediately called the phone number in Washington, D.C., that was provided in the letter. The woman on the phone said, "Sir, according to our records, you are not qualified to have the TSA Global Entry card."

After several phone calls to Washington D.C., I found out that Customs and Immigration officers at the POE had written in their investigative reports that I entered the U.S. illegally through the POE and was arrested by the officers. The records stated I was

295

a *Border Jumper* because I crossed the border illegally from Mexico into the U.S. without identifying myself when entering the POE.

I told Washington, D.C, that I did not identify myself as a DEA agent until later because of the corruption at the POE.

I did eventually receive the TSA Global Entry card.

The DEA Agents They Wanted to Kill

Marco Oscuro and Flaco el Pulpo were present, along with my CIs, during one of the "Oompa" parties (Mexican parties with bands) at Jaime's mansion. Jaime boasted to Santo and Angelito, saying, "DEA will never be able to touch me because of my connection with CIA and what I've done for them. The CIA comes to me for information. So, I'm pretty much protected by them."

The following week Santo and Angelito told me that when they were at one of the Oompa parties, Joselito was bragging about the DEA agents he tried to kill. Joselito said, "Don't worry, I can get anyone or anything across the POE. I have a niece and a nephew who works at the border. I can get whatever information I need to find out what the DEA is doing and who is working for DEA."

296

I received information from my SOI that the Garcia brothers harbored a "hit squad" in San Luis, Mexico. They instructed the sicarios to kill DEA agents.

I asked the SOI, "Who instructed the 'hit squad' to kill the agents?"

The SOI said he didn't know.

The brothers have been linked with a host of threats and murders, primarily against CIs, PIs, SOIs, and DEA agents in the U.S. and Mexico.

A DEA source said that the Mexican Federal Attorney in San Luis, Sonora, Mexico initiated federal arrest warrants against the Garcia brothers and their criminal associates. The arrest warrant was because of their involvement in the shooting of two DEA agents in San Luis, Mexico.

I was thinking, hopefully; Now, maybe I can get a source inside the Conqeladora (Ice House) in Mexico to get more information on the 'hit squad.'

Mexican Federal Army asked for $3-million

I was getting hard factual evidence for AUSA Fly to prosecute the Garcia brothers, and I was getting excited again.

Santo and Angelito were helping me to make the drug connections with undercover drug buys from traffickers that worked for the brothers.

This is what I've been working toward. Everything's taking shape here! Don and Roy, I'm going to get the brothers!

If I could arrest some of the drug traffickers and connect them directly to the Garcia brothers and their family members' dope business, then I could develop the link analysis. There was a vast pool of other CIs I needed to develop to help out with the case.

Hopefully, new informants could come from the Los Angeles area where Javier's shrimp trucks were headed. I needed some more business types of CIs living in Mexico to help me. I already had Santo and Angelito, but, still, I needed a CI inside San Luis POE. *But can I trust the other CIs?*

FBI Agent Stone contacted me and said, "An unknown female called the FBI to report Jaime was kidnapped by the Mexican Federal Army. Jaime failed to pay the Mexican Federal

Army for facilitating a large shipment of heroin up to the border of Arizona. The Mexican Federal Army asked for $3-million for Jaime's release."

I told Agent Stone that my SOI said Jaime owed the money to the Mexican Federal Police, not the Mexican Federal Army, for his protection from moving *dope* to San Luis POE.

FBI Agent Stone showed me a local Mexican newspaper with Jaime's photo and the story of his kidnapping and ransom fee. He later asked Jaime's produce partner, Franco Finca, if he was the U.S. contact for the Garcia brothers' narcotics activities. Finca denied any involvement but was aware of the drugs moving through a suspected underground tunnel into the United States at San Luis POE. Agent Stone and I were no longer working jointly on the Garcia brothers' drug activities because FBI Stone was afraid of the corrupt NTF cops and corruption at the POE. However, FBI Stone continued to provide me with information on Jaime's kidnapping.

Agent Stone focused on Jaime's kidnapping but didn't provide me with any details about Jaime's brothers.

According to my sources, Joselito Garcia paid the ransom to the Mexican Federal Police for Jaime's release, not the Mexican Federal Army.

30 Kilos of Cocaine; $14,500 a Kilo

The DEA in Phoenix provided me information that a drug defendant squealed like a rat to DEA on the Garcia brothers' trafficking organization in San Luis, Mexico. The defendant said Jaime was the owner of more than 500 kilos of cocaine waiting to move into the U.S. through San Luis POE. The defendant also said he could arrange for a DEA undercover agent to purchase 15-20 kilos of heroin every 15 days from Jaime's traffickers. The defendant further said there would not be any problem for the heroin to cross the POE into the U.S.

After receiving this information, I received a call from Santo telling me, "Jaime and Joselito are ready to sell me 30 kilos of cocaine for $14,500 a kilo. Joselito said that his brothers have a lot more of it and can sell it to me real cheap."

I told Santo to purchase a one-kilo sample before he negotiated the price for the 30 kilos with Jaime and Joselito.

300

I said to myself: I want to make sure I have one kilo of cocaine from the brothers for AUSA Fly in Phoenix to prosecute when the time comes.

On the day set to purchase the one-kilo sample of cocaine, Angelito called and said, "Santo is in jail for a Driving Under the Influence (DUI)." He added, "I can't talk to Marco Oscuro, Joselito's trafficker, without Santo. I can't meet with him alone. Can you find someone to replace Santo and negotiate with Oscuro to buy the one kilo? I need someone to help me with Oscuro."

I said, "Look, Angelito, I can't speak Spanish fluently with Oscuro to buy the one kilo. But I do have someone that can help you negotiate to buy it from Oscuro. Her name is Kathy. She is from Europe. Kathy knows how to negotiate the price for the one kilo and the other 30 kilos, and hopefully, the 500 kilos later. You can introduce Kathy to Oscuro, and she will get the kilo of cocaine, even if she has to meet him or Jaime in Mexico."

Angelito wasn't comfortable making the one kilo buy from Oscuro without Santo. He trusted Santo to make all the decisions when purchasing dope from the brothers. Santo was in jail, and he was just a bodyguard.

301

Angelito didn't know Kathy or if he could trust the woman from Europe. He wanted to talk to Santo before Kathy talked to Oscuro and make the buy.

A few days later, Santo called me from the Phoenix county jail. I said, "Santo, I have someone from Europe that can buy anything that is for sale. Tell Angelito not to worry; the woman can talk to Oscuro and buy the kilo without sticking a knife in Oscuro's fat belly and taking it for free. She has the money to buy only one kilo. She'll have the rest of the money to buy 30 more kilos if the price is low enough to move it to Europe."

Santo told me he would call Angelito about the woman.

Santo told Angelito on the phone, "You need to talk to this woman because she's behind the 30 kilos deal with Agent Hardin. I think she is an informant from Europe who works with Agent Hardin."

Later that day, I asked Kathy, "Can you help me buy a kilo of cocaine and hopefully negotiate 30 kilos more with a trafficker in Mexico? After you buy the 30 kilos, I want you to talk about the 500 kilos with him."

She said, "Sure. I'll buy it for you and the other 30 kilos."

302

"Okay, come with me. I need you to speak with Angelito. He works for me. He is going to introduce you to Marco Oscuro, who wants to sell one-kilo cocaine and then the rest of 30 kilos later to Angelito."

The next day in Yuma, Kathy and I met with Angelito in a parking lot behind a grocery store. Kathy told him, "Don't be a chocho (sissy) when you talk to Oscuro. Do you want me to talk to Oscuro, or can you set up the purchase for the sample kilo of cocaine with him?"

Angelito said, "No, I can talk to Oscuro."

Kathy said, "Angelito, you don't have the cajones (balls) to make a buy with Oscuro. I need you to set it up to buy the kilo for $14,500. Can you handle it? Call Oscuro!"

Angelito listened to her and called Oscuro. Kathy discussed with Angelito where she could meet Oscuro later to finalize the deal to buy the one-kilo sample.

With Kathy telling Angelito what to say to Oscuro, Angelito finally convinced Oscuro to sell a kilo of cocaine for $14,500 to Kathy.

Angelito spoke to Oscuro to set up the deal. Oscuro said, "Okay, tell that girl from Europe. I can deliver the kilo of cocaine to her in Phoenix. Then, I'll deliver the other 30 kilos to her when she is ready."

Angelito told Oscuro that Kathy wants the 30 kilos if the price is less than $12,000.

Oscuro said, "I have to talk to Jaime."

Later, Oscuro agreed to sell the 30 kilos and to follow up with the 500 kilos of cocaine to the woman from Europe after she approves the one-kilo sample.

After the telephone conversation ended between Angelito, Kathy, and Oscuro, I told Angelito, "Set up the deal to buy the sample kilo from Oscuro now. I am going to Phoenix to get help from DEA to surveil this sample buy once you get the location from Oscuro."

Later, he called me and said, "Oscuro has a kilo of cocaine waiting in Phoenix! Kathy can meet with Oscuro at Denny's."

I told him, "Angelito, you have to help to make the kilo buy from Oscuro. The woman can't be there at Denny's to meet with him. Kathy will send someone else to buy it from him."

304

The next day in Phoenix, the undercover DEA Hispanic agent was not too sure if he could buy a kilo sample of cocaine from Oscuro by himself. I told the young agent, "Don't worry. Angelito will help you. Just let him do the talking."

The DEA undercover agent bought the one sample kilo for $14,500 from Oscuro with Angelito's help.

Later, I field-tested the white powdery substance, and everything appeared to be authentic. It was a kilo of cocaine.

Several days later, I traveled to Phoenix to meet a Judge that could help release Santo from the county jail. I explained to the Judge that Santo could help me buy 30 kilos of cocaine from the Garcia brothers and later 500 kilos. I explained to the judge the brothers tried to kill two DEA agents.

The judge said to me, "Okay, Santo will be released, but you will be responsible if he commits another crime or gets another DUI."

Once Santo was released, Santo and Angelito said they would set up the buy for the 30 kilos from the Garcia brothers when I was ready with the money.

305

I told Agent Stone that I bought a one-kilo cocaine sample for $14,500 from Marco Oscuro in Phoenix.

"Oscuro told Santo the kilo sample is from the 30 kilos of cocaine; follow up with 500 kilos. He is ready to sell the rest for a lower price of $12,000 to him."

Santo was attempting to obtain from Oscuro and Jaime the rest of the 30 kilos of cocaine for $12,000 a kilo to develop credibility or possibly buy even more from Jaime.

I asked Agent Stone again, "Will you help me buy 30 kilos? I need $360,000. Can *FBI* help to pay half?"

Agent Stone said, "Yes."

He also told me he could help out with my investigation into the Garcia brothers' organization.

I asked him, "When can you help me buy the 30 kilos from the brothers?"

"Soon. I need to talk to my boss."

Agent Stone was going to help me make the big purchase. Later, Santo would negotiate another purchase of 500 kilos from Oscuro and Jaime. I started gathering more information on how the brothers were successful in moving cocaine across the border at San Luis POE and into the U.S.

I worked by myself, following the Garcia brothers in the Yuma community, restaurants, churches, schools, and grocery stores. I followed their cars, produce trucks, and other family members throughout Yuma and near to the POE, keeping a low profile.

With the help from FBI, I would purchase the 30 kilos from Jaime's traffickers. After buying the 30 kilos, I could negotiate the purchase of 500 kilos from the brothers, following up with the arrest warrants for Jaime and Oscuro.

"Make sure that your character is free from the love of money, being content with what you have; for He Himself has said, 'I WILL NEVER DESERT YOU, NOR WILL I FORSAKE YOU" (Hebrews 13:5 New American Standard Version).

Mexican Trafficking White Heroin

PI Jeff Pearce and PI Randy Torgerson told me that el Pulpo, the manager at the maquiladora furniture company, had a lot of information on the company's computer in his office about suspected heroin activities of the Asian's and the Garcia brothers.

A few days later, I mentioned to FBI Agent Stone that the Asians might be involved with the Garcia brothers trafficking white heroin. The PIs had learned the information from their source, who worked at the maquiladora with Flaco el Pulpo.

I have everything I need on el Pulpo. He was the weak link to the Garcia brothers' family. Greed for money, women, and power are the downfalls of any culture. I discovered this was el Pulpo's weakness.

I heard from the PIs that Agent Stone contacted them about the Asians and the brothers working together. Agent Stone said to the PIs, "We would like to set up a deal where we can go into Mexico with you to search el Puplo's computer at the maquiladora furniture company. We want to go into el Pulpo's office at the maquiladora and download his computer."

I was thinking; Who does Agent Stone mean when he says, "We? He never mentioned it to me."

Agent Stone never gave me an explanation for why he wanted to review el Pulpo's computer or why he was now interested in the connections with Asians.

Up until the late 1990s, DEA could work in Mexico under no specific conditions from the Chief Legal Counsel in Washington D.C. DEA can carry their weapons and conducted surveillance in Mexico without the Mexican officials knowing what they were doing. The FBI was not allowed to work in Mexico without the Mexican Federal Police support. It was illegal for Agent Stone to travel in Mexico without notifying the Mexican Federal Police.

This is highly unusual.

The PIs were willing to work with Agent Stone, but they wanted him to give them a copy of the information on el Pulpo's company computer. He agreed. The PIs were wondering why Agent Stone was so nice to them now. He was a Mormon and didn't drink beer or participate in dirty jokes with other agents. Agent Stone made it evident to me that he never liked the PIs. But now he wants to work with them.

Several days later, I went to the San Luis border with the PIs. Shortly after midnight, we met with Agent Stone and an

309

unidentified female agent from Washington, D.C., near San Luis POE.

She only identified herself as an Information Technology (IT) Specialist but didn't give her first name. She just smiled when I asked her a question but wouldn't answer. She would not communicate with me.

Is she working with NSA or CIA?

PI Torgerson and I stayed at the border near San Luis POE. Agent Stone, the IT Specialist, and PI Pearce went into San Luis, Mexico, to search el Pulpo's computer at the maquiladora furniture business.

Everything changed that night after Agent Stone and the IT Specialist returned with PI Pearce back to the U.S. border. Once they arrived, I agreed to meet with Agent Stone and the IT Specialist at the Yuma FBI office. At the office, I only met with Agent Stone, and I was wondering; *What happened to the IT Specialist? She is not here for this meeting.*

Agent Stone said, "She downloaded a lot of great information from el Pulpo's computer. She will get copies for you and the PIs of everything she took from the computer."

The next day, PIs Jeff Pearce and Randy Torgerson met me at the coffee shop at the Best Western Hotel. PI Pearce said, "It was incredible how the IT Specialist retrieved the information so quickly from el Pulpo's computer. I saw photos and email documents of Asians with el Pulpo and Javier Garcia in the IT Specialist hands."

After several days, I thought it was strange that I never got any information on el Pulpo's documents from Agent Stone. I never saw the IT Specialist again or received the copies that Agent Stone promised to give me.

PI Harry Fresno contacted me about the information retrieved from el Pulpo's computer. I finally tracked FBI Agent Stone down at his office and said, "Dude, what's up? What happened? You need to return the phone calls to PI Fresno. What about the information you have from el Pulpo's computer?"

I went to revisit Agent Stone and asked him about the copies from el Pulpo's computer. He told me that the IT Specialist had the copies. Then Agent Stone added, "Look, there's nothing there, and I can't tell you anything else. It's just a bunch of numbers."

He said, "FBI has refused to work with you or the PIs on the Asian and Garcia brothers' investigation. They also do not want to help you to purchase the 30 kilos of cocaine from Jaime Garcia."

Something happened the night when they searched el Pulpo's computer at the maquiladora furniture company.

Later, at the DEA Yuma office, Agent Stone told me he no longer wanted to be involved with the Garcia brothers' case. He never gave me a reason why.

I asked, "Why the sudden change?"

He refused to explain.

I knew someone higher up in the FBI must have stopped him from working jointly with DEA on the investigation.

I told Agent Stone, "Tell your boss I need your help to purchase the 30 kilos form the brothers."

He said, "I will talk to him again, but my boss is going to say 'No.'"

He did not want to talk about the brothers and did not want to work with PIs Jeff Pearce and Randy Torgerson.

I met with the PIs at Skyview Hotel in Yuma and told them what Agent Stone said. PI Pearce told me, "I saw what was downloaded from el Pulpo's computer. A name of a Chinese Seafood Company! Agent Stone has the copies that the IT Specialist made from the files in el Pulpo's office. I gave him a document that showed shrimp loads, accounting, and communications. I even provided him a photo I found inside el Pulpo's desk that shows Javier meeting with Asians in El Golfo."

PIs Pearce and Torgerson thought the female IT Specialist who got all the information was an unwitting partner in the search with Agent Stone. Agent Stone told her to get the information from the computer because it was for something big. PI Pearce believed that she didn't realize it was more of a cover-up type of action for another agency.

PI Harry Fresno told me, "In DEA and FBI there are government-appointed people, elected people, and agents. There are witting and unwitting circumstances where agents know why they're doing something, and others don't. Agent Stone and the female IT Specialist were just told to do something, and they did it."

Agent Stone stopped communications with the PIs, and eventually with me.

313

It's clear to me that the brothers and Asians were running narcotics out of the brothers' shrimp business. I knew this was big! White heroin and Mexicans don't usually mix. The Garcia brothers have their black and brown heroin distribution in the United States. Something was not right here! I asked myself:

A lot of law enforcement officers in Yuma didn't like the FBI or DEA. FBI Agent Stone was a jerk and not very cooperative with other agencies in Yuma. Some of that might have been DEA versus FBI. There was often a lot of friction back then over cases between the two agencies.

I was thinking, Agent Stone and the IT Specialist searched el Pulpo's business in Mexico. Whatever happened down there changed the nature of the case and FBI support.

Cocaine and Heroin with Frozen Fish and Shrimp

According to my CIs and SOIs, the Conqeladora (Ice House) was where the brothers' dope traffickers brought fish and shrimp loads from the barquitos, fishing boats. The traffickers picked up the heroin with frozen fish and shrimp in El Golfo. The white heroin was from a Chinese ship off the coast. The brothers'

314

employees would take the drugs and shrimp, size ten jumbo shrimp, to the *Ice House*.

Santo and Angelito told me, "The shrimp were huge! Big enough to hide drugs in a cavity cut under the tail."

I met with Santo and Angelito behind a clothing store location in Yuma. I told Santo, "Start talking about computer chips [slang for drugs] in your shrimp trucks, anything that can make extra money. The brothers know you're Colombian, and Colombia is known for cocaine, heroin, and marijuana. Throw it out there again to the brothers that you're interested in getting some extra money because your shrimp business is failing. Just mention it casually."

It took time for Santo and Angelito to earn Javier's trust, and time to get the "big fish." It was the time I could wait to give Don and Roy justice.

Santo and Angelito met with Javier's brother-in-law, el Pulpo, at Javier's grocery market in Mexico. They later provided me a five-kilo box of Javier's Tiger shrimp. Santo and Angelito were right about the tails. They were huge.

315

Chinese Seafood Company Wants to Meet with Santo

I got a message from Santo that he was invited to Los Angeles with Javier to visit the Chinese Seafood Company in Chinatown and meet some of the owners.

I wondered; Why do the owners of the Chinese Seafood Company in Chinatown want to meet with Santo? Did the FBI or the IT Specialist say something to CIA about the information from el Pulpo's computer?

I told Santo, "You've got some activity going on between the brothers and the Chinese. I want you to go with Javier and learn as much as you can about the owners of the Chinese Seafood Company in Chinatown. I want to know more about what's happening with Javier and his friends in Los Angeles with their shrimp business."

A week later, Santo got on a plane with Javier at the Yuma International Airport. I had the airport under DEA surveillance. As soon as I saw them get on the flight and departed to LA, I called DEA Agent Luis Short, the Asian Gang NTF case agent in Los Angeles, about the Garcia brothers' connection with the Chinese Seafood Company in Chinatown. "Agent Short, I want you to protect my CI (Santo) if he needs it and gather information on the meeting with the Asians in Chinatown."

He said, "I'll have DEA agents in the Los Angeles Asian Gang NTF meet at the Los Angeles airport and follow your CI and Javier to Chinatown."

He said to me, "I'm going to come out to Yuma and see you later when this is done."

PI Jeff Pearce was on his way home from Yuma to Los Angeles Airport (LAX). He would then transfer to another flight to Fresno, California. He happened to be on the same flight to LA as Javier and Santo.

PI Pearce was going berserk! Why was Javier on this flight to Los Angeles?

He decided to follow Javier. He was going to see where Javier and the other guy were heading in the LA area.

I got a call from PI Pearce's boss, PI Fresno. "What are you doing? You should have told me Javier was on the plane! I've got one of my guys on that plane."

I said, "Harry, you need to calm down. Nothing is going to happen with PI Pearce. The guy with Javier is a *shadow*."

317

Santo and Javier arrived at LAX, and PI Pearce was ready to follow them. He immediately saw Agent Short at the airport. He went over to Agent Short and told him that Javier was on the plane traveling with another guy.

Agent Short said, "Agent Hardin has already contacted me. You come with me. I want you to drive, and you and I will follow the CI and Javier Garcia."

After Javier and Santo met with two Asian men at the airport, they went directly to a Chinese Seafood Company in Chinatown. Javier introduced Santo to the older Asian man at the Seafood Company. Santo didn't get his name. Santo and the Asian man only shook hands and exchanged greetings. The meeting didn't last long, and then the two Asian men took Santo and Javier back to LAX.

Once in Yuma, Javier never mentioned to Santo again anything about going to the Chinese Seafood Company in Chinatown.

Santo told me that nothing happened in Chinatown. There had been no discussion of Santo's shrimp business with the Asian Seafood Company.

318

After the trip to the Asian Seafood Company in Chinatown, Santo noticed Javier's behavior toward him changed, and he wasn't sure what was happening.

I suspected the two Asian men might have observed Agent Short, PI Pearce, and the DEA surveillance team following Santo and Javier from LAX to Chinatown. I sensed the Asians were aware that Santo might be working with the government, even if they weren't sure which one.

Agent Short called me and said, "It's highly unusual for the Asians to meet with Mexican traffickers in Chinatown. Can I come over to meet with you?"

He kept questioning, "How did the Mexican brothers hook up with the Asian group?"

I briefly filled him in about the connection of the Chinese Seafood Company and a meeting Javier arranged for the CI.

In the next few days, I decided to go and meet Agent Short. I flew to LAX and had a meeting with him near the Federal Courthouse. It was very private and secure. He didn't talk a lot about the surveillance of Santo and Javier's meeting at the Chinese

319

Seafood Company. There wasn't even a DEA written report on the surveillance by Agent Short.

I knew something wasn't right.

That evening we went to Chinatown for dinner. He knew the Asian manager and waiters and spoke to them in their native language.

I asked him for further information about the seafood company's possible connections with the CIA. The agent was focused on himself and his DEA career, hoping to work in Hong Kong or somewhere in China. He drove around with local LAPDs in the Los Angeles County area to gather intelligence on Chinatown's criminal drug trafficking network. That's about all he did.

He wasn't interested in discussing the Chinese Seafood Company. I didn't mention it to him again that night.

I learned later that a DEA agent at the Consulate Office in Hermosillo and another agent out of Washington D.C. were working the Asian organization, especially the Chinese Seafood Company in Chinatown.

Employees & Young Girls Sexually Abused

On one occasion, when Santo and Angelito couldn't find Javier at his grocery store in Mexico, they met with Ana Blanca at a local bar. After a few drinks, Santo asked her if she knew about the relationship of Javier with the Asians. She explained to Santo that Javier's small shrimp boats in El Golfo would go out to meet the other larger boats. On one occasion, she saw an Asian ship in El Golfo who gave Javier a lot of shrimp. Javier would move the shrimp to the Ice House before moving it across San Luis POE.

Ana told the CIs about how the girls, who were employees, placed tin foil bindles inside open shrimp tails. On one occasion, Santo and Angelito accidentally saw this while visiting the Ice House. They watched Javier's employees cut the shrimp tails open and put small tin foil bindles inside each tail. The CIs knew it was white heroin but couldn't prove it.

Santo and Angelito continued to see young girls sexually abused at the shrimp factory and the ice warehouses. Santo and Angelito begged me to help the young girls escape from the Garcia brothers. I talked to AUSA Fly in Phoenix without telling my group supervisor, GS Juan Antonio Moreno, about what was happening

321

to the young girls at Javier's shrimp facility. He pretended he didn't hear what I said and ended the phone conversation.

Later, GS Juan Antonio received word from the AUSA regarding Javier's employees and my conversation with AUSA Fly. He said the DEA in Phoenix wanted me to *back off* about pushing the AUSA office to do something about the young girls at the shrimp facility in Mexico. As the GS put it, "You don't want that kind of relationship with the AUSA office looking into sexually abused girls within the Garcia brothers' organization's family in Mexico. Do you understand, Larry?"

Don't Snort Cocaine nor Have Sex with Young Girls

Several weeks later, Santo told me, "I met Joselito again. He scares me, and so does Marco Oscuro."

Nobody outside the DEA office knew of Santo and Angelito meeting with Jaime, Javier, and Joselito Garcia in Mexico; only the agents at my office were in on it. During the next several months, the CIs met with Javier about the shrimp business.

Javier questioned Santo, "My brother, Joselito, tried growing coca plants to produce coca, but it didn't work out. What's

322

the method you use in Colombia to produce coca? Do you think we can grow coca plants here in Mexico?"

Santo told Javier, "I don't know the method for growing coca, but maybe I can move it in my frozen shrimp boxes into the U.S. at San Luis POE."

Javier thought this was funny because it was an idea that hadn't yet been discussed.

Santo and Angelito turned out to be the best CIs I ever worked with. When CIs worked for me, I kept them close and told them not to violate any laws of doing dope and having sex with young girls. Santo and Angelito were paid CIs, and therefore protected by me as long they followed directions and didn't violate United States law.

Did I trust Santo and Angelito? Heck, no! But there were a lot of law enforcement officers I didn't trust either.

A few weeks later, Santo and Angelito met again with Javier in San Luis, Mexico. They just talked about the shrimp business. After the meeting in Chinatown, there was no conversation about drugs connected with the Asians, just shrimp with Santo. Javier was very cautious with who he could trust to

323

know about his brothers' organization. The brothers were behind several killings in Mexico, including the attempted murder of two DEA agents. The CIs had to be careful.

Santo was excited that these brothers were big-time dope criminals. He wanted to get things rolling to buy more dope from the brothers.

Tiger Shrimp Tails

While waiting to meet with Javier at his small ice house in El Golfo, Santo and Angelito witnessed again two women placing a white powdery substance in tin foil bindles. The women would filet the shrimp, cut out a pocket right in the middle of the shrimp tails, then put the tin folds inside and close the tails.

The shrimp was loaded in kilo boxes that were iced and placed on racks. Then Javier's employees loaded the shrimp boxes into Javier's refrigerator truck.

Once Santo and Angelito entered Arizona from Mexico from San Luis POE, Santo called me. He said, "I believe the tin foil bindles contained white heroin that Javier's employees were putting in the shrimp."

324

"The white heroin is being moved soon through the POE in Javier's shrimp truck," said Santo.

He provided me all the information I needed to stop Javier's shrimp truck when it came across the U.S. border. I convinced GS Juan Antonio Moreno that I needed to search Javier's truck.

GS Juan Antonio told me, "Larry, if we don't find drugs inside the shrimp, this is going to cost DEA a lot of money because you are going to destroy all that shrimp."

"The white heroin is there. Santo and Angelito saw it with their own eyes!" I told him.

I was watching Javier's shrimp truck enter San Luis POE from Mexico. I knew it was loaded with drugs, and I was going to be the first DEA agent to get white heroin from the Mexicans. I was excited, knowing that the Mexicans and Asians were smuggling white heroin into the U.S., and I was going to catch them.

I was watching the truck at the POE stop for an inspection.

I haven't seen the Customs officer search Javier's shrimp trucks in the past. What is going on?

I thought I had tight control over who I could trust, and no corrupt official at the POE was going to interfere in searching Javier's shrimp.

The Customs officer opened the shrimp truck door. The officer walked up to the opened truck door with his dog; the officer turned around, closed the door, and walked away with his dog.

Why didn't the narcotics dog alert to the drugs inside the truck?

Later, with agents from my office, I stopped Javier's truck away from San Luis POE. I had two Border Patrol agents I could trust with their drug-sniffing dogs to help locate the white heroin inside the truck.

The Border Patrol agents' narcotics dogs alerted to drugs when they searched outside the shrimp truck. I called for another dog from Customs to help smell for any drugs on the truck. A third dog did the same thing and alerted me there was something inside the truck. I told the driver of the truck to follow me to a cooling facility company in Yuma.

When we arrived at the cooling center, I had two dogs from the Border Patrol and one dog from Customs to help search the

326

shrimp truck at the cooling center. Once again, all three dogs alerted that there were drugs inside the truck.

Why, didn't the Customs officer's dope dog alert to the shrimp boxes inside the truck at the POE?

I had to make sure there were drugs inside Javier Garcia's truck. If I didn't find anything, DEA would have to pay for the damage to Javier's shrimp. There was too much money being spent to break open the frozen shrimp boxes, not to find dope.

The other DEA agents and I took out slabs of five-kilo boxes of jumbo shrimp. With the slabs of five-kilo boxes of jumbo shrimp laying outside the truck, the agents' three drug dogs went crazy, sniffing the suspected dope inside the boxes of shrimp. One of the dogs was taken around the slabs, and then the dog alerted to two particular ones. The two slabs were towards the back and in the middle of the shrimp truck.

Man, I got white heroin! I got it, guys! I finally made the case against the brothers!

With the help of GS Juan Antonio and two DEA agents from the office, we cracked the frozen boxes open and broke the shrimp tails. All the colossal shrimp were lying there on the cooling

327

floor. These beautiful, jumbo tiger shrimp, there was nothing inside the tails!

I'll be damned. Only a very few in my office knew about me stopping Javier's shrimp truck. But someone leaked it to Javier or at the POE. Without a doubt, I believed that Javier Garcia had switched the shrimp load on that truck in San Luis, Mexico, so that when it came across, there was nothing! Someone from the POE saw me and had warned Javier I was going to search his truck.

I could see it in the DEA agent's eyes, GS Juan Antonio, the Border Patrol agents, and the Customs agent with their three dogs. There was no dope inside the shrimp tails!

I was surprised. The Border Patrol agents said to me, "Hey, we want the shrimp lying on the floor."

I couldn't take the destroyed shrimp, so I let the Border Patrol agents and Customs agent have it. Rumor has it; that night, the Border Patrol agents had a nice shrimp barbecue feast at their homes.

I got a call from Santo at the DEA office telling me that shrimp was going to another Chinese Seafood Company in Phoenix, not to Chinatown in Los Angeles. Why did Javier's shrimp truck suddenly change and move the shrimp to Phoenix, not Los Angeles? I couldn't prove it, but I was sure someone inside law enforcement, someone close to me, must have contacted Javier Garcia.

The Customs officer who searched the truck at San Luis POE called me, "Why did you stop that shrimp truck? I went in and out of that truck with my dog. I put some marijuana spray on the truck tires. I wanted to test my dog out."

I was thinking, Bullshit! How did the Customs officer know I was the one who stopped and searched the shrimp truck?

I asked him, "Why would you call and tell me that? Why did you target that particular shrimp truck and that moment to train your dog? That day and at that time?"

The Customs officer hung up on me.

When the names of the Garcia brothers were mentioned, everybody in Yuma law enforcement knew who they were; the brothers had many connections with individual family members and law enforcement in Yuma and at San Luis POE.

I started to worry about Santo and Angelito's safety from corrupt law enforcement, not the brothers.

329

I got a call late that night from Javier's wife, who said, "You destroyed my husband's shrimp."

I said, "Yes. I destroyed a lot of shrimp. I am sorry."

She continued to give me a hard time about why I destroyed her husband's shrimp.

"Mrs. Garcia! I'm going to hang up now. I will meet you tomorrow."

The next day, I met Javier's wife at her residence in Yuma. I told her she could contact DEA in Phoenix about the incident of her husband's truck.

Mrs. Garcia said, "You destroyed over $70,000 worth of shrimp. I have seen you before in town, and I know you are DEA."

Without a doubt, some corrupt cop took a photo of me and gave it to the Garcia brothers' family.

I immediately said, "Have I met you before, Mrs. Garcia?"

I was thinking what she is saying is strange, as I listened to Mrs. Garcia; I never heard from Javier about why DEA stopped his truck, and the shrimp being destroyed. Javier already knew the reason I searched his truck. Why is his wife calling me instead of him?

330

I learned from CIs and SOIs that Mrs. Garcia went to the Catholic church on Sundays. She was very connected with the Yuma community. *Was she aware that her husband was moving drugs into the United States?*

An SOI said that every year, Mrs. Garcia would get a brand-new red Cadillac for Christmas with a big red ribbon from Tommy Pescado, the used car dealer in Yuma. The SOI said Tommy was a nasty guy, married to a girl from the U.S. post office in Yuma. They were both very connected to the Garcia brothers' family.

Destroyed $70,000 of Frozen Tiger Shrimp Tails

A few days later, Santo and Angelito said they met with Joselito at Jaime's home in Mexico. I asked them, "Did Joselito or Jaime say anything about Javier's truck that was stopped and all the shrimp that was destroyed?"

Santo told me, "Joselito never mentioned DEA searched Javier's shrimp truck. Even Javier didn't mention DEA destroyed his Tiger shrimp to the CIs."

331

DEA was obligated to pay out over $70,000 for the load of shrimp I destroyed. However, Javier never asked DEA for the money, nor did his wife called me again.

I found out later from a Border Patrol agent at the Office of Personal Responsibility (OPR) in Yuma that two Border Patrol agents were suspected of getting money "under the table" from narcotics traffickers in Mexico. The Border Patrol agents were the two dog handlers I used on Javier's shrimp truck.

"Do not conform any longer to the pattern of this world but be transformed by the renewing of your mind. Then you will be able to test and approve what God's will is – his good, pleasing and perfect will" (Romans 12:2 New International Version).

Karaoke Night in Colorado Springs

I was going to meet with PI Jeff Pearce in the morning at the Colorado Springs DEA office to go over the information about the Garcia brothers' family member arrested for trafficking drugs in Colorado.

Since my meeting at the DEA office wasn't until the next morning, I decided to go down to the hotel bar and have a beer and meet with PI Pearce. He was dressed up and wearing suspenders. I was thinking; *He looks like a lawyer looking for a job.*

Half the people in the bar were Air Force cadets. There were also some young girls walking around looking for future military husbands. I am sure the girls weren't looking for him or me.

It was karaoke night, and PI Pearce decided to go up on the stage and sing. The singing sounded like Grandpa Hardin yelling for cows to come to the barn. While he was singing or shouting a song I never heard before, the cadets in the back of the bar started making fun of him. PI Pearce was almost drunk or at least, getting there and said, "What are you bald-headed punks laughing at? Shut the fuck up!"

After he drank a few more beers, I said to him, "Don't get yourself in trouble!"

"How about you?" he asked.

I'm a DEA Federal agent. What kind of trouble could I cause?

PI Pearce kept on singing (yelling) for the cows to come home, but the cadets wouldn't shut up.

333

After he finally stopped singing, he returned to the table. He was just sitting there at the table, really depressed, telling me that he wanted to impress the young waitress who was waiting on him.

Oh, boy, here he goes! He's trying to sing and pick up a girl and wondering why he can't.

I said, "Here, buddy, you take my DEA badge, go over and show it to the waitress. Tell her you're a cop, not a PI, and you want to get to know her!"

Sure enough, he went over with my badge. He flashed the DEA badge and came back, smiling like a canary bird who just swallowed a fat worm.

He said to me, "I didn't get the waitress, but I was really pleased with how the badge worked."

He wanted to keep the DEA badge for a while. Jeff looked at me and said, "Can I have it?"

I took it back from him and said, "Sorry, buddy, I can't let you keep it."

The waitress came over and flirted for a few minutes with PI Pearce. She finally let him know she had a boyfriend and was getting married.

334

I said, "What? You have a boyfriend, and you're flirting with my buddy?"

"Yeah, my boyfriend is very good to me."

"Then, why would you flirt with someone like him if you have a boyfriend you are planning to marry?"

"Who are you to say who I should flirt with?"

I flashed my DEA badge and said, "I'm an authority on the subject."

The waitress just walked away.

PI Pearce went back up to the mic to sing another song, and while I was sitting there listening to him screaming, things started escalating between him and the cadets. The Airforce Cadets were yelling at him, "What are you doing? You can't sing."

He continued singing anyway.

The Cadets continued to hassle him, "Who do you think you are? Frank Sinatra? You've got to do better than that."

He suddenly stopped singing and pulled on his suspenders. Then, he smiled at the cadets and turned to me and said, "I heard that the Colorado Springs law enforcement was called."

PI Pearce and I then walked out to the lobby, where some of the cadets were waiting.

Two Colorado Springs law enforcement officers came over to me and said, "Is everything okay?"

I said, "Yeah, I'm DEA, and I'm going to bed."

"Okay!"

And, that was the end of that ordeal.

They Killed a DEA Agent

DEA agent Richard (Richie) Fass was killed while working undercover in Phoenix, Arizona. Vasquez Mendoza, a Mexican citizen, planned it; the killing of Richie Fass.

Richie Fass

Later the same day, Arizona Department of Public Safety (DPS) Highway Patrol officers stopped and detained Augusto Vasquez Mendoza's pregnant wife and her brother traveling to Yuma to cross into San Luis, Sonora, Mexico. DEA Phoenix had information from their CIs that Augusto was involved in the murder of Agent Richie Fass.

336

Augusto's wife and her brother, Mexican citizens, were trying to escape into Mexico to avoid DEA. Agent Saul Morales took custody of Augusto's wife and her brother from the DPS officers, and I pushed them into the back seat of my car.

While driving to San Luis, Augusto's wife and her brother refused to answer questions when I asked about the whereabouts of Augusto. She was almost nine months pregnant and continued to rub her huge belly and complained to me of sharp pains. She started crying out loud.

I said, "Shut-up."

I was so mad I wanted to slap her across the face. I was wishing and thinking; *If only I had the corrupt Mexican* Commandanté *with me. She and her brother would have to talk.*

Her brother was crying and begging to stop because of the intense questioning from me. I told Agent Morales to pull over to an isolated area next to a lemon grove a few miles away from the entrance to the Mexican border. Agent Morales stopped, and I reached for a ketchup baggie from the glove compartment.

I opened the door and whispered to Agent Morales, "I'm taking this girl into the lemon grove. I'll handcuff her to a lemon

337

tree. Then I'll shoot one round from my little Sweet Pea .38-revolver into the air and smear the ketchup on my face and chest.

When I returned to the car without her, her brother will think I have his sister's blood on me. Then I'll jerk him out of the car, pointing my Sweet-Pea at his head, and he'll tell me where Augusto is. Her brother will be peeing and pooping in his pants."

As I got out of the car, dragging the screaming pregnant girl by her arm, her brother started crying and screaming for help. I told him to stop screaming, or I'll shoot his sister in the face right now.

Agent Morales yelled at me, "Don't Larry. The girl could have a miscarriage and lose the baby."

I thought about the way her husband had planned to kill Richie. I looked at Agent Morales with anger, "She and her brother helped kill Richie."

I took her back to the car and pushed her into the backseat next to her crying brother. They were both screaming and crying.

I told her, "I am taking you and your brother over to Mexico because the Mexican law enforcement cops can get the answers I need from you both."

She finally told me that Augusto was already in Mexico and hiding in San Luis. *Wow. Augusto is where the brothers controlled the corrupt cops.*

I dropped Augusto's wife and her crying brother off at a trailer Augusto rented near the Mexican border.

I immediately had Officer Daniel Blackman help set up listening devices on the trailer. The next day, Augusto's wife and her brother disappeared into San Luis, Mexico. Augusto's wife and her brother were never seen again.

Joselito told Santo and Angelito the brothers knew Augusto's wife and her brother were in San Luis, Mexico, but Augusto was not with them.

Santo asked, "Who is Augusto?"

Joselito said, "We don't want DEA to focus on us."

Joselito mentioned to Santo, "Augusto's wife and her brother are no longer in San Luis. We didn't want the shooter who helped kill the DEA agent in Phoenix to come to San Luis looking for his wife and brother-in-law. We don't want DEA to focus on us, while they're looking for Augusto. The DEA might think it was us behind killing the agent in Phoenix."

339

Augusto Vasquez Mendoza became one of FBIs most wanted fugitives. With DEA pressure on the Mexican government, Augusto was finally captured and prosecuted in the United States.

I was wondering; What happened to Augusto's wife and her brother. Did the Garcia brothers make them disappear in the hot Mexican desert near the Path of the Devil mountains?

The Dark Battle of the Drug World

I needed to get the Garcia brothers indicted quickly because more cops in the law enforcement community were getting involved in my investigation. Suspected corrupt Customs and Immigration officers at San Luis POE were *catching wind* of the work I was doing to indict the brothers and their family members. The corrupt officers knew that once I arrested the brothers, I would find out who the officers were at the POE.

Things were happening very fast at the AUSA's office in Phoenix to bring the case to closure. The PIs were in Yuma every week working on the brothers' case and identifying suspected corrupt cops. PIs Jeff Pearce and Randy Torgerson provided me with lots of intelligence to use to build the case against the brothers

340

using produce and shrimp trucks to smuggle drugs into the U.S. at San Luis POE.

I'm thankful I had my wife close to me. I lived in Yuma, so I was at home most nights. PIs Pearce and Torgerson were away from their homes in California and more easily drawn into the dark battle of the drug world to access information on the drug activities. I worried about what it could do to the PIs if they met the Garcia brothers without me.

Arizona State Senator and The Garcia Brothers

The PIs told me, "Listen to what we've got here!"

It was a tape recording captured between Ed Pastor, the Arizona State Senator, and Jaime Garcia. They were discussing on the recorder Jaime's agricultural produce business and how it was doing in Mexico.

I called FBI Agent Stone about the tape recording between the Senator and Jaime Garcia. Agent Stone immediately came to my office and picked up the recorded tape. Two weeks later, when I hadn't heard anything, I called Agent Stone and asked, "What's going on with the tape recording I gave you?"

341

Agent Stone told me he *ran this up the pole at FBI,* and nobody in the U.S. government wanted to touch it. So that just fizzled out.

Photo of a DEA Agent

Agent Saul Morales asked me to go with him to meet with the Mexican Federal Commandanté Fernandez in San Luis, Mexico. Commandanté Fernandez called about a small stolen American Cessna aircraft that crashed in the desert in El Golfo near the fishing village where Javier had his shrimp business.

The Commandanté said the small plane was loaded with cocaine. I knew from the CIs and SOIs; the Federal Commandanté Fernandez was a corrupt law enforcement officer who worked closely with the Garcia brothers.

Agent Morales said he'd met the Commandanté Fernandez before in San Luis, Mexico. He had given the Commandanté several boxes of 45-caliber ammunition. On one occasion, he gave Commandanté Fernandez an apple pie in exchange for information on drug traffickers in Mexico. I was wondering; *Why would this DEA agent trust a corrupt Commandanté?*

342

We arrived at the Mexican Federal Police station in San Luis, Sonora, Mexico, and met with Commandanté Fernandez. He told me he would take us to the crashed plane near El Golfo.

While I was at the police station, I observed a young man being slapped in the face several times by the federales. Blood was dripping out of the man's nose. I couldn't believe the man never cried or screamed when the cops slapped him several times in the face. The man's wife or girlfriend was crying as she watched the federales beating her husband. Then the federales moved her to another location inside the building.

I had heard from informants and witnesses that corrupt Mexican cops would take advantage of a woman for sexual pleasure. Unfortunately, I knew what this couple was about to experience. *I hope she has some Vaseline with her.*

The Commandanté said, "Let's go!"

Agent Morales and I jumped into the back seat of Commandanté Fernandez's black SUV. The driver was traveling very fast through the town of San Luis, Mexico. Several black SUVs with armed plainclothes federal police followed.

343

Agent Morales, I, and the Commandanté finally arrived at an isolated desert area where the stolen Cessna plane had crashed. I noticed the plane was burned down to the metal.

The Commandanté laughed and said, "The American plane carried cocaine, but someone must have unloaded it before we arrived."

Commandanté Fernandez was smiling as he spoke of the disappearing cocaine from the plane.

I was thinking to myself; What's really going on here? Without a doubt, the corrupt Commandanté knows where the cocaine is and who has it.

The Commandanté had a small black box camera in his hand and wanted to take a picture of me, no one else, as he told Agent Morales in Spanish. I was thinking to myself; *How dumb! Here I am, at a desert crash site in the middle of nowhere looking at a burned-out plane with a corrupt Commandanté. I can't even speak Spanish fluently, especially the Mexican slang.*

I looked directly at Commandanté's Fernandez bulging black eyes. I said to Agent Morales, "I want Commandanté Fernandez to understand that if he wants a picture of me, then his officers, all 12 of them, are going to take their shirts off and we'll all take a picture together, like a big family. You know, like a big happy family out in the middle of the 120° F desert."

Agent Morales nervously translated what I said to Commandanté Fernandez. The other Mexican officers laughed, and the Commandanté smiled. He then started to laugh and put the camera on his face.

He gave an order to his officers for everyone to take off their shirts, including Agent Morales and me. I was the last one taking off my polo shirt. I took my shirt off thinking; *I'm the only white-skinned dude out here in this desert!*

The Commandanté took several pictures, focusing on me standing next to the stolen crashed plane.

After taking several photos of me, Commandanté Fernandez invited me over to Javier's Cantina in El Golfo for lunch – the only restaurant in the small village. How could I say "no" to the Commandanté in the middle of the desert, surrounded by armed federales without their shirts?

At Javier Garcia's Cantina, "We are all eating tiger shrimp!" announced the Commandanté.

345

I was wondering; Who'll pay the bill? It's not going to be Commandanté Fernandez or me.

At the restaurant, I drank one Corona and ate two of the biggest shrimp I'd ever seen. The Commandanté shouted again, "The shrimp is tiger shrimp. The best!"

I wanted to pay for my corona beer, but Commandanté Fernandez told me, "No."

No one paid the bill; it was all free.

Agent Morales and I finally arrived back at San Luis POE border late that night. I thought to myself; It's a beautiful feeling to cross into the U.S. from Mexico. Thank God, I'm alive, and now, the Garcia brothers have a picture of me.

At the POE, an Immigration officer told me a young Mexican male was just arrested for having a kilo of cocaine hidden inside his pants.

I said to the Immigration officer, "Why are you telling me?"

He said, "The Mexican male said he is working for DEA."

"This is bullshit! All the traffickers tell you guys at the POE the dopers are working for DEA. Officer, listen very carefully to what I'm saying to you. You take care of the Mexican male and give the kilo of cocaine to the other Customs officers at the POE."

Did Commandanté Fernandez have something to do with telling the corrupt Immigration officer about the kilo of cocaine? Maybe it is one of the kilos stolen from the crashed plane in El Golfo.

The brothers and their dope traffickers have a photo of me without my shirt on standing next to a crashed plane. Now, the Garcia brothers will be able to recognize me when they see me follow them in Yuma and near the Mexican border. Because of the photo, it was extremely dangerous for me to go back to Mexico. I could be kidnapped and killed.

I wasn't afraid of the brothers and the other criminals. I was more cautious with my government and working with other agents and law enforcement that might be corrupt. I wasn't thinking of the officials in Mexico or the brothers, but my own people in the law enforcement community.

Sometimes, I would see PIs Jeff Pearce and Randy Torgerson follow me around on both sides of the border. I asked them to keep me in their sights. They would follow me, and I would

347

follow them. It was all about staying alive, not getting killed by corrupt cops.

Shot Several Times in Vietnam

Working undercover, PI Harry Fresno introduced me to a former U.S. Marine officer, Benito Bravo, who worked as a drug guard for the Garcia brothers. Benito was a war veteran who was shot twice in Vietnam while out on patrol and once by a sniper.

According to military records, Benito was a real hero who was wounded twice in Vietnam, saving the lives of his Marine buddies. He was an enlisted Marine promoted to a field commissioned Lieutenant.

He told PI Fresno, "Larry is a CIA agent. I saw him before in Mexico."

Benito did not want to talk with me about the Garcia brothers. I immediately thought, *Why did Benito say I work for the Spooks? Maybe the brothers also believe that?*

PI Jeff Pearce told me later that the former Marine knew Charles Blacksmith, a friend of the brothers, who was working for the *Spooks*. PI Pearce also said to me that Charles Blacksmith owned a shrimp business in Mexico.

Who is Charles Blacksmith?

I heard the name popping up with other law enforcement sources and my CIs. I didn't want to deal with the *Spooks*.

I told Santo if he could locate Charles Blacksmith's shrimp business in Mexico, I wanted him to arrange a meeting to get information about the Garcia brothers' shrimp business.

Santo and Angelito later met with Charles Blacksmith in Mexico to discuss their shrimp business. Blacksmith told Santo to be careful with Jaime Garcia. He discussed nothing else with Santo about the brothers. Then, I told Santo and Angelito to stay away from Charles Blacksmith. That was the CIs' last meeting with Blacksmith.

The Murders and The Corrupt Cops

I often said, "Law enforcement in Yuma and San Luis always knew where my CIs, PIs, and SOIs were, in Mexico or out on the streets in Yuma. I protected my CIs, PIs, and SOIs because I was DEA. No one in the law enforcement community wanted any

349

problems with me or DEA. PIs Jeff Pearce and Randy Torgerson did hard work in identifying corruption and took more risks in this case. I was unable to focus 100% on protecting them from corrupt cops. I was working on other criminal investigations at the same time.

There were times I'd be doing surveillance by myself on the brothers and other cases, and PIs Pearce and Torgerson followed me around. They were protecting me because they always felt like something was going to happen to me. There was a lot of law enforcement corruption; the PIs thought I was vulnerable.

I just wanted to stay focused, with blinders, on the Garcia brothers' organization, the murders, and attempted killings. I couldn't do that because I kept hitting one roadblock after another from the U.S. Attorney's office in Phoenix to end the case as I tried to continue the Garcia investigation.

A Former DEA Administrator

I was sitting in my office reading, leaning back in my chair with my feet up on the desk, and the phone rang. I answered, and the voice said, "Hello, this is Robert Bonner. I represent a client in

LA. I understand you're targeting my client's furniture trucks coming across San Luis POE at the Mexican border."

I don't like a lot of lawyers, even when they're on my side, especially Public Defense lawyers. Those working for the dopers tend to lie a lot and can be brutal in the courtroom, convincing the jury that cops and DEA agents are liars. It's a game of chess with a lot of them.

But, I was startled hearing the name, Robert Bonner. The name was familiar, and I asked, "Who are you?"

"My name is Robert Bonner."

"Did you ever work for DEA?"

"Yes, I'm a former DEA administrator."

Bonner was my DEA administrator a few years ago. He was well-known and well-liked by everyone in DEA.

My feet hit the floor! "Sir, why are you calling me?"

Mr. Bonner stated in a soft voice, "I'd like to come out to Yuma and meet with you."

We agreed to meet at a hotel in Yuma. I advised my GS Juan Antonio Moreno about the meeting, and he immediately called the DEA Phoenix office.

GS Juan Antonio got back to me and said, "No, you're not going to meet with Mr. Bonner in Yuma. Instead, you'll meet with him at the DEA office in Phoenix."

I tried to explain that Mr. Bonner didn't want to go to Phoenix to be around all that DEA hoopla. Mr. Bonner wanted to focus on the Garcia brothers' investigation.

GS Juan Antonio refused to let me meet Mr. Bonner in Yuma. When I arrived at the DEA office in Phoenix, there were two other guys wearing suits in the elevator with me. I didn't know who the two men were or why they were going to the same floor. They looked at me, I looked at them, and I knew there was going to be a problem. I had the feeling the CIA knew I was focusing on a Chinese Seafood Company in Chinatown and the connection with the Garcia brothers. Once off the elevator, I asked the secretary who the two guys were.

"CIA from Los Angeles," she said.

Why is the CIA meeting with my big bosses in Phoenix? Maybe they're friends of Mr. Bonner? Or were they here for something else?

352

DEA Phoenix management had control of the meeting. The two guys from the elevator were sitting in the meeting when I walked into the meeting. So, when Mr. Bonner and I finally met, we weren't able to talk about the brothers' case. Instead, we made small talk. Later, Mr. Bonner went outside the office to smoke in the parking lot. I followed him.

I was standing in the parking lot with Mr. Bonner. He and I were disappointed because we didn't have a chance to talk about the investigation. The only thing he said to me was, "We will talk later."

"Yes, sir!"

A lot of people from other law enforcement agencies were involved here. It wasn't just about the Garcia brothers. It was also about the Chinese. I was thinking about the two CIA agents I met at DEA Phoenix. It was becoming very personal to me why the CIA was involved in the case.

I gave Mr. Bonner my respect because he was my former DEA administrator, even though he was now a private attorney. I met Mr. Bonner again with PI Harry Fresno at the United States Attorney's office in Phoenix.

353

I was working on other cases at the same time and could have let this one end. But, how could I after the relationships I'd built with the PIs, CIs, and SOIs? How about Don and Roy almost losing their lives because of the Garcia brothers? The PIs, CIs, and SOIs were giving me all kinds of information and intel to support my case to arrest the brothers.

United States Attorney's Office in Phoenix

Mr. Bonner came to Phoenix to try to convince U.S. Attorney Janet Napolitano and her staff of AUSAs that I had a good case against the Garcia brothers and corruption at the POE. Mr. Bonner seriously wanted Napolitano's AUSAs to prosecute the brothers. Ms. Napolitano was not present at the meeting. She let her AUSAs run the meeting with Mr. Bonner, PI Harry Fresno, and me.

The way they sat at the large dark brown wooden table and treated PI Fresno and Mr. Bonner was terrible. The AUSAs were so rude, telling Mr. Bonner, PI Fresno, and me there was not enough evidence to present the case to a Federal Grand Jury to indict the brothers or the corruption at the POE.

354

I was distraught because Mr. Bonner was my former Administrator, and the PI was a former Sheriff Lieutenant. They both came from good backgrounds in law enforcement and deserved some respect from the AUSAs.

Mr. Bonner, PI Fresno, and I knew from DEA Chief Legal Counsel; the case was ready to be presented to a federal grand jury. Don and Roy deserved to have a grand jury review the evidence I had gathered against the brothers and the corrupt cops at the POE.

I eventually got to know Mr. Bonner and PI Harry Fresno throughout the Garcia case. They are both great men in their own profession.

Strange, I had enough evidence on the Garcia brothers for DEA Chief Legal Counsel. The case was ready for the AUSA in Phoenix to indict. Also, the Yuma County attorneys were prepared to indict the brothers if the AUSA in Phoenix declined to prosecute federal violations.

Snorted Cocaine and Sex with Young Girls

Meeting the AUSA

AUSA Robin Fly in Phoenix wanted to meet with Santo and Angelito. I told the CIs to dress in suits and not look like they were criminals working for DEA. I said to Santo, "I want you and Angelito to smell nice and look professional because you are going to go in front of the Federal Grand Jury and will be testifying at the hearing."

I arranged the meeting; Santo, Angelito, and I met with AUSA Fly at his office in Phoenix. The CIs looked and smelled good. Santo was a very classy individual and always looked good. On that day, Santo wore a dark blue suit with a red tie. He owned his own shrimp business in Mexico and did very well speaking to a higher authority. Angelito did not wear a suit, but he was dressed in black pants, wore a red polo shirt, and worn-out brown boots.

Santo and Angelito told AUSA Robin Fly details about the brothers' dope business and the corruption at San Luis POE. The AUSA started backing off when he heard how the CIs learned so much about the brothers trafficking organization, the corrupt officials at the POE.

356

He said to me, "Larry, you don't have enough to prosecute Jaime and Javier for conspiracy to transport narcotics into the U.S. nor their statements of trying to kill Don and Roy in 1975. Joselito is a possibility for a federal indictment."

"How about Javier and his relationship with Chinese Seafood Company?" Santo asked AUSA Fly.

AUSA Fly looked as if he hadn't heard the name of the Chinese Seafood Company. He then asked Santo and Angelito, "How were you so successful in penetrating the Garcia brothers' family?"

During the meeting, I found out Santo and Angelito were snorting cocaine with el Pulpo and the brothers. I had no idea they were doing drugs in Mexico, and I especially didn't like them having sex with the young girls. Santo told me the girls were over 18 years old, and they were the brothers' employees. AUSA Fly asked Santo, "How did you know for sure if the girls were 18 years old? Did you ask the girls their age?"

Santo said, "No."

The brothers were having sex with young girls. Santo and Angelito were definitely part of the brothers' group. Their lives

357

depended on how they socialized with the brothers. AUSA Fly was freaking out that Santo and Angelito were snorting drugs in Mexico and having sex with young girls.

Santo remarked, "We had to snort cocaine and have sex with the young girls whenever we met with the brothers. The brothers know DEA agents and law enforcement officers can't do drugs nor have sex with young girls. Only bad law enforcement agents."

I immediately told AUSA Fly, "I never instructed Santo and Angelito to use cocaine, only to stay alive."

Then I said to him, "Damn it, it takes a crook to do a crook."

He said, "I can't do this. I can't prosecute the case."

He didn't want to indict the Garcia brothers, but only charge Marco Oscuro, the mule for the brothers, for the one kilo of cocaine sold to an undercover DEA agent in Phoenix.

I was thinking to myself, He, now, only wants to indict the mule, Marco Oscuro, not Joselito or the other brothers. He can't do that! The CIs bought a sample kilo of cocaine, and Jaime set it up with Santo and Angelito to buy 30 kilos and later, another 500 kilos.

358

I yelled, "This is bullshit!"

Santo looked directly at him and told him angrily, "Why did I go to prison for five years for helping a DEA undercover agent buy an ounce of cocaine? I was charged with conspiracy and never saw the cocaine. I called my friend who sells cocaine and told him that a guy wanted to purchase some stuff from him. He's ready to deal! Look at all Angelito, and I did for this case! "

I quickly thought; That wasn't smart for Santo to talk to the AUSA like that.

I looked at AUSA Fly and said, "You son-of-a-bitch! You can't do this! You've got the Garcia brothers all over this corruption at the POE. The brothers already spoke with Santo and Angelito about how they were involved in the attempted killing of the DEA agents, Don and Roy. It's on the tape recordings. I have evidence."

"This is a conspiracy! At least let me arrest the brothers and put them in jail for a few days. You can get the brothers indicted with the Grand Jury."

I said, "Let me bring the three brothers in and start squeezing them about the corrupt cops. I can even separate the brothers, find out who is going to talk first about their dope business and who the corrupt officials are working at San Luis POE.

His response was, "I can't prosecute this case."

I looked at Santo and Angelito and told them, "Let's get the hell out of here! This son-of-bitch is not going to prosecute Joselito, Jaime, or Javier."

I was thinking with anger; He is trying to find a way to sabotage the case.

I told Santo, "You should never have mentioned the Chinese Seafood Company to him."

Santo looked at me strangely when we walked out of the office. I told him, "I'm going to lose my job with DEA because I called the AUSA a, 'SOB (Son of a Bitch).' You can't talk like that to an AUSA. They have so much political clout and so much power to shut down this investigation from ever getting the brothers indicted for their drug activities and trying to kill Don and Roy."

The CIs were distraught because they thought AUSA Fly was looking for an easy excuse to get out of indicting Jaime, Joselito, and Javier.

360

The CIs had put their butts out there. I was thinking about how Santo and Angelito were following my instructions to target the Garcia brothers in trafficking drugs into the U.S.

The brothers never knew the CIs were working for me. But then you have an AUSA who tells you he doesn't have enough to prosecute! It just isn't right! I understand why Santo and Angelito don't trust some of the officers at San Luis POE anymore nor AUSA Fly, after meeting with him.

Remember, it takes a criminal to do a criminal.

DEA Can't Touch me

The case needed to come to an end before the CIs got hurt by the brothers or corrupt cops. There were too many leaks with the few people I was working within the law enforcement community. I had tight control of the case, but I never could figure out how exactly the Garcia brothers knew what I was doing at the POE.

Santo and Angelito continued to meet with the brothers several times in Mexico, but Javier became less friendly with them. I kept wondering who was behind this leak.

361

I could never put my finger on the agent or cop who was leaking my information to other corrupt agents at San Luis POE.

When my CIs were with Jaime and Joselito snorting cocaine, they listened to the brothers brag about their connections at the POE. The CIs reported to me that the brothers talked about the CIA knowing about the same drug smuggling routes from Mexico into the U.S. as the Garcia organization.

Jaime made the statement, "I don't care what DEA does. They can never be able to touch my brothers or me. I'm connected to the United States Government."

Ana Blanca, Javier's mule and sex partner, later told Santo that Jaime thinks they are DEA agents!

Santo told me, "Blanca once said Javier is seriously addicted to drugs."

The CIs were getting worried the brothers might learn that they worked for DEA. Santo wanted to stop meeting with the brothers and any of their traffickers because of the corrupt Customs and Immigration officers at San Luis POE.

According to my SOIs, the Garcia brothers were the cartel's *gatekeepers* at San Luis POE for narcotics entering the U.S. They were also informants and assets for the Mexican government, in the same way as the Chinese Seafood Company in Chinatown.

I thought, That's why I was running into all these problems getting prosecutions against the brothers.

After delving into the case further, the AUSA's office in Phoenix sent me a letter. AUSA Robin Fly was very appreciative of the hard work I was doing on the case. He wrote, "Your dedication to the case is outstanding, and hopefully, your efforts will begin to bring dividends."

The letter is political bullshit written for AUSA Fly's boss, U.S. Attorney Janet Napolitano.

He continued to encourage me to close the case. He wanted to bring this case quickly to an end. I was feeling uneasy because the United States Attorney's office, Janet Napolitano, and I were not on the same page to indict the brothers.

AUSA Fly did not know I was working with DEA Chief Legal counsel in Washington, D.C. After the first year of the Garcia brothers' investigation, with the help of my CIs, PIs, and SOIs, I was sending fantastic information back to DEA Chief Legal counsel in Washington D.C. about the brothers' involvement in the attempted murder of DEA agents Don Ware and Roy Stevenson.

You've got Another new AUSA

After another meeting with AUSA Fly, the Garcia brothers' case started coming to a close because once again, the Chinese Seafood Company was involved with the brothers. The CIs also didn't want anything further to do with the case because of him. He didn't have the *guts* to prosecute the brothers because of the corruption at the POE and the Chinese connection.

Santo and Angelito were still around helping me, but they didn't want to go back to Mexico and meet the brothers again.

I got a call from DEA Phoenix, "You've got a new AUSA."

The new AUSA was Nay Whitehouse, a real young guy, very naïve, and very liberal when it comes to prosecuting narcotics. AUSA Whitehouse thought the federal drug charges were too harsh on traffickers, especially the poor mules. He was the third AUSA assigned to the Garcia brothers' case.

AUSA Fly went back to prosecuting low-level cases but never worked again on the investigation. He didn't want anything to do with it because of the corruption.

Like the other AUSAs, I invited AUSA Whitehouse down to Yuma and across the border into Mexico to see the Garcia brothers' homes. Then, of course, he also got excited about the case.

I wanted him to have a clear visual picture of what I was talking about, the miniature white houses with marble pillars imported from Italy. I explained to him that the larger home is Jaime's, a produce farmer, and yet, he wasn't moving much produce. The other house was owned by Javier, who was providing shrimp to the Chinese Seafood Company in Los Angles, California and Phoenix, Arizona.

As it turned out, AUSA Whitehouse didn't understand why charges were so severe for cocaine trafficking against the brothers and their traffickers. I explained to him that federal drug laws were that way; the States played it their own way in prosecuting drug cases. In Miami, a kilo of cocaine would get a lesser charge for prison time than in Kentucky.

California is off the market. The liberal views by the public toward narcotics distribution meant that most of California state attorneys and federal attorneys were no longer enforcing sentencing guidelines to prosecute drug traffickers. Also, there was so much cocaine being sold and moved throughout California. The jury selection in California was also a major problem for attorneys. The attorneys were dealing with the majority of the citizens that were very liberal and not able to find a poor mule guilty of drug trafficking violations.

I started to see that the new AUSA didn't want anything to do with the Garcia brothers. He just wanted the mule, Marco Oscuro, for selling the one kilo of cocaine, not the brothers. I didn't want to let the brothers get off that easy.

There was plenty of evidence to indict the Garcia brothers.

Who's Protecting the Chinese Seafood Company

Later, DEA Agent Luis Short called me and said he was coming out to Yuma with an agent from DEA headquarters in Washington, D.C. The agent from D.C. was assigned to work with

Asian drug trafficking groups and was working with Agent Short on intelligence in the Chinatown area of Los Angeles.

DEA Agent Luis Short wanted to discuss the Chinese Seafood Company and the Garcia brothers. I was surprised to hear the agents from LA, Washington D.C., and an agent from the U.S. Consulate office in Hermosillo, Mexico, were coming to Yuma because of the Asians and Mexicans working together to move shrimp and drugs into the U.S.

At the meeting in Yuma, I presented the case to DEA Agent Short, an agent from D.C., an agent from Hermosillo, Mexico, and AUSA Whitehouse.

I showed the agents from DEA in LA, Washington, D.C., and Hermosillo direct evidence tying in with the Chinese Seafood Company meetings with the Garcia brothers in El Golfo, Mexico, and later in Chinatown. They all said the brothers were prosecutable, except AUSA Whitehouse. He didn't say anything.

I sensed the DEA agent from D.C. working with Agent Short was there to protect the Chinese Seafood Company and to get the brothers away from the Asian organization. I couldn't understand why the agent from Hermosillo was at the meeting. I

367

could tell AUSA Whitehouse just came down for one reason; to see what I was going to share about the brothers' criminal activities at the meeting with the other DEA agents, but not to do anything about it.

I couldn't understand what AUSA Whitehouse really wanted from the case. If I could get the brothers, then I was going to find out who were the corrupt cops and those in the Asian organization and what the brothers and Asians were all about.

Agent Luis Short knew a lot about the Chinese Seafood Company activities in Chinatown but wasn't going to tell me anything. He was strictly an intelligence guy. That was my last meeting with him, the agent from D.C. and the agent from Hermosillo, Mexico.

PIs Jeff Pearce and Randy Torgerson couldn't sit in the meeting, but they were around outside, waiting for all of us and especially AUSA Whitehouse to come out the front door.

I want to do this for Don and Roy

I gathered all the evidence, notes, and a copy of the Garcia brothers' investigation letter from DEA Washington, DC, and the

368

review from the Department of Justice/DEA Chief Legal counsel. The Chief Legal counsel had reviewed the case, laying out the federal charges and the indictment against each of the brothers.

The brothers' tape-recording bragging to the SOIs and CIs about trying to kill the agents, Don and Roy. The CIs (Santo and Angelito) recorded the brothers boasting. But AUSAs Fly and Whitehouse didn't care.

Later, I told the Chief Legal counsel, "You have the same evidence against the brothers I gave the AUSAs in Phoenix."

DEA Chief Legal counsel knew, without a doubt, that I had what I needed to prove the case because I had some great information from the PIs, CIs, and SOIs. The case was already prepared! It was ready for the Federal Grand Jury, based on the evidence and information provided.

The Chief Legal Counsel in Washington, D.C. said to me, "Larry, the case is already done – whoever gets it at the US Attorney's office in Phoenix, they don't need to do anything! It's ready to go! It's all written out, and you've got the evidence to back it up."

369

He added, "You need to indict these brothers with all this evidence."

I responded, "I want to do this for all of us, especially Don and Roy."

Later, Chief Legal counsel sent me a letter stating, "This is the best case ever on the Garcia brothers. Keep up the good work. You have enough to prosecute the brothers and go after the corruption at the POE."

This was unbelievable; I had enough to prosecute the brothers for the attempted murders and their drug activities in the U.S.

My new Yuma DEA GS Peter Cotton saw DEA Chief Legal counsel's letter and stated, "You have the brothers indicted."

With all this information, I felt I had the proof for the second AUSA Fly and later, the third AUSA Whitehouse, to present the case to the Federal Grand Jury in Arizona. I had the brothers on audio recordings and drug evidence purchased with the help of Santo and Angelito.

When the SOIs and PIs came on board, I had several sources targeting the brothers. I had a close relationship with Santo and Angelito, especially Santo. I was already well into the case when PI Fresno and his PIs, Jeff Pearce and Randy Torgerson, were giving me so much information that kept me going deeper into the brothers' drug activities and the corrupt officials at the POE.

I got emotionally involved in it. I was told directly by the AUSAs in Phoenix to stop the investigation and indict only the mule for the kilo of cocaine, but it was too late. I knew there was corruption in Yuma and at the POE. But I just didn't know how much. I had lost all trust in AUSA Fly and now with AUSA Whitehouse.

I kept pushing to indict the brothers, even though I was being told by GS Cotton and the AUSAs office not to continue the case. But, how does the AUSA office or my GS say to me to back off the brothers? How do you do that without explaining the reason?

GS Cotton may not have known the truth; he was just told from his higher-ups in DEA management at the Phoenix office that I had to back off this case to indict the brothers because of someone at AUSAs office said so. At some point, they couldn't really tell me to back off on the case without having to explain national security

371

issues. So, GS Cotton just tried to divert my attention by transferring me from Yuma to Phoenix.

The next thing I knew, I was still the case agent, but the Garcia brothers' case was coming to an end. It was a slow *death*.

The end of the case occurred one day at AUSA Whitehouse's office during a meeting. I was upset about not getting help in Phoenix from the AUSAs office to prosecute the brothers. One of the attorneys at the meeting that I'd never met before took the case file and said, "The AUSA office can't do anything else," and slid the case file over to AUSA Whitehouse.

There were some people at their office doing things covertly and overtly. I was deeply upset and thinking, *Does this mean they can't do anything?*

At this point, I was instructed by AUSA Nay Whitehouse, in a roundabout way, to put the case to rest. Now I understand why AUSA Fly was removed for unknown reasons to no longer work the case. The AUSAs office in Phoenix had everything I provided them on the brothers. I knew in my heart that I had the Garcia brothers. Especially when an attorney from the Department of

Justice, DEA Chief Legal counsel in Washington D.C., told me, "You've got the brothers!"

The Chief Legal counsel sent everything back to me, showing all the charges and who should be indicted in the Garcia organization.

Later, AUSA Whitehouse asked me to meet him again at his office in Phoenix. He told me at his office, "We can indict Marco Oscuro, Jaime's right-hand man, for the sale of the kilo of cocaine to the DEA undercover agent, but nothing else."

I sensed something was wrong when I was at the office, and he didn't want to prosecute the brothers.

I was thinking; Who is "we" at the AUSA office? Someone is pressuring him to indict the trafficker, Marco Oscuro, but not the brothers.

I jumped up from the chair and told him, "I'm going to take the case to the Yuma County prosecutor's office. The County Attorney wants to process it, indict these Garcia brothers, and expose the corruption at the border!"

He yelled, "Larry, you can't take this case to Yuma County, it's a federal investigation, not at state investigation."

373

I yelled back at him, "Not anymore."

I told him, "You're wrong, buddy. I'm going to take it to Yuma county attorney's office because they're going to do it. They are going to indict the brothers and everybody on that list."

He told me, "It won't happen!"

Then I yelled back as I was leaving the office, "The damn brothers tried to kill two DEA agents, Don and Roy. That's a no-no. You don't get to do that! Those agents are part of my family."

This was a big letdown! The meeting ended without agreeing to indict the Garcia brothers.

As I was walking out to my car, I thought to myself, Why does he only want a mule when everything's documented, and it becomes discovery? DEA Chief Legal counsel laid out all the evidence and facts on the brothers to be indicted for attempted murder and drug trafficking.

Nothing's going to happen with this case! I'm not going anywhere with the brothers. I'll never get them because the Phoenix AUSAs office said I don't have enough evidence right now. Is the CIA involved in this investigation?

But I had a strong belief that I was going to get the brothers for attempting to kill Don and Roy. Maybe, the Yuma County Attorney's office will help me. I already bought a sample kilo of cocaine and negotiated for 30 kilos more from Jaime and Joselito. Later 500 kilos from the brothers. And the third new ASUA in Phoenix would only indict one mule, Marco Oscuro, the brothers' right-hand man. Oscuro was a close associate of the brothers and was always at the meetings with Javier, Joselito, and Jaime when Santo and Angelito were there.

AUSA Whitehouse didn't want to hear about the DEA Chief Legal counsel decision on the case. I walked out of the office and returned to my DEA Office in Yuma.

The Black Plague

Usually, there were only two agents in the DEA office at one time. I never did have a partner. Sometimes, I worked with other agents in the office on their drug investigations. The agents were all were good people to work with, and I didn't believe there could be a leak. But I had to be careful working on the case with Santo and Angelito.

375

I found out later from the PIs Jeff Pearce and Randy Torgerson that one of the agents from my office was the leak, indirectly. I couldn't believe what the PIs were saying that an agent in the office was leaking information about the brothers. They didn't believe the agent was intentionally sabotaging the case. They did discover the agent was telling some Customs officials outside the DEA office what I was doing and what was happening in the investigation.

I sometimes felt someone from the AUSA office in Phoenix and the corrupt officers at San Luis POE were always behind the scene watching me as I focused on the brothers' drug activities. I'm surprised I didn't get killed by a corrupt cop, but if I did, DEA would go crazy; my family would go crazy to find the killer or killers. I'm amazed the PIs, Santo or Angelito, or SOIs weren't killed, either.

When the Garcia brothers' produce trucks were waiting to cross into the U.S., I asked for help from a very few selected agents from Border Patrol and U.S. Customs with their drug dogs to assist in the searches.

Later, it was almost like I had the black plague. No one wanted to work with me because of the Garcia brothers – no one except my CIs, SOIs, and the PIs.

Focus on the Facts before the Conspiracy

I'm the kind of guy who can put facts, evidence, and intelligence together for federal and state prosecution. You give me the bits and pieces of evidence, and I'll pull it together so the AUSAs office in Phoenix can prosecute the brothers.

When the drug trafficking ties into something as big as the Chinese Seafood Company and the Garcia brothers, I want to focus on the facts and not the conspiracy to develop the drug trafficking connection. You might not get the guy who is making the hand-to-hand drug deal, but you've got to get the guy setting up the dope delivery.

I wanted to tell the PIs, CIs, and SOIs so much about the Garcia brothers' investigation, but I couldn't because they weren't agents, they were private citizens.

I commented to my wife, "I'm telling you; I feel very comfortable with the PIs, CIs, and SOIs providing me information

377

because they have my back, and I have theirs. I'm constantly fighting battles, not only in my DEA office, but also with the AUSAs office in Phoenix, and other agents in Yuma. When I get close to arresting and prosecuting the brothers, I know the PIs, CIs, and SOIs will be great witnesses!"

The PIs, CIs, and SOIs couldn't believe I was only one DEA agent working this case. I was *burning out* because of so many long hours working other criminal investigations and fighting the AUSAs office in Phoenix and my GS about the case.

It was getting to the end of the case, and enough was enough. PI Harry Fresno encouraged me, "Stay focused, man. You're doing this for the American public and the common good. You have to stop the corruption at the border."

Dealing with Corrupt Cops in Yuma County

There were several times when Lieutenant (Lt) Danny Elkins of the Arizona Southwest Border NTF would travel to San Luis POE Arizona and Mexican border with me. He and I worked well together on other drug cases. We had the same goal to put the Garcia brothers in prison.

Lt Elkins wanted to put the brothers in jail as much as I did. He couldn't believe the Asians were involved with the brothers. He also knew I was dealing with corrupt cops at the POE and in the Yuma county communities.

Don't Trust the Mexican Cops

I told the PIs, CIs, and SOIs, "It's not safe for any of you to go down to Mexico. If the Garcia brothers thought, you were DEA – it's hard to say where you'd be now."

DEA Agent Kiki Camarena trusted the local Mexican cops, and that trust cost him his life. It was corruption, plain and simple. Corrupt law enforcement cops found him and helped torture him to death. His Mexican cop buddies were the ones who knew he'd been tortured.

The Wife of a DEA Agent

I enjoyed working with the PIs, CIs, and SOIs because I felt comfortable that they were not corrupt. I really did. I never felt that way with some of the agents and cops in the community. Some agents and cops didn't like the PIs, my CIs, or my SOIs.

379

One night when PI Jeff Pearce was at a party in Yuma, he met a drunk woman bragging about her husband being a DEA agent in Yuma. PI Pearce was trying to talk her into having sex but decided to call me first before he laid her down on the bed. He said the woman's name and the name of her husband. He asked me, "Is this gal the wife of a DEA agent?"

"Yes, leave her alone. You don't want to get involved with her! You don't want to *dance with the devil* tonight."

I said, "PI Pearce, the grace of God has got you here for a reason to help me put the brothers in jail. Don't let the devil play with your mind. The devil plays with your soul. Leave the agent's wife alone."

The County Attorney's Office will Indict

I met with Lt Danny Elkins to see if he would help me prosecute the Garcia brothers in Yuma County.

He was so excited to have a case against the brothers. He couldn't understand why the AUSAs office in Phoenix didn't want to prosecute the brothers, but only indict the mule. He told me, "I want you to talk to the County Prosecutor here in Yuma. She's in charge of the narcotics unit. I've already called the County Prosecutor about your case. She's as excited as I am that the Garcia brothers are going be charged for their crimes, and maybe stop the corruption at the border."

I told him that I sent everything I had on the case to Washington, D.C. Department of Justice (DoJ) DEA Chief Legal counsel and that I received a response from him stating, "We've reviewed the case. Great job. You have the evidence. Just get it prosecuted!"

I told Lt Elkins, "I'm excited to get this done and plan to meet with you later. I want to show you the letter from Washington D.C. and to the Yuma County Attorney's NTF office."

The next day, the Lt and I met with the Yuma County Attorney. The County Attorney knew about the Garcia brothers and their criminal activities. She was well aware of how dangerous it was working so close to the border and the corruption. I presented her with the case review from DEA Chief Legal counsel. She was speechless when she read that Chief Legal counsel recommended the case should be submitted to the Phoenix Federal Grand Jury.

After our long meeting, the County Attorney was excited to assign the case to one of her young, new Yuma County Attorney assistants to present to a State Grand Jury. I told her, "I'm ready now to meet in front of the Grand Jury."

The young County Attorney's assistant was from the East Coast. He was a clean-cut guy and was freaking out because he really wanted this kind of case. This would be a big feather in his cap. Based on the evidence, the County Attorney's office was sure the Grand Jury would indict the brothers on State charges for attempted murder and their drug activities.

I continued to meet with Lt Danny Elkins and talked about our work together on the Garcia brothers' case.

Wow, the Officer is one of the Corrupt Cops

Soon after, GS Peter Cotton told me, "Larry, you need to talk to San Luis Police Officer Pedro Vaca about the Garcia brothers' case. He has been assigned to help with your investigation. You have got to bring him on board because he's going to be working the border in San Luis."

When I met Officer Vaca, I explained the Garcia brothers' investigation, but I did not mention my CIs. I thought to myself; *I don't know this Officer Vaca. Is he corrupt? Why is my new GS pushing me to work with him?*

That night, when I was driving back to the Yuma office after meeting with AUSA Whitehouse in Phoenix, I realized it was to be the last meeting I would have with Janet Napolitano's attorneys.

I decided I would continue to meet the Yuma County Attorney and the new attorney assistant the following day. I was ready to tell the County Attorney's office, "The case is finally yours."

As I was driving towards Yuma, I got a message from GS Cotton that he wanted to talk to me right away in his office. Once I arrived in Yuma, I went straight into the DEA parking lot. When I walked into the building, GS Cotton called me into his office. There he was sitting, behind his big oak desk, with the Yuma County Attorney and the new assistant prosecutor sitting in front of him. I was wondering; *What's going on? Aren't we supposed to meet in the morning?*

383

GS Cotton said, "Larry, you need to sit down."

I wondered; Is this about the meeting with AUSA Whitehouse in Phoenix?

"No, I'm going to stand up," I told GS Cotton.

I had just been driving for three-and-a-half-hours from Phoenix.

GS Cotton said to me, "San Luis Police Officer Vaca went to Yuma County Attorney's office."

The County Attorney said, "Yeah, Officer Vaca came to our office today and said there would be threats against us because we are targeting the Garcia brothers and their family members."

I told them, "You know, I have been working the case for several years, and now I've found one of the corrupt cops. Let's think about what just happened today."

I looked at GS Cotton and said, "Officer Vaca went to the Yuma Attorney's office, behind my back, behind everyone's back in this office, and told the County Attorney, if you take this brothers case, there's a chance you and your new assistant attorney will get killed."

I was angrily thinking; I can see it in their faces. Officer Vaca scared the hell out of them!

Then, I said out loud, "The reason Officer Vaca scared you was that he knows the Garcia brothers. Damn it! Officer Vaca must be one of the corrupt cops working for the brothers."

I then turned my attention to the County Attorneys and said, "He is either corrupt or crazy."

GS Cotton said, "I will contact the FBI tomorrow and report Officer Vaca's threat."

"It is too damn late. Officer Vaca did his job threatening the attorneys. The case is done."

The new Yuma County Attorney assistant nervously said, "Larry, I have a wife and a newborn baby."

According to the PIs and SOIs, it was suspected that Officer Vaca was a corrupt cop. Now I could prove it, but I had to be cautious when I met Officer Vaca again. That night, I warned the DEA agents in my office to stay away from Officer Vaca, "You don't want to meet or talk with Officer Vaca, he's corrupted."

The next morning GS Cotton immediately removed Officer Vaca from our office. He was not surprised about leaving. He didn't

385

ask GS Cotton why he was removed from the case, and he could no longer enter the DEA building. The County Attorney's office didn't move forward to indict the brothers. The case went downhill from there.

Within a week, two FBI agents from Phoenix interviewed Officer Vaca for corruption and threatening the County Attorneys. After meeting with him, the FBI agents reported to GS Cotton. They wanted to meet with my GS alone, and I was not invited.

I told GS Cotton, "I need to be involved in meeting with the FBI agents because I am the case agent, no one else. I want to know why Officer Vaca waited so long to make those threats. Who encouraged Officer Vaca to go to the Yuma County Attorney's office; was it the brothers, someone at FBI, CIA, or the AUSAs?"

Why wasn't the County Attorney or I invited into the FBI meeting, only GS Cotton?

After the meeting ended, GS Cotton said to me, "You know what, FBI agents can't do anything with Officer Vaca. The FBI agents told me that he is kind of mentally deranged and mentally sick."

When I heard that, I said, "Yes, but corrupt, too. You wanted him to work with me on the case. What the FBI said to you about Officer Vaca is bullshit, and you know it."

The way the FBI agents handled Officer Vaca's threat against the County Attorneys worried GS Cotton. GS Cotton started to realize that something might be stopping me from indicting the Garcia brothers. *Perhaps GS Cotton was really worried about his safety?*

GS Cotton knew that the two FBI agents from Phoenix, who talked with Officer Vaca, ended my investigation against the brothers. A thought came to me; *Did the AUSAs office in Phoenix say something to FBI to make it go away to protect the brothers?*

PI Randy Torgerson later said, "I believe it's not Officer Vaca that threatened the Yuma County Attorney office. I think it was FBI that put Officer Vaca up to threatening the County Attorneys."

I was wondering; Why did the police officer threaten the attorneys for working the Garcia brothers' case? And my GS and the FBI aren't going to do anything about the corrupt cop? If Officer

387

Vaca is mentally deranged and mentally sick, then why is he still working on the streets and at the border."

Five-shot Revolver

I was with another DEA agent, sitting in our pick-up trucks out in the hot desert, waiting for a load of drugs to come across into an Arizona Indian reservation from San Luis POE. The Indian Tribal Police were nowhere around to help us. *I wonder why?*

GS Peter Cotton came out to meet with me in the desert in his grey Mercedes sedan to talk about ending the Garcia brothers' investigation. He wanted to tell me what I should and should not do with the case. He wanted me to close it and focus on other major traffickers, not related to the brothers.

I asked him, "How about Don and Roy? They almost died in Mexico because they happen to be DEA agents. The brothers wanted to kill Don and Roy. You know GS Cotton, I'm a senior agent. I was in the Yuma office as an acting GS before you arrived at the office. I knew what I was doing when I targeted the brothers."

I looked directly at him and said, "Do you know I always carry a backup gun in my ankle holster, a snub nose five-shot revolver little Sweet-Pea .38? A .38-revolver saved Don and Roy from being killed by the brothers. You know, boss, I can take my little Sweet-Pea from my ankle holster. I can stand here next to you and play with the .38, and you know what? I might just drop this damn thing, and a round could go off and hit you in the damn leg. Boss, it's damn hot out here on the Indian reservation in the desert, Do you know that?" *I was thinking; Maybe the Indian Tribal Police are behind this drug deal moving into their reservation.*

He quickly looked at me. With my Sweet-Pea in my right hand, I looked at GS Cotton and laughed. He smiled nervously and got in his Mercedes and drove off. He probably thought I was crazy. The other agent smiled and said, "You just scared the hell out of him."

I really wasn't going to shoot GS Cotton with my Sweet-Pea.

I questioned myself; Why can't GS Cotton let me do my job today? The young agent and I are waiting on a group of Indian traffickers moving drugs onto their reservation.

Narcotics Officers Lt Danny Elkins and

Sgt. Mike Crowe are Assassinated

On the morning of July 5, I decided to go for a three-mile run along the water canal next to the orange and lemon trees to enjoy the desert landscape. I ran there, regularly, to reduce stress from work and focus on how blessed I am to be alive.

About halfway into my run and meditating on prayers, a Deputy U.S. Marshal agent rode up to me on his bicycle and said, "Jack Hutchinson killed Danny Elkins and Mike Crowe last night at the NTF office."

The Arizona Southwest Border NTF has about 22 members who investigate drug activities in the Yuma area, where the borders of Arizona, California, and Mexico meet. The NTF group has Customs agents, Department of Public Service (DPS) officers, Border Patrol agents, Deputy Sheriffs, Yuma Police, Indian Tribal Police, and other local law enforcement agencies.

Lt Danny Elkins

Danny Elkins was a Yuma PD Lieutenant, and Mike Crowe was a Sergeant (Sgt) with the Department of Public Safety (DPS). Jack Hutchinson was a Yuma County Deputy Sheriff officer. Danny, Mike, and Jack were assigned to NTF.

On July 5, I went to the crime scene at the NTF building, but Yuma Police Homicide Unit wouldn't let me inside the public parking lot. I later talked with the NTF custodian of drugs and weapons evidence who was with Lt Elkins and Sgt. Crowe last night. The custodian told me some of what happened.

Sgt Michael Crowe

The drugs and weapons were stored in a secured evidence vault in their own NTF building. With Lt Elkins' approval, Officer Daniel Blackman installed a video camera in the evidence vault. Before he left on his fishing vacation with his son, he knew someone inside the NTF group was stealing drugs and weapons from the evidence locker.

391

He said, "Officer Blackman was reviewing the video when he observed Officer Jack Hutchinson entering the evidence vault. Officer Blackman identified Officer Hutchinson as he was going into the vault. Officer Blackman called me to say it was Hutchinson who was stealing the seized drugs and weapons from the evidence vault. He had installed a hidden video camera in the vault because he learned that someone working at NTF was stealing guns and drugs from the vault.

The custodian told me, "I told Officer Blackman to stay put at the other site. I wanted to call Lt Elkins. I also told him that Lt Elkins and I were coming over, and we're going to talk about this. We've got to do something about it now because everyone from NTF is out for the Fourth of July. Some are watching the fireworks at the Marine Corps Base."

Lt Danny Elkins had just come back from his fishing trip with his son. He met with Officer Blackman and the evidence custodian to review the video. He finally learned from the video that Officer Jack Hutchinson was the person involved with the missing drugs and weapons evidence.

After reviewing the video, Lt Elkins called DPS Sgt. Michael Crowe.

Lt Elkins and the custodian then drove over to the NTF back-parking lot behind the building.

At the back parking lot, Lt Elkins and the evidence custodian noticed Mike and Jack's cars were there. He and the custodian exited the car and entered the building without their guns.

The building was shaped like a box with windows only at the front entrance. This was how the building conserved energy from the summer desert heat. The building was very secure with razor wire fencing around the front and back parking lots. Several agents and cops worked in the building where they parked their cars and trucks in the secure back parking lot. From the NTF building's back entrance, you have to walk through a long narrow hallway before entering the agent's and cop's office spaces. There was no other way out of the building to the parking lots.

In the front, there was a public parking area with a trash dumpster. The public went in and out at the front parking lot.

393

Location NTF Officers Back
Parking lot

The agents and cops who worked there had weapons, but when it got hot, most of the cops and agents would leave their guns and shotguns in their cars and trucks in the back parking lot while they were in the building. That night, Lt Elkins and the custodian left their guns in the Lieutenant's car.

Once inside the NTF building, Lt Elkins noticed Sgt. Crowe was talking to Officer Jack Hutchinson. Hutchinson had a red bandanna wrapped around his head, wearing black pants, a black shirt, and was carrying bolt cutters.

Lt Elkins immediately saw Officer Hutchinson looked up at a hole in the ceiling. Lt Elkins was also sure Officer Hutchinson noticed the hidden camera at the evidence vault. He turned around and started to walk down the narrow hallway to the back parking lot. Sgt. Crowe approached Officer Hutchinson, who refused to stop and talk with them. Officer Hutchinson continued to walk outside to the back parking lot.

394

While he walked into the back parking lot, Lt Elkins and Sgt. Crowe thought he was leaving the NTF building and not coming back. They knew Hutchinson was seen on the video entering the drug and weapons evidence vault. Now, he was trying to do something to make it look like somebody else from NTF had been stealing the drugs and weapons from the evidence vault.

Suddenly, Officer Hutchinson entered the narrow hallway and started shooting his automatic handgun. He was a retired staff sergeant in the Marine Corps, and he knew how to finish a job. But his gun jammed for a moment, and then he continued shooting. Without their guns, Lt Elkins and Sgt. Crowe ran away from him and into the office room. Officer Hutchinson knew there was no way in or out of the cop's room. Lt Elkins and Sgt. Crowe were trapped. The custodian was still in the hallway and stood his ground as Hutchinson approached him.

The drugs and weapons custodian said that Hutchinson had the eyes of Manson: dead, nothing there. Officer Hutchinson pointed his weapon straight at the custodian. Click, click. He was out of ammunition. The custodian watched him go down the hallway and out into the back parking lot.

Lt Elkins and Sgt. Crowe ran out to the hallway to see if the custodian was okay. The custodian yelled, "Let's go out the front door."

As the custodian ran out to the front public parking lot, he heard more shooting inside the building. He said he jumped behind the trash dumpster in the public parking lot. Hiding behind the trash dumpster, he looked up and saw Sgt. Crowe coming around the building, running towards the dumpster. Behind Sgt. Crowe was Officer Hutchinson, shooting at him.

NTF Public Front Parking lot; Trash Dumpster far left

For some reason, Sgt. Crowe, then, tried to crawl under a car, a Jeep Cherokee that had been left there all night in the public parking lot. Officer Hutchinson grabbed Sgt. Crowe by his feet, pulled him out, away from the Jeep, and shot the Sgt. in the chest. As Hutchinson was killing Sgt. Crowe, Lt Elkins had come into the front reception area and got on the phone to call Yuma Police for help.

396

Officer Hutchinson walked away and then Sgt. Crowe scooted up behind him, sitting on his butt. The Sgt. wasn't dead. He was crying. Officer Hutchinson came over and shot him again. It's like going hunting; you never know if you've killed your animal until you put a bullet in his skull.

With Sgt. Crowe now lying on the ground, Officer Hutchinson went back inside to look for Lt Elkins and the custodian.

Later, an NTF officer said that Lt Elkins fought for his life. The videotape showed everything that happened. The partitions inside the office room were about four inches off the floor. Lt Elkins took his shoes off and put them next to the partitions.

He grabbed Officer Hutchinson when he came to look for him. They must have been fist-fighting because the Lt's watch was found on the floor. Bullet rounds were sprayed all over the partitions and the ceiling. Lt Elkins tried to get the gun out of Officer Hutchinson's hand because there was a lot of the Lt's blood on the floor and on Officer Hutchinson. Lt Elkins knew he had to move quickly to take the gun away from Officer Hutchinson.

With Officer Hutchinson's weapon on the floor, he took out a second gun, a 45-automatic, hidden behind his back, and came around as Lt Elkins was trying to pull himself up from the floor. Officer Hutchinson shot the bullet right in the Lt's spine. Lt Elkins went down to the floor, and Officer Hutchinson shot him again, almost blowing the Lt's head off.

Officer Hutchinson went outside to the back parking lot and saw Yuma Police. They had their guns pointed at Hutchinson and said, "Get your hands up!"

As Hutchinson was walking towards his car, he was on the phone talking to his wife, "I have to give up. If I don't, they're going to kill me!"

Sgt. Crowe made it to the hospital. He was fighting to stay alive and was anxious to see his pregnant wife. He died later during surgery.[38 39 40 41 42]

Officer Hutchinson never got the death penalty, but he got life in prison because he was under the influence of methamphetamines.

I thought, That was a horrible death! Sgt. Mike Crowe was my neighbor, and his wife was pregnant and ready to have a baby.

398

The last time I saw Mike, he was holding his wife's hand while walking past my house.

Lt Danny Elkins was married with a son and daughter. He was also in charge of the NTF. The last time I saw him alive, he told me at the DEA office he was going fishing with his son.

I believe Lt Elkins and Sgt. Crowe's deaths were a tragedy to all of us in the law enforcement community.

Danny Elkins was a trusted friend. Hopefully, his death was not connected to the Garcia brothers' case. I could never prove it.

Targeted Twice for Illegal Activities

I had targeted the Garcia brothers' operations and finally learned the brothers had become *untouchable* by the Department of Justice and other law enforcement agencies. I told the PIs, CIs, and SOIs, "Do you see what's going on here in Yuma?"

The abuse and corruption in our law enforcement are in the wrong hands of evil people working as cops and agents, like the brothers' niece, working at San Luis POE border as an Immigration officer.

I told the PIs, "The AUSAs office in Phoenix, local cops in Yuma, and the officers at the POE have targeted you twice for illegal activities."

Most AUSAs in America would die to have a case with a DEA agent, making a hand-to-hand buy from one of the mules who worked directly with the Garcia brothers. I had all the pieces of factual evidence for them. Santo had everything recorded on tape: the conspiracy and facts about the brothers trying to kill the two DEA agents, and the phone calls going back and forth from the brothers' homes.

The AUSAs office in Phoenix had all this factual evidence and details against the brothers, and the attorneys are not going to indict the brothers?

Santo told me again, "I went to prison for making a phone call to a guy to meet with a DEA agent. The agent wanted me to help him buy some cocaine."

I told Santo and Angelito, "My hands are tied. Everything I have is discovery, and it will be released through the judicial due process to indict the mule, Marco Oscuro. The brothers and the Chinese Seafood Company will see everything in the discovery that

400

happened in this investigation because Oscuro will have the right to see the evidence against him."

One morning when I went to go to the office, I had a flat  tire on my SUV. Someone had put a spike into one of the tires. I found animal guts in a plastic bag in my backyard. My

SUV rear window was broken

undercover SUV rear window was smashed.

I was angrily thinking; The corrupt cops won't leave the PIs and CIs alone. They were coming after all of us; myself, the PIs, SOIs, and CIs!

Yuma Police set up temporary surveillance on my home to see who was behind these incidents. *What a joke.*

GS Cotton told me, "It's time to go, Larry. Enough is enough! I want you out of the office! Get out of here, get out of Yuma, get out of Arizona. Get a transfer to somewhere. You are too close to identify the corrupt cops. Do something!"

GS Cotton wrote to the DEA Phoenix office that things were getting worse for me with the corruption in Yuma. He told DEA Phoenix there were a lot of corrupt cops and agents in the law

401

enforcement community and at San Luis POE involved with the Garcia brothers' smuggling organization.

According to my CIs, the brothers learned from the corrupt cops that I was determined to arrest them. Santo and Angelito suspected the brothers knew what I looked like from the photo of me at the plane crash site that the Mexican Commandanté took.

Everyone is running away from this case. I'm sure the FBI and CIA are all over this thing. Without a doubt!

Later, as this case was coming to an end, Mr. Bonner asked me, "Larry, where would you like to go?"

"I'd like to go to Madrid, Spain."

"Okay, let me see what I can do. You know Larry, I never knew what the DEA agents were dealing with. I was always isolated from the problems you agents had," said Mr. Bonner.

AUSAs Wanted This to go Away

U.S. Attorney Janet Napolitano and her aide came to see me at the Yuma Office right before I was leaving Yuma for the Spanish language school for six months in Arlington, Virginia. She looked

402

me in the eyes and asked, "How can I resolve this case before you leave for language school?"

I could see it in Ms. Napolitano's eyes. I could see the political bullshit, and I was thinking to myself; This, is incredible. I am leaving for six months. She wants to help now. The AUSAs office wanted this case to go away because they have spent a lot of money, and it takes a lot of effort to protect someone or an agency connected to the Garcia brothers. DEA had two agents, Don and Roy, who were almost killed by the brothers. The brothers even later bragged about it!

In the DEA Yuma conference room, I showed Ms. Napolitano and the aide photos of the two miniature white houses in Mexico and talked about the tunnel between the brothers' homes. The aide said, "Oh, I've been to this home."

I was shocked and said, "You're telling me you've been to Jaime's house? A person doesn't go in that house without seeing Jaime snorting cocaine."

He responded, "Yeah!"

I zoomed into the aide like Grandpa's old coon dog, getting ready to bite and wanted to know why he had been there inside

403

Jaime's home. He knew he had done something wrong because my attention was now focused on him. I asked the aide again, "Why did you go into Jaime's house?"

He said, "Well, it was part of the work I did with Senator Ed Pastor. I went there for some conference connected to agriculture produce production in Mexico."

When Ms. Napolitano saw this interaction between her aide and me, she walked away to the other side of the conference room and left her aide and me alone. Suddenly, the aide ended the conversation with me. Janet Napolitano didn't mention the case again. I knew the brothers' investigation was closed for good.

GS Cotton asked me again to stop working on the investigation and transfer to the Phoenix office or somewhere else. But I declined the transfer.

Napolitano's aide and the Arizona Senator met with Jaime inside his home in Mexico. That proves the brothers were right to tell Santo and Angelito DEA would never arrest them. How about Don and Roy?

Stay out of Trouble and Just Do Your Job

I later received a phone call from DEA Headquarters offering me three positions to transfer out of Yuma: Instructor for Domestic Training, Instructor for International Training, both at Quantico, Virginia and Bogota, Colombia.

DEA Phoenix management and GS Cotton encouraged me, "If you go to Bogota, Colombia for three years, you could get your supervisor position back when you return to the states. But you've got to keep your mouth shut because it's very political there at the American Embassy in Bogota. You might see things that are morally wrong but stay away from it. Go down there to the Embassy, stay out of trouble, and just do your job. Don't get involved with the politics."

I knew DEA offered me the three positions to get me out of Yuma. My DEA career would be finished if I stayed there. I also knew my chances for promotion were over in Yuma, and anywhere else I would go.

I was once Acting Resident Agent in charge of Yuma and became a temporary GS-14. After fighting with the US Attorney's Office, the AUSAs, and DEA management in Phoenix, I quickly

405

lost my status as supervisor. There would be no more promotions for me in Yuma. Three DEA junior agents with less time on the job, later received their GS-14 promotion, jumping past me to become supervisors.

I told my wife, "It's time for me to go. The Garcia brothers' case is over!"

This was so sad because when I looked back on it, I did a lot of work on the case. I feel like I didn't do Don and Roy justice. I felt disgraced because I didn't get the brothers indicted. I had no one else working with me on this case, except the PIs, CIs, and SOIs.

DEA Headquarters' office in Washington D.C. transferred me to Bogota, Colombia, to jump-start my new career. I decided this was the best thing to do and possibly have another chance to be promoted to GS and someday Special Agent In Charge (SAC). Before I left Yuma, GS Cotton told me if I work well in my new position in Bogota, I'd get my supervisor promotion.

I knew it would be difficult for me in Colombia because I couldn't keep my mouth shut when I see corruption or misleading information. That's who I am. When I see a cop or an agent doing

406

something wrong, I speak my mind and tell them, but not necessarily to the DEA supervisors and management.

While waiting to be transferred to Colombia, I went to the Spanish language school for six months of training in Arlington, Virginia. When I came back to Yuma, it was unfortunate to see where the Garcia brothers' case was and how it ended. The case had been quickly shut down by the Phoenix AUSAs office.

After I left Yuma for good, the secretary from my office said the agents only arrested one person, Marco Oscuro, for the one-kilo cocaine that was the sample buy for the 30 kilos from the brothers.

I still had a hard time believing what the PIs told me about an agent in my office who was corrupt and leaking to suspected corrupt cops about the case.

When the brothers' mule, Marco Oscuro, was arrested, all the evidence became discovery. It went into the hands of the brothers and everyone else in Mexico, Colombia, and the Asians, the whole drug world.

I later learned in Colombia, that he served only less than a year in federal prison. For one kilo and negotiations for 30 kilos of

407

cocaine and then another 500 kilos. Oscuro was the right-hand man of the drug smuggling organization and got off with very little consequence.

It was hard for me to understand why the AUSAs office gave Marco Oscuro less than one year in prison for selling one-kilo sample to a DEA undercover agent and the negotiations for several more kilos with the CIs.

Where is the justice for Roy and Don?

"Let your eyes look directly ahead and let your gaze be fixed straight in front of you. Watch the path of your feet and all your ways will be established. Do not turn to the right nor to the left; Turn your foot from evil" (Proverbs 4:25-27 New American Standard Version).

Returning to San Fernando, Spain

Shorty, before leaving for Bogota, Kathy and I went back to our second home in San Fernando, Spain, to spend time with her family and friends.

Paco, a National Police Officer and close friend of the family, told Kathy that his friend was at the Spanish Embassy in

Bogota, working narcotics cases. His name was Jose Maria. Paco

wanted me to contact Jose Maria and take him out for a beer. He

was also a National Police Officer working in narcotics cases alone.

Paco said Jose Maria needed DEA's help.

As a DEA Agent in Bogota, Colombia

Learning How to Fight my Greatest Enemy: Myself

When I arrived in Bogota, Colombia, I immediately observed corruption and lying among some of the DEA agents and supervisors at the American Embassy. Some of the other agents and I struggled to stay away from it.

I didn't say anything about what I saw at the office, even though there were numerous investigations of false reports of DEA success fighting the war on drugs. I took the advice of my previous bosses in Phoenix and Yuma, who said, "Hardin, if you want to get promoted, keep your fucking mouth shut."

I took the advice of my GS in Yuma. At the Embassy, some of the Colombian women were beautiful, sweet, aggressive, and eager to have sex with Americans, especially anyone working at the American Embassy. Many married DEA agents fell into the trap of open sex, and some divorced their wives to marry younger Colombian women. Kathy worked at the American Embassy as a State Counselor officer and kept a close watch over me. Thank God, Kathy was my angel who protected me from the evil one.

411

The devil really worked on me with a lot of temptation in Colombia. It was Sodom and Gomorrah. I was learning how to fight my greatest enemy: Myself.

Later, after arriving in Colombia, I got a phone call from the Chief Legal counsel attorney's office at DEA headquarters in D.C. He wondered how things went with the Garcia brothers' case in Yuma.

I told him, "It's not going to happen, and I'm still not sure why the brothers will never be indicted for trying to kill two DEA agents. If you can do something to get the brothers prosecuted, that would be great."

He asked me, "What happened? We did the work for you at the Chief Legal counsel office. All you had to do was take the indictment packet to any AUSA in Phoenix, or the Yuma County attorney office."

I never heard from DEA Chief Legal counsel again.

I am a Consular Officer at the American Embassy and a U.S. Naval Officer. I am from Spain

Once in Bogota, Kathy and I went to the Spanish Embassy to meet with the Spanish diplomatic staff. Kathy's first contact at the Spanish Embassy was with Guardia Civil Julio Gomez. She told Guardia Civil Gomez that her father was a Guardia Civil and served in Franco's military during the Spanish Civil War. Kathy also told Julio, "My husband is a DEA agent."

Guardia Civil Gomez introduced Kathy to the rest of the Guardia Civil officers and some of the support staff. Kathy was welcomed immediately at the Spanish Embassy. Later, Kathy introduced me to him and the Spanish Ambassador at a party for the embassy employees. I brought a DEA hat for Guardia Civil Gomez, but when the Ambassador saw the hat, he grabbed it. The Spanish Ambassador gave Kathy a big hug and two kisses on her cheeks. The Ambassador then put the hat on his head and shook my hand.

He said to me, "Welcome!" in English.

I was wondering to myself when I looked at the Spanish Ambassador; *Where is my big hug?*

413

I could tell Guardia Civil Gomez liked the hat. I said, "The hat was for you. Next time we meet, I will have a better DEA hat for you, and I'll buy you a beer."

He hugged me and smiled.

Kathy told Guardia Civil Gomez, "My husband wants to contact National Police, Jose Maria."

At the Spanish Embassy's party, I finally met the narcotics police officer, Jose Maria. I invited him and the rest of his agents to the American Embassy to meet the DEA agents I worked with.

He asked, "What other agents? I am the only one working narcotics, here at the Spanish embassy. I want you to come to my party next week."

How Drug Cartels Learn about DEA Operations

After several weeks in Colombia, the Departamento Administrativo de Seguridad (DAS) police said they located a cocaine trafficker who was a former smuggler for Pablo Escobar. The DAS police said they were going to search Pablo Escobar's former smuggler's home in Bogota. DAS police, an intelligence and counter-intelligence state agency, worked closely with DEA at the

414

American Embassy to target Colombian narcotics traffickers smuggling cocaine into the U.S.

The DAS Colombian police knew that the DEA agent and I would assist in searching a cocaine trafficker's home in Bogota. Two DAS prosecutors would also be at the drug trafficker's home to document any criminal evidence seized by the DAS police. Once inside the trafficker's home, DAS Colombian prosecutors understood that I would be gathering additional criminal intelligence at the house related to drug activities into the U.S.

At the drug trafficker's home, DAS police interviewed the former trafficker for the Pablo Escobar's organization. The trafficker said to the police that he did not transport large amounts of cocaine into the U.S. and return to Colombia with millions in U.S. dollars for Pablo Escobar. The Colombian prosecutors were reviewing documents inside two large file cabinets in the trafficker's bedroom.

Then the prosecutors said, "Agent Hardin, look at the investigative documents in the file cabinets. That is how the cartels in Colombia know who DEA and other U.S. law enforcement are targeting drug cartels and their methods of moving drugs in the Central and South American countries to the U.S."

I looked into the files and started to review investigative documents written by federal agents and State officials describing how drug traffickers smuggled their drugs into the U.S.

Wow. I remembered a few years ago working the Garcia brothers' case in Yuma when I saw discovery evidence in boxes at a Mexican Prosecutor office. I reported it to the AUSAs office in Phoenix and the DEA Chief Legal Counsel office in Washington, D.C., nothing happened. Now, I was looking at the same problem in Colombia.

The reports in the file cabinets also contained how local state law enforcement officers were involved in ongoing investigative cases in their communities in the U.S. None of the names of agents, officers, inspectors, police, or informants were redacted on these written reports.

I said to the Colombian Prosecutors, "These written reports are called *discovery*. It is released through the due process to the defendant's attorney before trial. The defendant's attorney has a legal right to know what criminal charges there are against his client."

"Once the corrupt attorney representing his client receives the discovery of evidence against the defendant, the cartels use the written reports for their own intelligence on how to change the method of moving drugs into the U.S."

I asked the Prosecutors if I could take the written reports back to the American Embassy.

Again, I was told, "No."

Chasing American Stolen Planes in Colombia

Within a year in Bogota, I was assigned to help out with the Air Interdiction Group, who were chasing American stolen planes loaded with drugs and leaving Colombia for the shores of the United States. With the assistance of the CIA, NSA, and the specialized Colombian National Police, I observed

Stolen American plane loaded with cocaine crash-landed, Medellin, Colombia.

417

two planes forced to the ground by the Colombian Air Force. Once

Stolen American plane loaded with cocaine crash-landed, Cali, Colombia.

the American stolen planes were on the ground, the Colombian police were unable to arrest the pilot or seize the cocaine.

On these two separate occasions, I wondered; Why aren't we landing before the cartels take the cocaine and destroy the stolen planes.

I later learned from an SOI working for the Colombia National Police that once the pilots knew DEA was chasing their stolen American planes loaded with cocaine, they would land immediately, anywhere on the ground.

The SOI said it was the Revolutionary Armed Forces of Colombian (FARC) and the Colombian military unloading the cocaine and destroying the stolen American planes before DEA could arrive to arrest the pilots and seize the cocaine.

I remembered chasing a plane loaded with cocaine somewhere in the mountains of Valle de Calle, Colombia. The

418

Colombian military plane I was in felt like riding a roller coaster traveling up and down at high speeds to avoid the mountains and strong winds. I started praying for God to help me to quickly and safely land the plane on the ground.

The Colombian military plane was an Otter. It had a flexible wingspan for traveling around and through the mountains and valleys. After several hours of thinking the plane was going to crash into a mountain or a river, it finally landed somewhere in an open field. As soon as the plane door was opened, I jumped out, fell on my knees, and kissed the ground several times. I didn't care who was laughing at the American kissing the ground.

$500,000 Cash in Paper Bags

During a Christmas party, a Colombian bank employee saw a lot of U.S. dollars in four brown cardboard boxes at his boss's bathroom. The bank employee said he was looking for the bathroom when he found the boxes. The employee contacted his friend, who worked for the National Colombia police. With the help of his friend, the bank employee took the boxes to DEA at the American Embassy.

419

I was wondering; Why were the boxes opened and in plain view in the bathroom? This story doesn't sound right.

When the bank employee got to the Embassy, the DEA duty agent took the boxes from him. The employee told the agent on duty that he was not sure how much money was in the boxes. The DEA agent counted almost $5 million U.S. dollars.

DEA contacted the employee about the boxes of money. For the amount of cash seized by DEA, the bank employee was going to receive almost $500 hundred thousand dollars for his efforts, 10% of the $5 million.

At the American Embassy, I gave the bank employee a U.S. Treasury check.

He said, "I don't want a check from the United States. I want the cash in paper bags."

I started to laugh. But it hit me as I was thinking; *He doesn't trust getting a check from the United States.* So, I went to the bank at the American Embassy and got cash. I came back and gave it to him in paper bags.

I asked him, "What are you going to do with all that money."

420

He told me, "I am now a former bank employee. I am taking my family to Disneyland in Florida."

"I guess you want a U.S. visa for you and your family to enter the United States," I said.

And, then, I thought to myself, He is not returning to Colombia once he and his family are in Florida.

Where is Pablo Escobar's Son?

While at the American Embassy in Bogota, I started to focus my attention on the whereabouts of Pablo Escobar Junior, in Colombia, Argentina, and Spain. He was the son of Pablo Escobar. I read reports from SOIs and CIs, providing information about where Pablo Junior might be living and his family's activities. SOIs from the Colombia National Police reported that Pablo Junior was moving back and forth from Spain to Argentina.

He, his mother, and his sister were not trying to hide from DEA but from his dad's enemies in Colombia. The Cali mafia headed by Gilberto Rodrigues-Orejuela and Jose Santacruz-London wanted Pablo Escobar's family dead.

Pablo Escobar Medellin's cartel gained an international reputation for brutality and murder and had dominated the drug trade. National Police killed Pablo in Medellin.[43]

The day Pablo died, he was talking to his son, Pablo Junior, on his cell phone. DEA knew Pablo Junior was in Spain, and that his father would be talking to him.

Pablo Escobar was at his private home in downtown Medellin when National Police undercover officers, assisted by DEA, closed in on Pablo's location. Pablo Escobar and his bodyguard attempted to escape by jumping on the roofs of other homes. Both were shot numerous times by the Colombian National Police.

I heard from a National Colombia Police SOI, who worked at a "safe house" in Medellin, said on several occasions that Pablo Escobar trained his son, Pablo Junior, how to kill at an early age. In Medellin, a Colombia Police officer showed me a photo of Pablo Junior pointing a handgun at the head of a sicarios while Pablo stood beside him.

Billions of U.S. Dollars Provided to the Colombians

I found out later from my little brother in Kentucky that Senator Mitch McConnell and his wife Elaine Chao were traveling to Bogota. The Senator was scheduled to meet with the American Ambassador and Colombian government officials about several billions of U.S. dollars being provided to the Colombians to fight the *war on drugs*. Senator McConnell wanted to meet with me when he was in Bogota.

Several days later, my DEA boss asked about my connection with Senator McConnell. He told me the Senator wanted to meet with me when he arrived in Bogota, but my boss said that it might not happen.

I had already established myself at the American Embassy as someone who couldn't lie but would tell the truth that the "war on drugs" was lost in Colombia and back home in the United States.

My little brother called me to say that it might be a problem for me to meet with Senator McConnell. Then, my brother called again to say that the meeting with Senator McConnell was on, and it would be set away from the American Embassy. Later, my boss told me I would be meeting with Senator McConnell at a local restaurant in Bogota for lunch. He asked, "What kind of connections helped you to meet with Senator McConnell?"

I didn't answer him.

Kathy and I arrived early at the restaurant. Within a few minutes, Senator McConnell and Mrs. Chao and his security personnel entered the large dining area, followed by the American Ambassador, the Ambassador's staff, and two DEA supervisors. Senator McConnell and Mrs. Chao personally greeted Kathy and me. The Senator and I talked about life in Colombia as we entered a smaller dining area. At the large dining table, one of the DEA supervisors told Kathy and me to sit at the end of the table. I was approached again by an Ambassador's staff member that I needed to move to the end of the dining table.

As I was about to sit down at the end of the table, Senator McConnell asked me to sit across from him. Mrs. Chao moved to the end of the table to my chair, next to Kathy. I looked at my DEA Supervisors and the Ambassador's faces as the seating arrangements were adjusted. I knew I would need to be careful with my words during lunch.

Senator McConnell asked me about my Dad and family. He had kind words about them and talked about how my little brother helped him win the election in Kentucky. As the Senator continued to talk about my family, I quickly glanced towards Kathy at the end of the table. Kathy and Mrs. Chao were laughing and not paying any attention to what was going on at our end of the table.

The Senator looked directly into my eyes. I suddenly thought, Oh, no, here comes the political question from the Senator. He knows my family's reputation for telling the truth, and the Hardin's don't like corrupted politics. He asked me what I thought about the drug trafficking problems and the money that would be given to Colombia to fight the war on drugs.

Wow! I immediately looked in the Senator's eyes without thinking politically and said, "The Colombians don't care about our culture or our way of life. They only care about our money and what they can take from us."

Everyone at the dining table became quiet, except Kathy and Mrs. Chao. At the end of the dining table, Kathy and Mrs. Chao were not listening to what just happened.

I knew I failed to answer Senator McConnell's question correctly. I was in trouble. But I believed in telling the truth about why the Colombians should not get our hard-earned tax dollars just to waste it.

The Senator smiled at my bold statement of truth, without any political lies. I nervously smiled back at the Senator, and suddenly, the DEA supervisors interrupted to tell the Senator of all the wonderful results they had from dismantling the cocaine labs and disrupting the drug transport to the U.S.

The Ambassador followed by mentioning the excellent working relationships with the Colombian government. Senator McConnell continued to smile and looked at me while the Ambassador and DEA people talked about the great job they were doing in Colombia.

I was thankful Senator McConnell didn't ask me any more questions about the war on drugs in Colombia. I never said another word at lunch.

The Ambassador and DEA supervisors continued their political bullshit about why they needed the U.S. taxpayer's money to fight the war on drugs in Colombia. Senator McConnell and I

426

looked down at the other end of the dining table. My wife and Mrs. Chao were still talking and laughing.

Kathy was unaware that I just ended my chances of ever being promoted to a DEA group supervisor. Kathy and Mrs. Chao were oblivious about what had just happened between the Senator and me.

When lunch was finished, the Senator and I walked outside together with our wives. He asked me to stay in touch. I told him, "I'll never forget this meeting."

Senator McConnell and Mrs. Chao are a great couple. Kathy later received a Christmas card and a photo of us all together at the luncheon from Mrs. Chao.

Senator Mitch McConnell and wife, Elaine Chao

Today, Senator McConnell is the Senate Majority Leader, and Mrs. Elaine Chao is the U.S. Secretary of Transportation under President Trump.

427

DEA Agent Murdered in Colombia

While in Colombia, I was a duty agent for all calls from the

Young Frank Moreno

United States and any other drug activities outside the U.S. One morning at about 1:30 a.m. Kathy and I were awakened from a sound sleep when the phone rang. I was trying to wake up and picked up the receiver and just said, "Yes."

The voice said, "Agent Frank Moreno was killed in a Fuego [fire]."

I said immediately, "Who is this?" It was a Marine at the American Embassy.

I said to him, "What? Is this a joke?"

The Marine's voice repeated, "Agent Frank Moreno was killed."

I hung up the phone and called my boss to explain the call. My boss said, "Son-of-a-bitch! Larry, give me a few minutes to get the details. Call me back."

428

I decided to call Agent Moreno's wife. When I called, she said, "I don't know where Frank is! He's not answering his cell phone or his pager. I'm worried about him."

I didn't want to alarm her and thought it would be better to talk with her in person. I just told her, "When Frank gets home, have him give me a call. I need some help from Frank."

I called my boss back about the conversation with Frank's wife. Now, Kathy was sitting up in bed.

My boss told me, "You need to get to the hospital. You're going to meet the Embassy nurse. When you get there, go with the nurse. Frank's been shot."

I immediately jumped out of bed. Kathy was following me, grabbing her clothes.

I told her, "Stay home."

She said, "No, Frank's wife needs my help."

A 9mm bullet killed agent Frank. That bullet entered his chest, cutting his aorta and exited his back, hitting a young Colombian boy in the side of his neck. Frank died quickly. The boy passed away the next day.

Late that night, I watched four people examine Frank's body at the hospital. The medical examiners moved Frank's body from side to side on the table, locating the gunshot wound, taking photos. Frank's body laid there naked on the table while they moved him around, looking for other bullet holes in his body. As I watched, I was thinking; *Here lies my buddy who would steal my apple from my desk and always told me what was going on in the DEA office.*

Frank always had my back from gossip in the DEA office and out in the field doing operations when we were in Colombia.

The Colombian Medical examiner moved Frank's body to another location for the autopsy. At the other location where the autopsy examination was, Kathy and I observed a Medical Examiner, wearing a large black leather apron, black rubber gloves, and black rubber boots up to his knees. He asked us, "Do you want to observe the autopsy while I examine Frank's body?"

I said, "No."

That was Frank's body, and I didn't want to watch when the examiner cut him up like butchering a hog, back home on Grandpa Hardin's farm.

430

After a few hours, the Medical Examiner brought Frank's body out for me to examine. His body was a mess from his body fluids when they opened his chest, legs, arms, and skull. I told the examiner, "Damnit, can you clean him up? His body and his face? Comb his hair?"

The examiner later put a white Styrofoam cooler next to the body. I later learned that the cooler contained Frank's brain and organs. I will always remember that Styrofoam white cooler next to Frank's body.

Kathy had no words as she looked in horror at the white name tag wrapped around Frank's right big toe.

That night, one bullet killed two people, Frank, and a young Colombian boy. It was a Colombian known killer who murdered them both.

I helped take care of Frank's body for three days until he went home to Texas. His coffin had an American flag wrapped over it and the white Styrofoam cooler next to his coffin.

Soon after a meeting at the American Embassy about Frank's death, a DEA agent told me that Frank's death was a bump in the road, an end that could happen to any DEA agent. I suddenly felt like this was one big political lie with the war on drugs. I cried privately for Frank's death. I felt his life meant nothing to the DEA agents in Bogota.

Spain Guardia Civil Assassinated in Colombia

Less than a month after DEA agent Frank Moreno was murdered, Kathy received word that her friend, Guardia Civil Julio Gomez, was killed in a gun battle on the streets of Bogota. I was distraught. I had just finished taking care of Frank's body to fly back to the United States. I was still grieving, silently for my buddy, Frank.

Within a week, Kathy and I attended the funeral Mass for Guardia Civil Gomez. At the Catholic Mass, I met his son and his wife. I had a DEA hat for Guardia Civil Gomez but never had the chance to give it to him. I looked at his beautiful wife crying, and his son holding his Momma's hand. I looked down at Julio's son and gave him the DEA hat I had for his daddy. The boy proudly put on the hat.

There was no room to sit at the Catholic Mass, so Kathy and I remained standing in the back of the church. Most of the people
432

began to sing a song I had never heard. I asked Kathy, "What is the name of the Spanish song?"

She said, "Salve Rociera."

I found myself saying with the rest of the mourners, "Ole, Ole, Ole, Ole."

"Be strong and courageous, do not be afraid or tremble at them, for the LORD your God is the one who goes with you. He will not fail or forsake you" (Deuteronomy 31:6 New American Standard Version).

Pablo Escobar's Sister and Brother-in-Law

The State Consular officers at the American Embassy in the Visa Section knew I was looking for Pablo Junior. I later received a call from one of the Consular officers who I trusted. The Consular officer told me that she had Pablo Escobar's sister and the brother-in-law in her office. I told the Consular officer, "Don't let Escobar's sister and the brother-in-law know they will be meeting a DEA agent in the next few minutes."

Alone, I entered a small room. I had Escobar's sister and brother-in-law's Colombian passports in my hand. They were

433

sitting across from me at a small table. I had an angry thought as I looked at them; *This is Pablo's family. What a nice-looking couple, yet they're devils in disguise. They want to go to the United States to visit family and relatives.*

A U.S. Marine Embassy guard was standing in the doorway. I told the Marine he could leave the room. At the small table, Pablo Escobar's sister and the brother-in-law thought that I was a consular officer who would provide them their visas to travel to the United States.

I said, "Hello."

Reviewing their passports, I noticed they had traveled to a few other countries in South America and several times to Spain. My first thought was; *I can't believe that I have Pablo Escobar's sister and brother-in-law sitting in front of me. This is my golden opportunity to find Pablo Junior.*

I asked, "Are you related to Pablo Escobar."

I then displayed my DEA Credentials to them.

They suddenly appeared to be very humble and polite. I noticed their hands were shaking. Nervously, they started to move

434

from side to side in their chairs, as if they were trying to get up from the chairs and leave.

I asked again, "Are you the sister of Pablo Escobar?"

She said, "Yes" in English with no accent.

The brother-in-law immediately said, "I am her husband."

Without asking them any other questions, she told me Pablo was a very good brother. "He helped our family, the poor people of Medellin, the churches, schools, and the police."

I asked her husband, "What did you do for Pablo?"

He said, "I was his bookkeeper and lawyer. I took care of his business."

They both denied that Pablo was a drug trafficker.

I asked them, "Where is Pablo Junior?"

They dropped their heads without making eye contact and said they didn't know where he was.

I asked, "Why do you want to go to the United States?"

"To see family and friends," they said.

"Where do your friends live in the United States?"

They slowly got up from the chairs and said, "We want our passports; we're leaving now."

435

The husband was a lawyer and a bookkeeper for the Medellin cartel. The humble-looking lawyer knew I had no authority to arrest either of them. I had to return their passports and let them leave.

I was determined to find Pablo Escobar's son.

Retirement

After a short three years in Colombia, I moved back to San Diego, California.

Before I retired from the San Diego office, a DEA agent from Yuma talked to me about why I couldn't prosecute the three Garcia brothers. The Yuma agent said, "I want to finish where you left off to arrest the brothers."

I told him that he would never be able to prosecute the brothers.

Then he told me, "I'm going to come and see you."

Several weeks passed, and I got another call from the same DEA agent in Yuma. He asked again, "What happened? Why couldn't you arrest the brothers?"

I explained, "I laid all the criminal activities against the brothers out for the AUSAs office in Phoenix to prosecute. They told me they couldn't prosecute the brothers. It's over. It's done!"

I told the agent, "Washington, D.C., DEA Chief Legal counsel sent me a copy of the rough draft of the indictment about why the brothers should be indicted based on everything I outlined in my report. Look, I'm glad you want to look at the brothers again, but it's not going to get prosecuted."

The agent said, "I want to come to see you."

"Sure, I'll meet with you in San Diego or Yuma."

I didn't hear from him again, and that meeting never happened.

About two years after I retired, I got a call from a DEA agent in Phoenix. It was a different agent asking why the three Garcia brothers weren't prosecuted. I told him that since I was now a private citizen and retired from DEA, he needed to be careful.

The Phoenix agent understood and said, "Yes, but I need to ask you some questions about the case."

I asked him why he was reviewing my old case against the brothers.

"I was assigned to look at it by DEA management. All these Garcia brothers and the Asian people! What happened?"

"Those are good questions, but you might as well let it go. I'm telling you right now, take the Garcia brothers' case and close it for good. There's no reason to review it."

He told me, "I want to come out to San Diego and see you."

438

"You can call me or come here anytime."

He said, "Okay, I'll see you soon."

And guess what? I never heard from him again, and he never came to see me.

After not hearing from the Yuma and Phoenix DEA agents about the Garcia brothers, I decided to visit my family in Bardstown, Kentucky. When I returned to San Diego, I had three bottles of good Kentucky *Apple Pie* moonshine whiskey in my check-in luggage. When I finally arrived at the San Diego airport, I went to get my checked-in luggage at the carousel; I noticed two DEA agents, close friends of mine, standing near the pickup area. Both DEA agents were assigned to the Airport NTF.

I said in a whisper to one of the agents, "Hey brother, how are you doing? It's great to see you. I love my retirement from DEA."

He immediately said out loud, "Sir. I am a Federal Narcotics agent. I want to talk to you about your travel today."

I laughed, "What! Are you joking? We are buddies."

He said, "Sir. Can you consent for me to look into your luggage?"

439

"You know what is in my luggage. I always have moonshine Whiskey when I come back to San Diego. It is for our friends and retirement parties."

While I was talking to the one agent, the other agent quickly opened my luggage and found three bottles full of reddish liquid. The agent searching my luggage immediately took one of the bottles, raised it over his head so everyone in the airport terminal area could see it. "Sir. What is this?"

I angrily said, "Are you joking? You know what it is."

"Sir, I need to take this one bottle from you and test it for any illegal substance."

I said, "I can't give you a bottle. I promised one bottle for an IRS agent, a bottle for an NCIS agent, and the other bottle for an FBI agent. Brothers, you're embarrassing me in front of all these passengers picking up their luggage."

The DEA agent said, "Thank you, sir, for the bottle. I will leave the other two bottles in your luggage."

I later learned that the DEA agents loved the moonshine. The agents said they are looking forward to seeing me at the San Diego airport.

440

After retiring from DEA, I now share my experiences teaching classes to students majoring in Criminal Justice at a local university in San Diego and one of the European colleges. I also own a private investigation business and volunteer to visit military veterans, law enforcement agents, and police officers in hospice.

Adjunct Professor

Looking back at the Garcia brothers' case, the entire experience was incredible – probably one of the worst corruption cases I ever worked, not only in the United States, but also in Mexico and Colombia. In my DEA career, I never experienced anything like the kind of corruption involved in the case.

I felt so bad that I did Don and Roy wrong. I promised Don I would get the brothers for what was done to them. I believe there are only disappointments for the victims.

DEA defined me, not only as a person but spiritually. I struggled with determining the truth about life. A few people I knew personally were killed on the job; DEA agents Richie Fass, Frank Moreno, Lt Danny Elkins, Sgt. Michael Crowe, Guardia

441

Civil Julio Gomez, and my CI, Angelito. They were all hard workers and good people.

A time to be born, and a time to die. Ecclesiastes 3:2. Original King James Version.

Knowing the deaths of my brothers in law enforcement, killed in Arizona and Colombia, I think, is about understanding the truth and how they lived. What is the truth? I believe it is that I should enjoy every moment in life. Live your life now.

It's incredible what I learned from working narcotics on the streets for almost 24 years. On the streets, I had to stay focused and just try to do what I knew in my heart was right. I decided not to follow the path of the devil where there was only a battle with darkness and trying to find the light. That was my struggle working narcotics and in the shade of evil, the path of the devil. *Trust in the Lord with all your heart. There you can find the light.*

The triumph for me was keeping my faith. To stay focused on that was my biggest challenge *of Fighting my Greatest Enemy: Myself.*

Oh, Great Spirit,
whose voice I heard in the winds
and whose breath gives life to the entire world, here me.

I am small and weak.
I need your strength and wisdom.

Let me walk in beauty and make my eyes
ever behold the red and purple sunset.
Make my hands respect the things you have made
and my ears sharp to hear your voice.
Make me wise so I may understand
the things you have taught my people.
Let me learn the things you have hidden
in every leaf and rock.

I seek strength not to be greater than my brother,
but fight my greatest enemy myself.
Make me always ready to come to you
with clean hands and straight eyes,
so, when life fades, as the fading sunset,
may my spirit come to you
without shame.[44]

Epilogue

I had a great job with DEA. I enjoyed it. I believe I was in that job to work in Yuma for a reason: to target the Garcia brothers for what they did to Don and Roy. At the same time, I realized it was a dangerous atmosphere of corruption. I felt guilty about not getting to prosecute the Garcia brothers for trying to kill Special Agents Don Ware and Roy Stevenson. I had an opportunity to look into what the brothers were doing, and it felt like I could do something about it. I was determined. I kept to myself, and that's what helped to build my integrity.

PIs Jeff Pearce and Randy Torgerson talked to me about law enforcement skeletons in the closet in Yuma, Arizona. I didn't want to hear about any more corruption. I didn't want to know because I had to work with these agents and cops. I had to trust some of the corrupt agents and cops with my life. It's part of me and who I am. I knew I had to be very cautious about how I dealt with things in Yuma and at the Mexican border. It was like in Vietnam when some of the military officers took a bullet in the back from their own men that they lead into battle. The officers never made it back because one of their own men shot them.

I never got promoted in DEA. I wanted to become a Special Agent in Charge (SAC), which was as far as I could go in the agency. I had the personality and integrity. However, I never got the connections with the right people in DEA with the same integrity. Some of the guys with DEA and NTF stayed away from my PIs in Yuma because they were shaking the trees, and the rotten fruit was beginning to fall. Some of the guys in law enforcement were fearful of that falling fruit.

It broke my spirit when I had to let the case go and went to Colombia. I knew too much about the Garcia brothers' dope activities and the law enforcement corruption in Yuma. However, I was given a second chance in Colombia.

I lost some good friends in the law enforcement community, and I believe it might have been because of the work I was doing. I could never cross the line into corruption. I was so disappointed with myself for failing to honor Don and Roy.

I was confused about what I should do next with my career. I learned that corruption was deeper in law enforcement and politics than I ever imagined.

It became more apparent that some in DEA and the AUSAs office, with other agency involvement, didn't want the Garcia brothers indicted. It's almost like they wanted me to fail. My first GS didn't even say goodbye to me when he left Yuma. I was really frustrated. I was just trying to do what was right.

Look at what happened to AUSA Goodwill. He later went on to CIA. We had hit it off, and AUSA Goodwill encouraged me to go after these brothers. But then FBI and the other two AUSAs were all freaked out that I was getting too close to know everything involved with the brothers and the corrupt cops at the Mexican border. This had never happened before with other DEA agents, and it made me a threat to some in the law enforcement community if the public found out the truth about corruption at the border.

If the PIs; Harry Fresno, Jeff Pearce, and Randy Torgerson hadn't been involved, I probably never would have gotten so close to prosecuting the Garcia brothers. But it also wouldn't have been as stressful, because while I was working some other significant

447

cases, and the PIs got involved, they pushed me, and I pushed the AUSAs office.

Looking back, I think it's about knowing the truth, that I should enjoy every moment in life. I don't feel bitter about what happened with the DEA or the case. Some cases were easy to adjudicate, and some were difficult because of greed on both sides of the fence. It's amazing what money can do to people in the world of drugs and narcotics.

I was disappointed, not so much with the Garcia brothers' drug activities, but their connection to corrupt cops. The brothers were just a family operating a drug business at the U.S. and Mexican Southwest border. The brothers were giving a lot of the American people what they wanted, the dope. It was just a drug and sometimes a weapons business for the brothers. The brothers were out there pushing dope across the border into the United States from Mexico.

Sometimes innocent people got hurt and killed. It was the same in Mexico and Colombia. Working at the Mexican border and the POE, I didn't see a majority of white people coming across, but

448

I wasn't targeting Mexicans. I was targeting narcotics traffickers –
anyone involved with crime against the U.S.

I was meant to represent what is right, and yet I saw so
much evil working narcotics. This was more of a challenge because
I knew what was right. I knew the purpose of my career, yet the
evil I was going after was a powerful thing. The corrupted cops
knew what they were doing. The cops knew it was wrong and
immoral, but the corrupt cops tried to justify all of it to themselves.

Like DEA agents Richie Fass and Frank Moreno, Arizona
Southwest Border NTF Officers Lt Danny Elkins and Sgt. Michael
Crowe were murdered on the job. All hard workers, fighting the
war on drugs. Lt Elkins wanted to work on the Garcia brothers' case
with me. I blame the incompetent political lies, corrupt agents, and
cops who didn't want to prosecute the case.

Under the law, I could move on with new information the
PIs kept feeding me about corrupt cops. I could have kept going if
I wanted. If there were a conflict between what I could do and what
my GS told me I shouldn't do, I would go ahead anyway.

The burr in the saddle of this whole case was that DEA,
FBI, and the AUSAs office couldn't control the PIs. DEA and other

449

agencies couldn't tell the PIs to stop targeting corrupt cops and the brothers. The DEA GS could monitor me by not allowing me to continue working on the Garcia brothers' case, but the PIs didn't work for DEA.

The PIs were "go-getters" and knew how to get the information. PI Jeff Pearce was very young and emotional. He had just come out of the military and didn't have the civilian law enforcement background. This type of work was different than the military. He took it personally to see how the case came to an end. He began to lose his way following the path of the devil.

PI Pearce explained to me that he knew what he was doing. But he wasn't aware of all the ins-and-outs and the little tricks that he and PI Randy Torgerson learned along the way about how to deal with corrupt cops. They were learning new things on the job while working with me all the time. The hard part was learning that criminals are masquerading as good guys in law enforcement and the government. They did not learn how to deal with that kind of corruption.

Private Investigators weren't cops or agents, but I knew I could trust PIs Pearce and Torgerson. I had to be very careful not

450

to provide them with any DOJ/DEA documents. FBI knew PIs Pearce and Torgerson were shaking the bushes real hard for corruption. That's why they searched PI Pearce's home in Fresno, California, looking for DEA official documents that some corrupt official or AUSA said I provided to the PIs. Some AUSAs, including AUSA Nay Whitehouse, in the Phoenix office ultimately wanted to come after me, and they used the FBI.

The most dangerous thing I encountered while working narcotics was the temptation of lust, money, and sex. In a situation where money was found, no one could claim it. I made it through with the blessing of my faith, and for that, I worked hard. In a world like this, I was doing my job. I did put people in jail, but most of them were very poor and just trying to make a living. The poor drug traffickers had to rely on Public Defenders.

The triumph for me was keeping my faith in our Lord Jesus. Not with my wife nor my family, but with my confidence in God. I stayed focused on that. That was my biggest challenge.

I had to stay focused and just try to do what I knew was right in my heart. I decided not to follow to the dark battle, or as I would say: *Fighting my Greatest Enemy: Myself.* That was my struggle working narcotics.

DEA gave me a good career. I'm in good health, and I have an enjoyable retirement with a great pension. I made it.

I signed an agreement with DEA to wait five years before doing anything with the information I learned on the Garcia brothers' case or any other cases. I have written my first true story with the two PIs, Jeff Pearce and Randy Torgerson, called *Path of the Devil: Camino del Diablo.* This is the second and last, which is my true personal story: *Fighting my Greatest Enemy: Myself; Trust in God: Confia en Dios.*

I believe there were only disappointments for the victims and the families that the Garcia brothers hurt and sometimes killed. I will always remember that I lost the battle for Don and Roy, but I pray to see them later in heaven.

I struggled with determining the truth about life; "Live your life now."

I am sorry, Don and Roy. There was never a war on drugs.

A time to be born and a time to die, and with the grace of God, I am still alive.

452

References

"Media gagged from reporting drug test results of murder suspect." *Reporters Committee for Freedom of the Press: Feature.* September 25, 1995. Accessed April 23, 2018. https://www.rcfp.org/browse-media-law-resources/news/media-gagged-reporting-drug-test-results-murder-suspect.

Associated Press. "Arizona Deputy Charged With Killing Two Fellow Lawmen 'Exemplary' Narcotics Fighter Stealing Guns, Drugs From Evidence Room." July 8, 1995. Accessed April 23, 2018. http://www.spokesman.com/stories/1995/jul/08/arizona-deputy-charged-with-killing-two-fellow/.

Associated Press. "Agents Find Drug Tunnel to U.S. *The New York Times.* May 19, 1990. http://www.nytimes.com/1990/05/19/us/agents-find-drug-tunnel-to-us.html.

Attwood, Shaun. American Made: Who Killed Barry Seal? Pablo Escobar or George Bush (War on Drugs Book 2).

Campbell, Duncan and Tuckman, Jo. "Mexicans hand over drug-tunnel smuggler." *The Guardian: World News.* June 13, 2001. https://www.theguardian.com/world/2001/jun/14/Mexico.

Chief Yellow Lark, American Indian, Lakota, "The Great Spirit Prayer," 1887. Retrieved March 17, 2019 https://www.worldprayers.org/archive/prayers/invocations/oh_great_spirit_whose_voice.html

Department of Justice (DoJ). "Organized Crime Drug Enforcement Task Forces." *The United States Department of Justice: Criminal Division.* Updated, June 9, 2015. https://www.justice.gov/criminal/organized-crime-drug-enforcement-task-forces.

Ferranti, Seth. "The Story Behind an Infamous Escobar cartel Assassination." *Vice: Stuff.* March 27, 2016. https://www.vice.com/en_us/article/4w3mvw/an-fbi-agent-tells-story-behind-an-infamous-escobar-cartel-assassination.

Gallegher, Mike. "King of The Kingpins: The Mexican Federation." *Albuquerque Journal*. March 1997. https://www.abqjournal.com/news/drugs/8drug3-3.htm.

Golden, Tim. "Cardinal in Mexico Killed in a Shooting Tied to Drug Battle" *New York Times*. May 25, 1993. http://www.nytimes.com/1993/05/25/world/cardinal-in-mexico-killed-in-a-shooting-tied-to-drug-battle.html.

Grant, Will. "Mexico drugs: How one DEA killing began a brutal war. BBC News, Guadalajara." February 2012. http://www.bbc.com/news/world-us-canada-16920870.

Kraul, Chris. "From torture to terrorism: How DEA case let to extraordinary rendition." *Los Angeles Times*. February 26, 2015. http://www.latimes.com/world/mexico-americas/la-fg-dea-camarena-20150226-story.html.

Lisalus, Som. "Drug Tunnel Architect Faces 20 years." *Tuscon News Now: KOLD New 13*. Accessed August 9, 2017. http://www.tucsonnewsnow.com/story/4710820/drug-tunnel-architect-faces-20-years.

McFadden, Robert D. "Head of Medellin Cocaine cartel is

Killed by Troops in Colombia." Los Angeles Times. December 3,

1993. https://www.nytimes.com/1993/12/03/world/head-of-

medellin-cocaine-cartel-is-killed-by-troops-in-colombia.html.

Accessed June 20, 2019.

Merentes, Luis A. "Was the CIA behind 'Kiki' Camerena's Murder? Investigative Journalist and Congress Must Follow Up." Huffington Post. December 15, 2013. Accessed September 29, 2017.

Mora, Edwin. "DHS IG: Tunnels Along U.S. – Mexico Border 'Significant and Growing' Threat." *Breitbart*. Dec. 13, 2013. http://www.breitbart.com/big-government/2013/12/13/dhs-ig-tunnels-along-us-mexico%20border-significant-and-growing-threat/.

454

Multiple Authors. "Narcotics agent held in deaths of 2 Yuma officers." *Tucson Citizen: Local.* July 6, 1995. http://tucsoncitizen.com/morgue2/1995/07/06/99618-narcotics-agent-held-in-deaths-of-2-yuma-officers/.

Mydans, Seth. "Agents Seize 20 Tons of Cocaine In Raid on Los Angeles Warehouse." The New York Times. September 30, 1989. http://www.nytimes.com/1989-09-30/us/agents-seize-20-tons-of-cocaine-in-raid-on-los-angeles-warehouse.html?pagewanted=print.

Parker, Richard. "Mexico's Poor Trading Machetes for AK-47s." *Journal Washington Bureau: A Journal Special Report.* March 1997. https://www.abqjournal.com/news/drugs/.

Reel, Monty. "How El Chapo Builds His Tunnels. *The New Yorker.* August 3, 2013. http://www.newyorker.com/magazine/2015/08/03/underworld-monte-reel.

St. Clair, Jeffrey. "Air Cocaine: The Wild, True Story of Drug-Running, Arms Smuggling and Contras at a Backwoods Airstrip in the Clintons' Arkansas." *CounterPunch,* November 2016. https://www.counterpunch.org/2016/11/04/air-cocaine-the-wild-true-story-of-drug-running-arms-smuggling-and-contras-at-a-small-airstrip-in-clintons-arkansas/.

Stewart, Bob W. "United States May Ask State to Prosecute in *United Press International: UPI Archives.* July 14, 1995. "Police say evidence theft led to killings. http://www.upi.com/Archives/1995/07/14/Police-say-evidece-theft-led-to-killings/8785805694400/.

United States Court of Appeals, Ninth Circuit. "Michael Su CHIA, Petitioner-Appellant, v. Steven CAMBRA, Jr., Warden; Attorney General of the State of California, Respondents-Appellees. No. 99-56361." March 4, 2004. Accessed May 5, 2018. https://caselaw. findlaw.com/us-9th-circuit/1241789.html.

Wiedrich, Bob. "Acts of Heroism in Narcotics War." *Chicago Tribune.* June 18, 1975, page 28. http://archives.chicagotribune.com/1975/06/18/page/28/article/acts-of-heroism-in-narcotics-war.
455

Ybarra, Michael J. and Ford, Andrea. "Jury Finds Man Guilty in Murder of 2 DEA Agents." *Los Angeles Times*. November 2, 1988. http://articles.latimes.com/1988-11-02/local/me-573_1_three-dea-agents.

Notes

[1] **Antonio Lagares.** *Venta de Vargas. Una leyenda en el tiempo.* April

12, 2017.

[2] Mike Gallegher. "King of The Kingpins: The Mexican Federation." Albuquerque Journal. March 1997, Day 2. https://www.abqjournal.com /news/drugs/8drug3-3.htm.
[3] Ibid.
[4] Ibid.
[5] Jeffrey St. Clair. "Air Cocaine: The Wild, True Story of Drug-Running, Arms Smuggling and Contras at a Backwoods Airstrip in the Clintons' Arkansas." *CounterPunch* November 2016. https://www.counterpunch.org/2016/11/04/air-cocaine-the-wild-true-story-of-drug-running-arms-smuggling-and-contras-at-a-small-airstrip-in-clintons-arkansas/.
[6] Ibid.
[7] Ibid.
[8] Seth Ferranti. "The Story Behind an Infamous Escobar Cartel Assassination." *Vice: Stuff.* March 27, 2016. https://www.vice.com/en_us/article/4w3mvw/an-fbi-agent-tells-story-behind-an-infamous-escobar-cartel-assassination.
[9] Shaun Attwood. "American Made: Who Killed Barry Seal? Pablo Escobar or George Bush" (War on Drugs Book 2).
[10] St. Clair.
[11] Ibid.
[12] Ibid.
[13] Attwood.
[14] Ibid.
[15] Ibid.
[16] Chris Kraul. "From torture to terrorism: How DEA case let to extraordinary rendition." Los Angeles Times. February 26, 2015. http://www.latimes.com/world/mexico-americas/la-fg-dea-camarena-20150226-story.html
[17] Ibid.
[18] Ibid.
[19] Ibid.

[20] Randy Torgerson Interview

[21] Luis A. Merentes. Was the CIA behind "Kiki" Camerena's Murder? Investigative Journalist and Congress Must Follow Up. December 15, 2013.

[22] Kraul.

[23] Merentes.

[24] Kraul.

[25] Will Grant. Mexico drugs: How one DEA killing began a brutal war. BBC News, Guadalajara. February 2012. http://www.bbc.com/news/world-us-canada-16920870

[26] DoJ. "Organized Crime Drug Enforcement Task Forces." *The United States Department of Justice: Criminal Division.* Updated, June 9, 2015. Accessed August 14, 2017. https://www.justice.gov/criminal/ organized-crime-drug-enforcement-task-forces.

[27] Seth Mydans. "Agents Seize 20 Tons of Cocaine In Raid on Los Angeles Warehouse." The New York Times. September 30, 1989. http://www.nytimes.com/1989-09-30/us/agents-seize-20-tons-of-cocaine-in-raid-on-los-angeles-warehouse.html?pagewanted=print.

[28] Edwin Mora. "DHS IG: Tunnels Along U.S. – Mexico Border 'Significant and Growing' Threat." *Breitbart.* Dec. 13, 2013. http://www.breitbart.com/big-government/2013/12/13/dhs-ig-tunnels-along-us-mexico%20border-significant-and-growing-threat/.

[29] Som Lisalus. "Drug Tunnel Architect Faces 20 years." *Tucson News Now: KOLD New 13.* Accessed August 9, 2017. http://www.tucsonnewsnow.com/story/4710820/drug-tunnel-architect-faces-20-years.

[30] AP. "Agents Find Drug Tunnel to the U.S." *The New York Times.* May 19, 1990. http://www.nytimes.com/1990/05/19/us/agents-find-drug-tunnel-to-us.html.

[31] Monty Reel. "How El Chapo Builds His Tunnels. *The New Yorker.* August 3, 2013. http://www.newyorker.com/magazine/2015/08/03/underworld-monte-reel.

[32] Duncan Campbell, and Jo Tuckman. "Mexicans hand over drug-tunnel smuggler." *The Guardian: World News.* June 13, 2001. https://www.theguardian.com/world/2001/jun/14/mexico

[33] Tim Golden. "Cardinal in Mexico Killed in a Shooting Tied to Drug Battle" *New York Times.* May 25, 1993. http://www.nytimes.com/1993/05/25/world/cardinal-in-mexico-killed-in-a-shooting-tied-to-drug-battle.html

458

[34] Richard Parker. "Mexico's Poor Trading Machetes for AK-47s." *Journal Washington Bureau: A Journal Special Report*. March 1997. https://www.abqjournal.com/news/drugs/.

[35] Michael J. Ybarra and Andrea Ford. "Jury Finds Man Guilty in Murder of 2 DEA Agents. *Los Angeles Times*. November 2, 1988.

[36] United States Court of Appeals, Ninth Circuit. "Michael Su CHIA, Petitioner-Appellant, v. Steven CAMBRA, Jr., Warden; Attorney General of the State of California, Respondents-Appellees. No. 99-56361." March 4, 2004. Accessed May 5, 2018. https://caselaw. findlaw.com/us-9th-circuit/1241789.html.

[37] Bob Wiedrich. "Acts of Heroism in Narcotics War." *Chicago Tribune*. June 18, 1975, page 28. http://archives.chicagotribune.com/1975/06/18/page/28/article/acts-of-heroism-in-narcotics-war.

[38] Associated Press. "Arizona Deputy Charged With Killing Two Fellow Lawmen 'Exemplary' Narcotics Fighter Stealing Guns, Drugs From Evidence Room." July 8, 1995. April 23, 2018. http://www.spokesman.com/stories/1995/jul/08/arizona-deputy-charged-with-killing-two-fellow/.

[39] Multiple Authors. "Narcotics agent held in deaths of 2 Yuma officers." *Tucson Citizen: Local*. July 6, 1995.

[40] UPI. "Police say evidence theft led to killings." *UPI* Archives. July 14, 1995.

[41] "Media was gagged from reporting drug test results of the murder suspect." *Reporters Committee for Freedom of the Press: Feature*. September 25, 1995.

[42] Associated Press. "Arizona Deputy Charged With Killing Two Fellow Lawmen 'Exemplary' Narcotics Fighter Stealing Guns, Drugs From Evidence Room." The Spokesman-Review: Nation/World. July 8, 1995.

[43] Robert D McFadden. "Head of Medellin Cocaine Cartel is Killed by Troops in Colombia." Los Angeles Times. December 3, 1993. https://www.nytimes.com/1993/12/03/world/head-of-medellin-cocaine-cartel-is-killed-by-troops-in-colombia.html. Accessed June 20, 2019.

[44] Chief Yellow Lark, American Indian, Lakota, "The Great Spirit Prayer," 1887. Retrieved March 17, 2019. https://www.worldprayers.org/archive/prayers/invocations/oh_great_spirit_whose_voice.html

CPSIA information can be obtained
at www.ICGtesting.com
Printed in the USA
BVHW042140190623
666106BV00005B/38